Women and Soap Opera

Women and Soap Opera

A Study of Prime Time Soaps

Christine Geraghty

Polity Press

The right of Christine Geraghty to be identified as author of this work has been asserted in accordance with the Copyright, Designs and Patents Act 1988.

First published in 1991 by Polity Press
in association with Blackwell Publishers Ltd.

Reprinted 1992, 1999
Transferred to Digital Print 2003

Editorial office:
Polity Press
65 Bridge Street
Cambridge CB2 1UR, UK

Marketing and production:
Blackwell Publishers Ltd
108 Cowley Road
Oxford OX4 1JF, UK

Published in the USA by
Blackwell Publishers Inc.
Commerce Place
350 Main Street
Malden MA 02148, USA

ISBN 0–7456–0489–7
ISBN 0–7456–0568–0 (pbk)

A catalogue record for this book is available from the British Library and the Library of Congress.

Typeset in 10½ on 12 pt Times by Acorn Bookwork, Salisbury, Wilts
Printed in Great Britain by Athenæum Press Ltd, Gateshead, Tyne & Wear

Contents

Acknowledgements

No book can be written without discussion and argument with a host of people who hardly know of its existence. This is particularly true of a book on soaps since the very subject matter lends itself to innumerable conversations with friends, acquaintances and perfect strangers who offer their views with enthusiasm and knowledge. Such conversations have led both to unexpected insights and to confirmation that a previously disregarded thought would repay investigation. I am particularly grateful to two groups of people: firstly, to friends and colleagues at the National and Local Government Officers Association and particularly in the Health Section where I work for their patience and indeed interest in 'the book' which must have sometimes seemed to them to be a figment of my imagination; and secondly, to students on the British Film Institute/ University of London evening class in film study who each year allowed a session on television soap operas to interrupt their study of film narrative and frequently contributed to my own thinking on the subject. Other debts are obvious from the text but individuals whom I have pleasure in acknowledging include Jim Cook for his encouragment at a number of difficult points, Fiona Robertson, Marysia Lachowicz and Ruth Geraghty for their typing skills, Mark Finch for sparing the time to discuss *Dynasty* with me and Michael Geraghty for help with materials. As is appropriate for a book on soap opera, this book is dedicated to my family with thanks for their love, friendship and support and in particular to my parents, Ruth and Peter Geraghty, without whom, of course, none of this would have been possible.

January 1990

Introduction

For years, soap operas were scarcely noticed, trundling on in the corner, the same characters apparently going through the same traumas, watched only by the 'housewife' in the odd moments of her busy day. 'Soap' was a term of derision, an expression which implied an over-dramatic, under-rehearsed presentation of trivial dramas blown up out of all proportion to their importance. There was little here apparently to bring soaps to the notice of the general public or even media theorists.

But, as in the best soaps, things do change and this book examines the nature of that change. It is clear that the soaps themselves have widened their appeal: the glossy prime time soaps, *Dallas* and *Dynasty*, have become worldwide phenomena; in US colleges, the daytime soaps have keen followings among students; in Britain, playground conversations reflect the children's lively interest in both *EastEnders*, a British soap set in London, and *Neighbours*, an Australian soap set in the suburbs of Melbourne. Soaps in the eighties have become big news; *Time* magazine, in August 1980, took the question 'TV's *Dallas*: Whodunit?' and the shooting of JR was an item on the BBC's evening news on the evening it was shown in Britain. The tabloid papers made headlines of the characters' off-screen lives and speculated wildly about the outcomes of major stories. Rivalries were set up between *Dallas* and *Dynasty* or the British *EastEnders* and *Coronation Street* and the ratings were studied for indications of which programme was winning what became known in the British press as 'The Great Soap War'.

In the more rarified atmosphere of media theory, soaps were also being taken more seriously in the 1980s. This was due to the convergence of two emerging trends – a growing interest in popular television forms and an awareness, prompted by feminism, that

1

programmes enjoyed by so many women should not be ignored. Theoretical work on television began to look up from the news and current affairs programmes and to take more of an interest in other forms of drama, police series, situation comedies and quiz shows. In film theory, work on melodrama had rescued a despised genre and turned it into a legitimate object for study. US television theorists began to look at their own soaps in the same way and work on the importance of soaps in women's lives began to make a dent in the prejudice which surrounded them. The impact of feminism has been critical in creating an atmosphere in which the traditional skills and pleasures assigned to women could be re-evaluated rather than dismissed; this reassessment covered a range of cultural issues, from the apparently frivolous, such as the role of fashion and dress in women's lives, to the more obviously serious, as publishing houses discovered that the reissuing of long-neglected women's fiction could be profitable. In this changing atmosphere, it became possible to acknowledge the pleasures of soap operas and to argue that soaps are not inherently worthless but have been made to seem so. Jane Root has pointed out that the fact that 'soap operas are seen as female has helped to bring the whole form into disrepute',[1] but as feminism brought neglected genres such as the melodrama and the romance back into the centre of theoretical work so the potential importance of soap opera to women began to be recognised and argued about. This book is, I hope, a contribution to that process.

The soaps referred to in this book are not those which have always been defined as soap operas, particularly in the United States. I have concentrated deliberately on programmes which have been broadcast in the evenings but which, in their themes and presentation, seem to offer a space for women in peak viewing time. Research with audiences such as that of David Morley indicates that it is still difficult for women to control what is watched by the family in the evening and that prime time soaps are programmes which tend to be watched by women in the face of family opposition.[2] This book in its analysis of the US prime time programmes, *Dallas* and *Dynasty*, and of the British evening programmes, *Coronation Street*, *Crossroads*, *Brookside* and *EastEnders*, offers a case study of how far commercial popular programming can go in presenting strong female characters and dealing with issues from a point of view which is sympathetic to women. This appeal to women can be discerned in both the US and British soaps and explains some of their similarities but the way in which it is handled also reveals key differences and one of my purposes is to explore the range of pleasures offered to women in these programmes. But if these prime time soaps have a specific appeal to women they are also the programmes which are most under pressure to broaden their appeal to the whole evening audience and this book also seeks to explore how this necessity has affected their themes and structures.

This approach does not conform to some of the definitions of soap opera which are based on the traditional model of the daytime soap. The term is taken from US television where daytime programmes aimed at women were owned and produced by soap companies such as Procter and Gamble. It was used to describe (and denigrate) low-budget, daytime drama which to the outsider seemed slow paced and tacky, featuring families whose interactions produced stories of notorious complexity. Among American media theorists there has been some controversy as to whether prime time serials such as *Dallas* and *Dynasty*, with their more lavish production values and evening viewing slots, can be counted as soap operas. Thomas Skill argues that, 'for the most part, daytime is the province of the slower-paced, reflective drama compared to prime time's higher budgeted, action-orientated drama'[3] and George Comstock remarks that 'by definition, soap opera is a daytime program, broadcast several times a week with low production costs, as compared to prime time and attracts a predominantly, if hardly wholly, adult female audience.'[4] Other US writers have been more ready to include *Dallas* and even *Hill Street Blues* with soap operas. 'What unites them,' writes Horace Newcomb, 'and links them to soap opera is the sense of openness, the rejection of endings anticipated or already known.'[5]

What is important here is not so much to give the US prime time dramas such as *Dallas* and *Dynasty* the correct label but to recognise why there is a problem about definition. Clearly, as US critics have acknowledged, there have been changes in the daytime soaps themselves in the eighties. They have become more adventurous and outgoing both in their settings and their stories. They have received a wider share of publicity and, as Robert Allen has described, 'new groups have "discovered" soap operas, including millions of college students (nearly half of all undergraduate students in the United States), five million non-college-age men, and as yet uncounted adolescents.'[6] At the same time, some of their formal strategies for handling narrative and their thematic preoccupations have been recognised and taken over by prime time programmes from different genres. Police series like *Hill Street Blues* and *Cagney and Lacey* have strong serial elements in their format and a greater concern with the domestic and emotional life of the characters which has shifted them away from the more traditional police series; situation comedies like *The Cosby Show*, *Cheers* and *Roseanne* have allowed characters to develop in a way comparable to a soap, building on the audience's growing familiarity with a family's domestic dramas. In addition, prime time family dramas like *Dallas*, *Dynasty* and their offshoots have very strong thematic and formal links with daytime soaps but do not have the same scheduling format and make greater use of action and suspense. It is this blurring of the boundaries between soap opera and other genres which has caused the problems of definition.

The British context offers an even clearer example of the problems of attempting to work within a tight definition of soap opera. The different circumstances in which the British TV system developed meant that daytime soap operas could not be based on the US model since advertisers were specifically prevented from having that kind of direct input into programming. The limited number of channels (a commercial channel being first introduced as late as 1955 and a fourth national channel arriving only in 1982) and the more sporadic and piecemeal development of daytime television in the UK has meant that the demand for cheap, regular programmes has been much more limited. Generally the daytime needs have been met by obscure, home-produced serials like *Gems* or by Australian imports (*Sons and Daughters*, *The Young Doctors*) whose status is even lower than that of homegrown products. It would be meaningless, in a British context, to limit the definition of soap operas to programmes with a regular daytime scheduling. There has, indeed, been some hesitation in using the term at all in the British context. Granada, the production company for *Coronation Street*, has consistenly refused to describe its programme as a soap and indeed early critical work on it, such as the British Film Institute's monograph, *Coronation Street*, is restrained in the use of the term, preferring to talk about the 'continuous serial' or 'serial drama'.

Given the blurring of boundaries in the US context and the consistent use of prime time scheduling for the British programmes, it would be perverse to deny that *Dallas*, *Dynasty*, *Coronation Street*, *Crossroads*, *EastEnders* and *Brookside*, are soap operas in the interests of maintaining the purity of a definition. The programmes to which I refer, while maintaining certain key narrative strategies and thematic concerns, have extended the boundaries of soaps. Soap operas, as we shall see, has changed and it can now be defined not purely by daytime scheduling or even by a clear appeal to a female audience but by the presence of stories which engage an audience in such a way that they become the subject for public interest and interrogation. 'Who shot JR?' (*Dallas*), 'Should Deirdre leave Ken?' (*Coronation Street*), 'Will Den divorce Angie?' (*EastEnders*), 'How will Meg be written out?' (*Crossroads*) are, like it or not, questions which became part of the public arena, bringing to the fore two issues which will be extensively explored in this book – the capacity of soaps to engage their audiences in the narrative and their ability to open up for public discussion emotional and domestic issues which are normally deemed to be private. Stuart Hall has described this process well when, in commenting on *Dallas*'s popularity, he remarked,

> At a certain point, the programme attained a type of popularity that was not a popularity in terms of figures and ratings. I mean it had repercussions on culture as a whole. The viewers' involvement became something different. You couldn't help talking about the popularity of *Dallas*, because people were starting to refer to categories taken from the serial in interpreting their own experience.[7]

Part of this book's purpose is to explore how and why this happens. Individual programmes do not of course maintain at a consistent level the intense public interest which Hall describes but the soaps I shall be discussing have all shown this capacity to spread their hermeneutic entanglements well beyond the television set and to engage their audiences in the process of discussion which Hall describes.

One of the traps of work on a genre is the search for the perfect example. Genre theory then becomes a question of elimination and exclusion. The arguments against considering *Dallas* and *Dynasty* as soap operas smack of this, making it more difficult to recognise connections in the interests of preserving boundaries. This book is concerned to delineate the strategies and thematics which are shared by the soaps I am looking at but it is at least as important to recognise that their differences are also a source of pleasure and that we need to chart these differences as well as the similarities. In this context, it is essential to have a wide definition of soap opera, to see soaps as programmes in which similar issues are variously played out and which offer, within the same broad area, a spectrum of different styles and preoccupations. As we shall see, the viewer can then pick and choose between Colorado and Liverpool, glamour and down-to-earth ordinariness, fantasy and naturalism. Looked at this way, it is precisely because *Dynasty* and *Dallas* are different from the British serials that it important to look at them together. What is at stake is not the pure examples of a particular genre but a range of programmes which, taken together, represent a whole which can never entirely be consumed or played out.

In looking at this particular group of soap operas, therefore, this book has two purposes. It seeks firstly to examine the role of women in prime time soap operas and the pleasures and values which are offered to them as the implied audience for these programmes. It does not, however, focus exclusively on the representation of women in soaps but argues that their dominant role needs to be studied more broadly in terms of the thematic preoccupations of the programmes and the formal conventions which structure them. Very often, as we shall see, the powerful representation of women in soaps comes from the contradictory demands made of them by, for example, their role as the moral centre of the family which is set against the expression of their own personal desires and needs. Such contradictions are marked on a more formal level by the way in which the need for narrative action may be set against the demand for spectacle and glamour, the values of melodrama at odds with those of light entertainment. In looking at the role of women in soap operas, therefore, we need to examine the programmes' narrative organisation and aesthetic characteristics since it is the combination of certain thematic preoccupations with a particular kind of engagement with the viewer which forms the basis of soaps' appeal.

The book's second purpose, however, is to look at the way in which prime time soaps have stretched the boundaries of the genre, by introducing stories which are different from the traditional soap format, by giving more space and arguably more sympathy to male characters and by addressing issues of gender, race and class in a more overt and dramatic way. Such changes have had a considerable effect on the balance between male and female, the personal and the public, domestic life and work which is at the heart of soaps and I am concerned to explore the effect of these new issues and particularly the way in which women's pleasures in their programmes might be put at risk.

This book therefore begins with an analysis of the way in which soaps organise their narratives and demonstrates the position of simultaneous engagement and distance which is offered to the audience. This is backed up by an examination of the asethetic experience of watching soaps. One of the confusing things for critics of soap operas is the way in which they mix genres and work with elements of melodrama, realism and light entertainment. What is a problem for the critics is a source of pleasure for the audience and the different ways in which various soaps mix their generic factors is important in understanding their differences in approaching the major themes with which this book is concerned. Chapters 3, 4 and 5 are centrally concerned with the appeal soaps make to women and in particular with their validation of women's role in the personal sphere. The basic staple of soaps is the difference between men and women, between the public and personal spheres, between work and home. The complexity with which this motif is worked across the families and communities of the various soaps shows that it is still a major preoccupation although how it is articulated depends on the particular combination of setting and character, specific to each programme. Chapter 6 suggests how soap operas might be placed in the broader context of other women's fiction such as the woman's film and the romance, and contrasts the utopian possibilities of these popular genres. The final chapters are devoted to an analysis of soaps' capacity to handle difference and change and examine the innovations which have been brought about by the soaps' search for new viewers beyond the traditional female audience. Once again, women are central to these shifts although, as will be seen, some of the changes seem to be at their expense.

Most recent work on soap operas has concentrated on studies of audience response either to a particular programme such as *Dallas* or in the context of television viewing more generally. Such work has been important in shifting discussion away from more abstract theories which neglected the role of the audience or implied that the text controlled the viewer's response. The conditions in which I write do not permit me to undertake such systematic work (although as the acknowledgements make clear I am very grateful to all the people with whom I have discussed these programmes) but, in any case, it seems important that in the urge to speak to 'real viewers' the pendulum should not swing so much the other way that textual work which is sensitive to the positions offered to the audience is no longer feasible. It seems important still that the patina of authenticity which glows over the statements produced by audience research does not mean that this method becomes the only way in which the products of popular culture can be discussed. David Morley's identification of the very firm gender stereotypes which appear to mark family viewing needs to be pushed further if we are to understand why soaps are so clearly associated with women's viewing.

Writing about soap opera is a perilous business. There is no fixed object of study over which the critic can pore, hoping to extract a further nuance; the readers of this book will not be able to flick back and study the precision of my examples or the aptness of my descriptions. During the writing of this book, Pamela left *Dallas* and Fallon, via a space ship, came back to *Dynasty*; Angie and Den left *EastEnders* and the factory in *Coronation Street* was demolished; *Crossroads* was killed off and *Dynasty* came to an abrupt halt with

Alexis and Dex suspended for ever in mid-air. Despite all this, I believe that it is possible to map out the general contours of the soap terrain and would ask the reader to check my propositions against whatever is currently going on in the soap world.

1

Soap Stories

'Not another death. I don't believe this place. There'll be none of you left by Christmas.'

Lisa Lancaster, *Crossroads*

'I like a good gossip. It gives you an interest in life.'

Ethel, *EastEnders*

Lisa Lancaster's somewhat callous remark on the high death rate in the British soap *Crossroads* during the autumn of 1987 was, at face value, a comment which was in character and offered an opinion on what was happening in the narrative. For regular viewers, however, who participated in the gossip network established around the programme in the popular press, it had other resonances. They knew that the show itself was going to be killed off the following Easter and that Lisa's apparently casual remark was a rather bitter joke on what was happening outside the fictional world of the Crossroads Motel. The audience was thus expected both to feel strongly about the deaths and departures that were occurring in the storylines and to understand the external reasons which caused them.

This close relationship between soaps and their audiences, the intimate knowledge regular viewers have of the programmes and their identification with particular characters, is still a source of puzzled dismay to those who do not watch soap operas. Concern is expressed that soaps are a substitute for 'real life', that viewers believe that the characters really exist and think that Albert Square and Southfork are something more than sets grown familiar through repeated viewing. Such criticisms are, as I hope to show, ill founded but they do at least hint at the crucial relationship which soaps have with their audiences. This chapter will explore the nature of that

9

relationship through an examination of the formal narrative strategies which work to create it. Other TV programmes may deal with the traditional subject matter of soaps – personal problems, family life, relationships within a community – but only soaps invite the audience both to enter intimately into a fictional world and to stand back and view with dispassion the formal conventions through which that world is constructed. This double action of engagement and distance is the subject of this chapter. By examining the way in which soaps construct their stories and in particular the manipulation of space, time and characterisation in them, we shall be better placed to understand the particular pleasures of soap viewing.

Soap narratives and time

The organisation of time is one of the key distinguishing features of soap story-telling and allows us to draw a distinction between soaps and the related formats of the series and the serial. The differences between a serial, a series and a soap opera have become blurred in recent years as the success of the soap format has encouraged series programmes like *Hill Street Blues* and *Cagney and Lacey* to incorporate strong elements of soap. Nevertheless, there is a distinct difference between these formats which hinges on how far the organisation of time dominates the organisation of the narrative itself.

A serial tells a complete story but spreads it over a number of episodes, often using the device of the cliffhanger to pick up from one episode to another. Serialisation in this way has an honourable tradition in which the novels of Wilkie Collins and Charles Dickens feature. It is the format of many TV programmes, particularly the adaptations of classic novels for which British television has a reputation, and the popular mini-series (somewhat misleadingly named since they are not in fact series but serials) in which best sellers such as *Roots* and *Lace* are presented in three or four consecutive evening viewings. Thus serials, like soaps, use a set of unresolved narrative puzzles to carry viewers across the time gap from one episode to another but the length of the fictional time which is deemed to have passed between episodes depends on the demands of the narrative: it may be a minute, a month, a year; it may be no time at all if the following episode returns to the moment of drama on which the preceding episode ended. In addition, serials differ from soaps in having a final ending which provides a resolution to the problems which have been set up at the beginning of the story. This ending clearly subordinates the organisation of time to the resolution of the narrative strands. The series format, on the other hand, is like the soap in that it offers the audience a set of characters and very often a place (the police station, the hospital) with which we become familiar. In the traditional series format, however, like *The Rockford Files* or *Minder*, the organisation of time is dominated by the demand that the main story be resolved in a single episode. The classic narrative strategy of a stable situation which is disrupted and then restored through characters' actions is thus worked through for the viewer in one viewing and, while sub-stories may run across episodes, the audience is presented with a satisfactory resolution to a particular problem every time the programme is shown. The series, thus, lacks that sense of endless but organised time which characterises soap operas and which shapes the way in which we respond to their narratives. In soaps, stories are never finally resolved and even soaps which cease to be made project themselves into a non-existent future. The final scene of *Crossroads*, when, after nearly 24 years, it came to an end in April 1988, showed Jill Chance with her new lover, John, driving away to seek another motel, another 'Crossroads'.

This lack of resolution is both an effect and a consequence of the sense of a future which is another mark of the difference between soaps and serials and the traditional series. *The Jewel in the Crown* and *Rich Man, Poor Man* may be long, complex serials but we expect that in the end the significance of what we are watching will be revealed and each strand tied into a resolution. This is not to say that the resolution will always be effectively accomplished or that the story's pressures will necessarily be contained by its ending. It is the expectation of resolution which is important here. Soap operas do not encourage such expectations and the longer they run the more impossible it seems to imagine them ending. Instead of narrative time being subordinate to the demands of the story, it dominates the narrative process and enables other formal structures to be brought into play. Time rather than action becomes the basis for organising the narrative. At its most classic, a soap opera would appear daily and its organisation of time would be based on the yesterday, today and tomorrow of the viewer. Prime time soaps are not so strict in their adherence to 'real' time as this model suggests. Nevertheless, unlike the serial, the time which elapses between episodes of a soap is not dependent on the organisation of the story (what happens next?) but on some sense of time passing in the programme which parallels the time which has passed for the viewer between episodes. Characteristically, such soaps are introduced by the announcer inviting us to 'drop in on the Square' or 'find out what's been happening in the Street' as if life has been going on there without us. In addition, the passage of time is marked by references to the 'real' world of the viewer. The time of the year and the passing of the seasons are faithfully reflected; in *EastEnders*, plastic daffodils are planted in the Square when filming takes place in early March to ensure that the flowers will be correctly in bloom in April when the episode is shown. The appropriate festivals are marked; Sheila Grant visits Rome at Easter for the Pope's blessing; summer holidays are discussed and taken in July and August; the families of *EastEnders* and *Coronation Street* eat Christmas lunch and watch the Queen's speech along with the rest of the population. Important events in the 'real' world may also be referred to although this is more of a risk since cancellation or rearrangement between the date the episode is completed and its transmission could be embarrassing. A royal wedding can usually be safely marked and there have been references to political activities such as elections; the participation of fictional characters in such national events increases the sense of a soap world which runs parallel with the world outside the programme.

The organisation of soap time in a way that seeks to reflect the viewers' experience of time in their own lives may seem to be more characteristic of British soaps than of US programmes such as *Dallas* and *Dynasty* but it is one of the purposes of this book to show that it is not necessary for each soap to display to the same degree all the characteristics which they share. In this case, as in others, it is possible to see differences between the various programmes in the soap spectrum. Not all soaps mark out the passage of time as clearly as, for instance, *EastEnders* and *Brookside*. Even among the British soaps, *Crossroads* is much less likely to measure the passage of days between episodes and clearly the US prime time soaps do not use the strategy at all consistenly. Nevertheless, I would argue that they do the minimum to ensure that they operate as soap operas and not as series. Although the US prime time soaps are organised in terms of a season of programmes rather than appearing regularly throughout the year like their British prime time equivalents, the cliff-hanging departures at the end of each season ensure that the audience is more concerned with continuance than resolution. There is never, for instance, a sense that a resolution is possible or imminent. Even apparent narrative closures such as a wedding or a death merely offer the opportunity for more problems to fuel the narrative and stories are not resolved, as they are in a series, in a single episode. The US prime time soaps do also acknowledge, in however limited a way, the passage of time as reflected in events both inside and outside the programmes. The regular Ewing barbecue and the Oil Barons' Ball help to create a calendar in the *Dallas* year, while JR's excursions into terrorism and the lobbying of Washington over the price of oil would be examples of references to the outside world, as would the gubernatorial elections in *Dynasty*. Thus, within the spectrum of soaps, the organisation of time follows the same pattern even if there are differences in the degree to which it is the dominant factor.

Soap narratives and space

The way in which soaps handle the passing of time has implications for their organisation of space and setting. Soaps can run (potentially) forever and their lack of resolution can make them aimless and repetitious. One way of handling the problem of repetition is to make it enjoyable, to give the audience a sense of familiarity with setting and characters so that to return to them is pleasurable. The establishment of narrative space so that viewers know in a detailed and intimate way the layout of the setting in which the stories take place is thus a crucial consequence of the soap opera's use of time. Repetition permits a familiar geography to be established through camera-work and cutting which allows the audience to build up a sense of the fictional space.[1] This sense of space is almost inevitable in programmes that run for years when for economic reasons, if for no other, the same sets must be used again and again. Robert Allen argues that in daytime US programmes: 'the world of the soap opera is represented spatially through the close-up and the two-shot, a strategy that has the effect of focusing viewer attention almost exclusively on facial expression and figure relationships respectively.'[2] The close-up, which allows emphasis on an individual's face, and the two-shot, which enables the viewer to see two characters in the same shot, are used frequently in prime time soaps but a third shot is also important – the establishing shot, often the first in a scene, which establishes the geography of the programme's fictional world. In *Dallas* and *Dynasty* the regular establishing shot of, for instance, Southfork or the Carrington mansion is crucial, not only in fixing the location of a scene but also for alerting the audience to what is likely to happen. In both *Dallas* and *Dynasty*, for instance, particular decors are associated with specific characters and activities so that space and setting take on a narrative function. The Southfork patio offers a setting for the outdoor breakfasts which often set up future actions in *Dallas* and the regular use of the mansion staircase in *Dynasty* as a setting for Blake and Krystle made its appropriation by Alexis, when she took over the house, the more scandalous. What tends to be missing in the US programmes, however, is a sense of the geographical relationship between these familiar domestic settings or of the space between the interiors which represent office and home.

Such a lack of integration is not inevitable in US prime time soaps. *Knots Landing* showed how a sense of the geography of the programme could be established through the aerial shots in the credits and through the use of the public spaces between the houses for narrative events. It may be, however, that such an integration of space is more difficult when it is the public and the private, office and home which have to be linked. *Crossroads*, which paralleled the public work of the motel with the personal lives of its staff, had the least well-established space of the British soaps. Although the spatial link between the motel bar and the reception, for instance, was clearly elaborated, the position of the motel in relation to Jill's home or Di's cottage was much less clear. At the other extreme, the opening credits of the British soap *Brookside* clearly invite us into a geographical space, Liverpool with its cathedrals and municipal buildings, and then, in a series of shots, directs us to Brookside Close, the heart of the drama, clearly established by the street nameplate. Aerial shots give us access to the layout of the Close, the positioning of the houses and the relationship between the neighbours, and throughout the programme conversations and actions take place in the communal space between the houses. Similar care for geographical space is apparent in *EastEnders* and *Corononation Street*, where again the outdoor spaces of the streets provide an arena for narrative action as well as a link between characters' homes. The establishment of such space is in part a realist strategy for British soaps with implications which will be discussed in Chapter 2 but it is also critical in establishing the fictional world which the viewer is invited to enter.

Soap narrative and characters

The endlessness of soap time and the familiarity of its space has its effect on the construction of its characters. One of soap's most striking qualities is the way in which the audience becomes familiar with the history of certain characters and has access to knowledge which is well beyond that given in a particular episode. The audience may be aware for instance of traumatic events in a character's past which affect how they are currently behaving and can ascribe reasons for behaviour beyond that of dramatic necessity or the demands of plotting. Such awareness is based not only on knowledge of key events – that a woman has in the past lost a child or been married to a cruel husband – but also an understanding of the way in which a particular character fits in to the network of relationships which make up a soap. It is easy to underestimate the pleasure of predictability but very often the repetition of plots, so tedious to the casual viewer, is part of a pattern based on the well-established character traits of particular individuals. To see Cliff Barnes embark on yet another ill-fated attempt to foil JR, or Angie in *EastEnders* begin another emotional and fraught battle with her husband, Den, is to set off on a roller coaster whose ups and downs are reassuringly predictable because the viewer has been gaining knowledge of them for years. Familiarity with the characters allows the viewer to bring meaning to the narrative rather than having to rely on what is shown in a particular episode. It is the viewer who brings richness and density to material which on the surface can look thin and unrewarding.

If the presence of well-established characters leads soaps to value familiarity and predictability, the audience is also invited to relish change and disruption. The familiar world which soaps work so hard to establish is disrupted by new characters and changing story lines. What happens may be predictable but the interest lies in the many variations on how it will happen. A soap's endless future means that an ultimate conclusion can never be reached and soaps are thus based on a premise of continuous disruption. The stability of a conclusion is always threatened by the next event, the marriage by divorce, the unified family by the children's departure, the community celebration by quarrels and disharmony. Various formal factors contribute to this sense of the possibility of change. New characters are introduced on a short-term basis to feature in a particular story; long-term characters leave and their tracks have to be suitably covered. In US prime time soaps, an actor is replaced and the character is reworked to accommodate a new face. On both sides of the Atlantic, well-established characters change as the soap develops and the audience is offered a different perspective on them. Thus, in *Brookside* the treatment of Bobby Grant and his stubborn insistence on his role as head of the family became more critical and harsh and in *Dallas* Sue Ellen changed dramatically from an out-of-control drunk to a high-powered executive. Some of the most moving moments in soaps come when a regular acts out of character – JR remorseful, at least for a moment, at Sue Ellen's bedside or Mavis, in *Coronation Street*, summoning up dignity and courage to stand up, for once, for her rights. Such moments are brief but offer the regular viewer a different facet to a familiar character which can be drawn on in future episodes.

These moments of change and disruption are made possible by the interweaving story lines in which lacunae in plotting or characterisation conveniently go unnoticed. The British soaps traditionally run two or three stories together, sometimes linked by a common theme or counterpointing a serious story with a more comic one. These interleaving stories make it appear quite natural for characters to come and go, for regulars to disappear for a while and return, for new light to be shed on familiar characters. Even in US prime time soaps, where the dynamic of the narrative is more unified, the complexity of the overall narrative means stories can run parallel with each other. Thus Pam's search for her mother clearly had links with other stories in *Dallas* but was treated largely as a series of events which were separate from other elements in the overall plot. Such flexibility allows soaps to extend their range of stories, establish new characters and provide the audience with change and variety without losing the stability provided by the setting.

This ability to handle both repetition and disruption, familiarity and change is important in establishing the audience's relationship with a soap narrative and its characters. Soaps can survive major changes because the audience's commitment is engaged across a range of characters and stories and not dependent on one or two individuals. The importance of key characters, such as JR in *Dallas*, Den and Angie in *EastEnders* and Meg in *Crossroads*, can be overestimated. Certainly, as Dorothy Hobson has pointed out, the departure of a well-established character such as Meg Mortimer, the matriarch of *Crossroads*, arouses strong feelings in an audience for whom the change is just too disruptive.[3] Nevertheless, *Crossroads* did survive the departure of a major character and Angie's disappearance from *EastEnders* offered the possibility of new stories for her husband and daughter. Pamela Ewing's departure from *Dallas* meant that Bobby's relationship with Southfork was strengthened and also allowed his character to be available for new romantic encounters. The organisation of space, time and character means that the audience is engaged with the programme as a whole, with its overall narrative and its established space; it is no accident that the titles of soaps refer to a geographical area or group of people (*EastEnders, Dallas, Dynasty, Coronation Street*) rather than one or two individuals :*Kojak, Cagney and Lacey, Bergerac*). While the viewer's engagement with particular characters is clearly important, it is perhaps more diffuse than is usually recognised. Identification is decentred; it is invited across a range of characters not with a particular central figure. It is thus possible for regular viewers to be torn between two characters, to endorse the position of some characters but not others and indeed to find some tedious as well as dislikeable.[4]

One striking consequence of the decentred identification offered by soaps is the range of women characters in the programmes, occupying different social positions and having a variety of functions in the narrative. In mapping out character types in *Coronation Street*, for instance, Marion Jordan identified a range of positions held by women in the programme including grandmother types, married women and 'marriageable women', breaking down the latter into 'mature, sexy women', 'spinsterly types' and young women.[5] In each category, she was able to place up to four characters suggesting that the viewer is offered a number of variations within each position. Similarly, *EastEnders* was careful to establish from the start a range of women characters from the grandmother, Lou Beale, to the schoolgirls, Michelle and Sharon. More frequently than other TV genres, soaps feature women characters normally excluded by their age, appearance or status. Thus, *EastEnders* offers a remarkable number of elderly women (Mo, Dot, Ethel, Marge) or middle-aged women (Pauline, Hannah, Kathy, Pat), together with a high proportion of women characters who are living on their own or without a male partner. The other British soaps, *Crossroads* and *Coronation Street* in particular, are similarly careful to present a wide spectrum of female characters.

It cannot be said that the US prime time soaps provide the same range of women characters although their number is still striking. The emphasis on middle-aged women is worth noting and the attention given to their stories rather than to those of younger girls is comparable to the British soaps. The US prime time soaps also share with their British counterparts an unusually high number of narrative positions undertaken by women characters. Thus *Dynasty* offers Alexis as the active, scheming manipulator and Krystle as the passive moral arbiter, with a number of other women – Sammy Jo, Amanda, Kirby, Fallon – negotiating between the two poles. Similarly, *Dallas* has Miss Ellie as the moral centre while around her are placed a range of women who occupy different family positions (wife, mother, daughter), different work roles (executive, secretary, shop owner) and who have a variety of narrative functions, frequently initiating action as well as suffering from the actions of others. The role of these women characters will be discussed more fully in later chapters but for the moment it is important to note that the range of characters allows the audience a whole set of possible identifications which are not mutually exclusive. A viewer who is a wife, daughter, mother, may find herself engaged with three different characters who are caught up in those positions. More generally, rather than following the narrative action of a single hero as in most series, the viewer is able to identify with Alexis *and* Krystle, with Sue Ellen as JR's victim *and* Pam as his opponent. It is this multiple identification with a number of characters which is a strong element in a soap's ability to engage us so powerfully.

The formal pleasures of soaps

This capacity to engage the audience tends to be associated with a belief that the audience cannot distinguish between fact and fiction, a view which is reinforced by stories of viewers sending Hilda Ogden a new mac or applying for jobs at the Crossroads Motel. The ability of the audience to distance itself from the programmes, to step back and comment on how the fiction is created, receives less attention. Any consideration of the audience's relationship with soaps must, however, note how the programmes play with their own conventions and narrative devices in a way that parodies and comments on the fictional nature of the world they present.

Such attention to form is recognised as an important element in high culture and an awareness of conventions is understood to be part of the pleasure taken in a work of art. The reader is invited to appreciate the rhythmic patterning in a poem or the intertwining of theme and symbol in a novel, to understand the form as well as the content. In film theory in the 1970s, it was argued that the practice of drawing attention to form could be given a political edge as one of the ways of challenging the notion that cinema is a 'window on the world' which enables the audience to see reality more clearly as the narrative unfolds to its conclusion, the moment which reveals the truth. Independent film-makers of this period, working with such theoretical models, sought to set up a different relationship with the audience, one which emphasised defamiliarisation and the interrogation of issues rather than identification and the satisfaction of a conclusion.[6] Perhaps because of this history, theoretical debates about the formal qualities of soaps have tended to concentrate on how far their formal overtness made them, at least potentially, more progressive than other TV formats. As Jane Feuer puts it, 'serial form and multiple plot structure appear to give TV melodrama a greater potential for multiple and aberrant readings than do other forms of popular narrative. Since no action is irreversible, every ideological position may be countered by its opposite,' although she goes on to warn that 'the "openness" of TV texts does not in and of itself represent a salutary or progressive stance.'[7] Tania Modleski also argues polemically that 'soap opera may be in the vanguard not just of TV art but of all narrative art'[8] but, as we shall see in chapter 3, she tends to work with the notion that the audience is largely unaware of the processes of soap opera narrative, which somewhat undermines the more radical possibilities she sees in such an argument.

If we are to understand the relationship between soaps and their audience, we need to look more closely at the viewer's quite conscious participation in the processes of soap fiction. This participation is achieved in a number of ways. The conventions of establishing space, time and character, for instance, become so familiar that they are recognisable to soap audiences as formal strategies. The gap between episodes brings the audience up against its own inability to control the telling of the story and draws attention to its fictional construction; the establishment of the truth, the aim of most narratives, is, in soaps, subject to conventions which quite overtly postpone resolution, making us aware that fiction is not the inevitable and uninterrupted revelation of the truth. The audience learns to be aware of the rhythms of the narrative. The device of interweaving stories draws attention to the processes of narration, disrupting the cause and effect chain of one story with parallel scenes from another. The viewer knows that a character who has featured strongly in a story over a number of episodes will take a back seat for a while and that new characters who may appear to be taking on a prominent part are likely to have a fairly limited life in the programme. This familiarity with the conventions means that the soap audience has the ability to recognise the way in which the soap narrative is constructed and is able to enter into the play of that process by predicting future events through a reading of internal conventions.

The other way in which viewers recognise the conventions of soaps is the readiness with which they can be stretched, parodied and broken. Death in the US soaps generally has long been recognised as being by no means irretrievable. A US poll on 'Who shot JR?' revealed strong support for Sue Ellen's lover Dusty who was, at the time, dead though his resurrection was later effected. This possibility of returning from the dead was parodied in the appearance in later episodes of Wes Palmer, claiming to be Jock Ewing. The plausibility of his claim had little to do with lie detector tests and his knowledge

of the Ewing past and much more to do with the audience's acceptance that, in defiance of realist conventions, US prime time soaps
had adopted their own narrative premise that death, certainly one
without a body, is not final. Bobby's reappearance parodied even
this since he had 'died' on screen and his absence had had considerable consequences including a new husband for Pam. The retrosepc-
tive dream which suddenly rendered a whole season of narrative
action 'inoperative' could be seen as cheating by the engaged audience which had wept at Bobby's death. It is better seen as a
recognition that, in soap opera, conventions can be stretched to
breaking point precisely because they are understood to be conventions and that it is part of the fun for the audience to see how the
programme can get out of the narrative web it has woven for itself
and the viewer.

British soaps, because of their greater dependence on realism, are
less daring in displaying their own fictionality. Nevertheless, they do
break their own conventions, often in the interests of increased
drama, and in doing so draw the viewer's attention to that disruption. Both *Coronation Street* and *Brookside*, for instance, have
abandoned the usual organisation of time in soaps by allowing the
actions of the story, in exceptional circumstances, to dictate the
passage of fictional time. In *Coronation Street* the crash of a lorry in
the Street and in *Brookside* the siege in the Close were shown in
considerable detail over a number of episodes and the convention
that time continues to pass unrecorded between each episode was
broken. Similarly, the British soaps have occasionally chosen to
devote a single episode to one story rather than follow the characteristic device of interweaving stories. Thus *Brookside* devoted a whole
episode to a scene set in a working men's club in which Bobby Grant
and his workmates discussed their future, the possibility of redundancy, the effectiveness of trade unions and the morality of moving
away from their roots. *EastEnders*, similarly, gave its audience what
was perceived as a *tour de force* when a half-hour episode was
entirely devoted to Den and Angie, arguing, fighting and weeping
over their marriage. Only the occasional appearance of the window
cleaner, vainly eavesdropping as the couple moved from room to
room around the pub, gave any relief from the single story and in
some sense replicated the viewer's own voyeuristic relish. In both
cases, the concentration on a single story drew the viewer into the
drama and potentially forced an emotional engagement with the
positions being so dramatically taken up. At the same time, the
deliberate avoidance of the normal narrative construction was striking and drew attention to qualities of setting, acting style and

rhetoric which themselves betoken performance and the creation of a fictional world. It is this double vision, this combination of enagement and distance, which is so characteristic of soap opera's relationship with its audience.

If the regular viewer builds up a knowledge of the internal mechanisms of soaps, s/he also has access to a vast range of knowledge of the external pressures on soap stories. Jean-Luc Godard began *Tout Va Bien* with credits featuring the cheques paid to all those involved. The keen soap opera viewer can have this information and much more and is actively aware of how the story line has been constructed around such material factors. The reader of the popular press and/or women's magazines is provided with details of future stories, facts about actors' contracts and their financial and emotional situations with the added complication that the reader must know how to interpret the popular press which has its own priorities and standards of accuracy. Rows on the set, the desire of a leading character to leave, the death of an actor are all fed into the fictional world of the soap and become part of how its narrative is understood. Patrick Duffy's departure from *Dallas*, for example, became an exercise in narrative logistics as the viewers speculated on how his well-publicised death was to be effected. On a broader level, when *Dallas* and *Dynasty* were dropping in the ratings, viewers knew in advance of the changes in story line and cast which it was hoped would improve the statistics. Similarly, it became impossible to understand the stories in *Coronation Street* in the mid-eighties without some knowledge of the deaths and departures of the programme's actors, since it was clear that the story lines were having to be constructed around such events. However much a viewer was engaged with the stories of the fictional Elsie Tanner, for instance, s/he was simultaneously aware of the desire of the actress, Pat Phoenix, to leave the show and the need for the narrative to enable that to happen.

The double process of emotional engagement with a soap and acute awareness of the devices of its narrative process can be seen clearly in press interviews with soap actors. Much is made of the interest the press takes in soap characters, in terms both of the actors themselves and the characters they play. Certainly, the interest in soaps is sustained by a seemingly endless supply of articles which promise revelations either about future story lines or more frequently about the characters. In fact, the press is merely replicating, rather more crudely, what the soap audience has consistently enjoyed – participation in the soaps' narrative. The basis for such press interviews is often the exploration of the similarities and differences between the actor and the character but it is a task which breaks down in confusion since soaps' narrative strategy is to play with, though never entirely blur, these boundaries. One example from a wealth of such material gives an indication of how such pieces work.

Readers of *Woman's Own* in January 1987 are lured with the headline 'Why I've got to leave Dirty Den', to find beneath it an article based on an interview with Jane How who played Den's mistress, Jan, in *EastEnders*.[9] Since Den was divorcing his wife to be with Jan, the headline appears to deliver a surprising revelation although it merely confirms what regular viewers will have already deduced. As it turns out, Jane How the actress does not know how the story is going to develop around the character she plays – 'I really *don't* know what is going to happen.' What she does know is that her contract is due to expire and, as the magazine puts it, 'one thing is for sure; come April when her contract expires, Jan won't be there to nurse Den through the day-to-day traumas of life in Albert Square.' The article goes on to compare what Jane and Jan have in common – a middle-class background, emotional warmth and sympathy – with their differences – Jane is married with a child while Jan lives on her own. The actress distances herself from the part – 'I couldn't imagine living Jan's life, not staying with a married man that long' – but at the same time claims authentic knowledge of the character – 'There's one thing I can tell you though, she really does love him.'

The division in the piece between the presentation of the actress speaking both for herself and on behalf of her character is typical of the writing on soap opera in the press. In exploring the gap between them, the article maintains the fiction of the character, Jan, trying to sort out her own life and priorities in the face of Den's unreliability and her own needs. The one hard fact we glean is that Jane How's contract is to end and that therefore change is on the way. The viewer is able to link that fact with internal evidence from the programme in which Jan has been shown to be uneasy with Den's East End, working-class lifestyle.

Material like this is cited as evidence of the audience's inability to distinguish fact from fiction, a failing to recognise that the characters in soaps are not real. I would argue that far from confusing the audience, such material picks up and expands on the activity in which the viewer is already engaged – an informed speculation based on 'evidence' from inside and outside the programme. When writing about *Coronation Street*, I described this process as a 'delicate balancing act of discussing characters as if they were real people with histories, motivations and futures while at the same time recognising the formal conventions of the serial in which they appear'.[10] The importance of this balancing act and the pleasure that it gives has been recognised elsewhere. Robert Allen, in his book on US daytime soaps, argues that 'to a greater extent perhaps than any other fiction, the soap opera text constantly walks the line between one that can be read as fiction and one that spills over into the experiential world of the viewer.'[11] We shall examine further in chapter 3 the implications of the audience's involvement with the characters' dilemmas and the nature of the spill-over into the 'experiential world of the viewer'. For the moment it is important to recognise that this tightrope walking is not just a matter of an audience wanting to think of *Coronation Street* or *Dynasty* as real but being forced every now and then into acknowledging that it is not. The narrative strategies described in this chapter simultaneously engage and distance the viewer; they allow us to be caught up in, for instance, the drama of Den, Angie and Jan while at the same time to be fully aware of the external factors (the end of a contract) which effect the fictional outcome. Conversations about *Dynasty* will be concerned with how Blake is to rescue himself from Alexis's machinations while at the same time commenting on Joan Collins's performance and her latest costume. In a similar way, the familiar practice of filling a friend in on last night's episode is likely to encompass a description of both what happened and how it was done. The pleasures of telling, rehearsing and predicting the mechanisms of narrative are very much part of soap opera's attraction.

The double process involved here can be underestimated. On the one hand, John Ellis has characterised TV viewing as 'typically a casual experience rather than an intensive one'[12] and argues that 'the isolation of the viewer implies a lack of involvement in the event portrayed.'[13] On the other hand, Tania Modleski, in her work on US daytime soaps, describes the viewer as 'constituted as a sort of ideal mother' of whom tolerance and sympathy are continually demanded;[14] 'the spectator/mother, identifying with each character in turn, is made to see "the larger picture" and to extend her sympathy to both the sinner and victim.'[15] In considering soaps at least. Ellis seems to underestimate the way in which narrative works to encourage identification and engagement but by contrast Modleski's rather helpless and bemused viewer seems to miss out on the more positive pleasures of enjoying fiction. The distance, created by knowledge of the soap and its clearly marked conventions, does lend enchantment to the view. The viewer understands that these are not her children and is therefore freed to speculate and gossip about the characters, knowing they are not her responsibility. The narrative work of soaps is to create that double vision, that oscillation between engagement and distance, which enables us to be both a concerned follower and an outside observer and which makes discussion of a soap almost as pleasurable as watching the programme itself.

2

The Aesthetic Experience

'I see you've taken my advice on dressing for success; red is a very good colour."

Alexis to Lesley, *Dynasty*

'It's not just you that finds marriage difficult. It's everybody.'

Rita to Brian Tilsley, *Coronation Street*

'She's a real Cockney.'

Dagmar yuppies to Angie, *EastEnders*

'Aesthetic' is not a word which readily springs to mind when thinking about soaps, nor is it much used in recent critical work on film and television. Hesitation about its use perhaps stems from an understandable desire to get away from the value judgements which have so blocked understanding of cultural works and have dismissed much popular culture as unworthy of sustained analysis. The notion that aesthetic qualities provide a source of pleasure in soap operas may seem unlikely but much of the criticism of soaps in this respect is based on a misunderstanding of the mixed nature of the soap genre. Just as the narrative organisation of soaps serves simultaneously to engage and distance the soap audience so the aesthetics of soaps work both to draw us into the programme and to permit us to stand back and comment on the effects. This chapter argues that soaps are not dominated by one aesthetic tradition but offer a range of experiences based on the different and sometimes competing values of light entertainment, melodrama and realism. It is only when the implications of this generic knot are untangled that it becomes possible to understand the nature of the aesthetic experience which soaps offer.

It is often assumed that soap opera aesthetics are entirely determined by financial considerations and the economic pressure under which soaps are made clearly does affect the way they look. Their *raison d'être* is, after all, to provide cheap and popular material for the television companies. Dorothy Hobson provides an absorbing account, in her book on *Crossroads*, of the strains of working on a low budget to produce a programme which is critically despised. '*Crossroads* is a very low-budget production,' she argues, 'and this is perhaps the over-riding factor in the final look and quality of the programme.'[1] The effects of this come through graphically in the words of an anonymous contributor who had worked on the programme:

> You get profound tackiness . . . I mean lines badly played because there isn't time to rehearse them, I mean shots not really well executed with bad lighting because there isn't time to relight and so on . . . It's outrageously bad, it's appalling, it's an insult to anyone who watches it, because the script is so dreadful.[2]

Compared with *Crossroads*, the other British soaps I am discussing operate with (slightly) less punishing schedules of two episodes a week (although, in autumn 1989, *Coronation Street* began to appear three times a week and *Brookside* started to do so in 1990); they receive more respect and care from their production companies but money is clearly limited. At the other end of the market, the US prime time soaps have the appearance of costing more money than their daytime equivalents but they still provide cheap drama for British TV companies. This is partly explained by their extensive export market (which enables costs to be spread over a larger number of buyers) but the marks of economy in the making of the programmes can be seen particularly in the limited number of sets and the constantly repeated camera positions. But the aesthetic experience of soaps cannot simply be explained by the economic constraints placed on them nor is it a question of watching soaps only for the story and trying to ignore the allegedly inadequate trappings. If we examine the programmes carefully we can see how soaps have drawn on different traditions to develop an aesthetic which offers pleasures within and perhaps despite the limits of economic restraints.

Light entertainment

Richard Dyer, in his book *Light Entertainment*, looks at the pleasures and values of a particular kind of television programme – the
variety show programmes 'akin to show-business, cabaret and musical comedy'.[3] Clearly, the light entertainment programmes he analyses, with their use of a host performer and guest artists, a series of
acts and frequently a live audience, are very different from soaps and
their traditions in music hall and variety led to a mode of direct
audience address which is not used in the narrative framework which
constrains soaps. Nevertheless, part of the appeal of soaps is the way
in which they use the values of light entertainment, sometimes so
excessively that they challenge the dominance of the narrative. In
outlining the values of light entertainment, Dyer looks at what he
calls the 'aesthetics of escape'; he describes the mechanism of
obliteration which offers, as a substitute for the experience of
reality, 'a world which is totally other than the real world, a completely fabricated, artificial separate reality. This is in itself so fascinat-
ing, so entrancing that the real world slips from consciousness.'[4] He
argues that the light entertainment aesthetic values colour, shape
and music over realistic representation and that, if ever totally
realised, obliteration would lead to total abstraction. In light entertainment programmes on television, however, these values are expressed not through abstraction but through a tendency to subordinate everything to spectacle; 'the basic principle [is] . . . the subordination of everything to the effect of quantity, expenditure, lavishness, extravagance, to "conspicuous consumption."'[5]

Although Dyer, in his monograh, is referring to a different form of
television entertainment, it is striking how readily such terms are
applied, often in a derogatory manner, to certain soaps. If soaps, as I
have argued, offer a range of styles, then US prime time soaps are at
the furthest end of the spectrum so far as light entertainment values
are concerned. Within the limits of the narrative (a constraint which
has much less effect in the variety show programmes to which Dyer
refers), soaps like *Dallas* and *Dynasty* relish the spectacle so that it
becomes the object of comment, separate from the workings of the
plot. The pleasure in lavishness and extravagance leads to an emphasis on glamour which underpins the use of locations and the
presentation of the stars. *Dynasty*, for instance, makes use of exotic
locations such as Hong Kong and while the spectacle is limited by the
constraints of a TV budget, the shots of scenery and the city,

together with the use of luxurious hotel rooms, enormous offices and expensive shops, offer the audience a deliberately artificial world. Great emphasis is placed on the Carrington mansion with its imposing staircase, elaborately furnished rooms and luxuriant grounds. The milieu appears to be a parody of the myth of English country living with its servants, its cholesteral-laden breakfasts, its riding stables and formal gardens. *Dallas*, although deliberately more down-market, still rates a swimming pool, servants, candlesticks on the table and extensive land and, significantly, when its ratings were falling it looked to more spectacular locations in Europe and the USSR to redeem its position.

In both cases, the settings provide an exotic backdrop for the characters themselves who are the main source of the spectacle of conspicuous consumption. It is on the women, in particular, that this spectacle is focused. They provide that slightly out-of-date glamour which is the hallmark of the programmes which Dyer described. There is always a sense of excess about their clothes because the decorative emphasis is so strong that their functional purpose is dangerously neglected. Their dresses are deliberately stylised and uncomfortable, the colours garish, the glitter out of place. They teeter on their high heels, the hair falling over the eyes as their walk is restricted by tight skirts. Tears do not affect the eye shadow, the lip gloss gleams through a passionate denunciation, a true flush never ruins the effect of the carefully applied blusher. This is particularly true of Alexis in *Dynasty*. The dress in which she conducts an emotional scene is almost as important as the dramatic implications of the scene for the narrative. This emphasis on make-up and dress gives women viewers the licence to look on the female stars of soaps as model objects of desire but the style presented to us is not simply to be admired. The women of US prime time soaps look and dress like light entertainment stars – Carol Channing, Shirley Bassey – even when down on the ranch and their excess pushes the programmes towards a parody of their own glamorous expectations. The clothes and hairstyles are to be mocked by the female viewer as well as envied. Who would really want to look quite like that – and yet who would not?

This emphasis on style as excessive to the narrative and as a source of pleasure in itself has played an important part in making stars of the characters/actors. Outside the programme, the tendency to parody is more likely to be lost and the discourse of consumerism becomes the more dominant. Selling the by-products of soap beauty is a serious business. Linda Evans, Victoria Principal and Joan Collins have traded in glamour and their appearance in the programmes is backed up by a whole range of endorsed products – perfume, workout tapes, books of beauty advice, health tips in magazines – which extend the conspicuous consumption out into the audience.

If light entertainment aesthetics can be most clearly demonstrated in the US prime time soaps, British soaps also have their elements of spectacle. Setting is not so important here and glamour is even more closely associated in the British programmes with certain women characters. This element can be seen most strongly in *Coronation Street* which has had a strong tradition of glamorous middle-aged women exemplified in the characters of Elsie Tanner, Rita Fairclough and Bet Lynch. Elsie began as a rather run-down and harassed mother but developed over the years her own style which aspired to a glamorous ideal well beyond *Coronation Street*. Unlike her US counterparts, Elsie's mascara did run but her bouffant hair-dos, stylish dresses and curvaceous figure referred back to a pre-sixties notion of glamour associated with stars such as Diana Dors. Other characters, such as Rita Fairclough who, appropriately in terms of the light entertainment analogy, was once a night club singer, followed this model, while the barmaid, Bet Lynch, took it to extremes of parody with the excesses of her hairstyles, earrings and tightly belted waist being subject to the same kind of comments as Alexis's ballgowns. Certain women in other British soaps carry the same kind of glamorous connotations – Angie, the publican's wife in *EastEnders*, was almost theatrically made up, while Nicola in *Crossroads* was specifically presented as the British version of the US female stars with her impeccable make-up and clothes which purport to be businesslike but which verge on the extravagant.

Melodrama

The values of light entertainment do not, however, go unchallenged in the soap aesthetic. While the glamour of light entertainment encourages the audience to sit back and relish the spectacle, the emotional drama of soaps also demands an aesthetic which will draw the audience in and establish the characters not only as objects of spectacle but as our emotional representatives. In understanding this phemonenon, we need to look at the way in which the elements of *mise en scène*, decor and performance operate in a melodramatic mode to engage the audience.

Critical theory on the aesthetics of TV melodrama is still not as developed as that on film melodrama and it is not possible simply to transpose debates within film study into the TV arena. Work on

Hollywood melodramas of the 1950s, for instance, argued that the aesthetic forms of expression stood in for or marked through formal excesses explosive emotional issues which could not be directly addressed in the narrative. Thomas Elsaesser comments on 'a sublimation of dramatic conflict into decor, colour, gesture and composition of frame, which in the best melodramas is perfectly thematised in terms of the characters' emotional and psychological predicaments'.[6] Picking up this notion of sublimation and using the analogy of Freud's definition of conversion hysteria, Geoffrey Nowell-Smith states that 'in the melodrama, where there is always material which cannot be expressed in discourse or in the actions of the characters furthering the designs of the plot, a conversion can take place into the body of the text,' into the *mise en scène* and performances.[7] Such analogies allowed fifties family melodramas to be read (and enjoyed) as critiques of US society and the bourgeois family, although it is unclear, as Christine Gledhill has commented, how far such 'radical readings' belonged only to the seventies critics rather than the fifties audiences.[8]

Looking at television melodrama, on the other hand, Jane Feuer has argued that this relationship in film melodramas between visual excess and the potentially subversive expression through visual signs of what is taboo in the narrative is much less evident on television. She goes on to describe how the melodramatic aesthetic in programmes like *Dallas* and *Dynasty* works *with* the narrative, rather than offering a critique of it, commenting that 'for *Dallas* and *Dynasty*, *mise en scène* would appear to function for the most part expressively'.[9] Far from undermining the logic of the narrative, various aesthetic devices underline and clarify it. Feuer thus points to the way that 'acting, editing, musical underscoring and the use of the zoom lens frequently conspire to create scenes of high (melo)drama.'[10] In this description, we can begin to see how the visual characteristics of US and British soaps – the close-ups of faces, of important objects, the deliberate movement of a character across a room, the lingering of the camera on a face at the end of a scene, the exchange of meaningful glances – work to make every gesture and action seem highly coded and significant, marking out emotional relationships and enabling the audience to understand the significance of every action. This is particularly important given the complicated nature of the stories being told. Soap narratives, like those of film melodramas, are marked by what Steve Neale has described as 'chance happenings, coincidences, missed meetings, sudden conversions, last-minute rescues and revelations, *deus ex machina* endings'.[11] These kind of stories can be seen in the whole range of TV soaps, *EastEnders* as well as *Dallas*, but Neale takes us further by commenting on the effect of such dramatic organisation. The 'course of events,' he argues, 'is unmotivated (or undermotivated) from a realist point of view, such preparation and motivation as does exist is always "insufficient." There is an *excess* of effect over cause, of the extraordinary over the ordinary.'[12]

It is this excess of meaning over motivation which lies at the heart of soaps' adoption of the melodramatic aesthetic as a way of drawing the audience into the programmes. On first examination, it would seem that TV soaps leave the audience too little work to do. They lack the satisfying sense of achievement of working out the ramifications of *Tinker Tailor Soldier Spy* or even *Miami Vice*. If the *mise en scène* is over-expressive, if the acting gives us signposts to the meaning and if (in the US prime time soaps at least) music underlines it even for the slowest viewer, what is there left for members of the audience to do? It is this sense that soaps are too easy to understand, predictable and facile, which is the source of many a critic's dissatisfaction. And yet Neale's analysis indicates that there is a space for the reader at key moments to provide an explanation for the excesses of the melodramatic aesthetics which are inadequately explained by the cause and effect process of the narrative. What is the reason for the welling up of music, the exchange of glances, the slamming of a door? Such spaces are most characteristically signalled by a close-up on a character after a dramatic confrontation – on Sue Ellen, drunkenly starting at JR, on Angie Watts looking unblinkingly into the camera as Den stalks away, on Sheila Grant, hunched in the corner of the sofa as her son Barry leaves once more. All these moments have narrative explanations but their intensity is more than the events of a particular episode warrant. They have to be filled in by the audience, those blank faces given a reason through the viewer's knowledge of the programme's past and a recreation of the feelings which the character must therefore be experiencing. It is this identification with heightened emotion through the filling of the space created by the excessive expressiveness of the *mise en scène* and performance which is the most important element in TV soap opera's melodramatic aesthetic. It enables the most unlikely characters to take on a representative role for the viewer – 'It's everybody' – and dramatically engages those who only a moment before may have been detachedly commenting on Joan Collins's latest dress.

Realism

If light entertainment and melodrama are important components in TV soaps, the British programmes are strongly marked by another element – that of realism. There is not space for a detailed discussion of this troubled term which has a host of definitions and has generated a specific history of its own in debates central to the history of film theory. And yet some discussion of realism is essential if only because it crops up so regularly as a criterion for British soaps and as a reason for their popularity. As Julia Smith, the original producer of *EastEnders*, remarked on a TV phone-in celebrating its second anniversary, 'We don't make life, we reflect it' and a number of the viewers ringing in congratulated her on the programme's accuracy.[13] It is this notion of realism as a plausible picture of everyday experience and its use as a justification in itself for what happens in the soap which requires some examination here.

The seemingly straightforward comment that *EastEnders* reflects life is actually somewhat disingenuous given that it was made in the context of complaints about excessive violence and sexual frankness in the programme. It avoids the question of whose reality is being invoked in justification, whose life is being reflected. It hides also complex relations between what is understood to be reality and its representation and the nature of the choices made by the producer as to what is appropriate to take on in a programme which is very popular with a young audience.[14] The comment similarly refuses to acknowledge the importance of conventions in forming our understanding of what constitutes realism and the way in which, as John Hill puts it,

> No work can ever simply reveal reality. Realism, no less than any other type of art, depends on conventions, conventions which . . . have successfully achieved the status of being accepted as 'realistic.' It is this 'conventionality' of realism which also makes its usage so vulnerable to change, for as the conventions change (either in reaction to previously established conventions or in accordance with new perceptions of what constitutes reality) so too does our sense of what then constitutes realism.[15]

The realist-documentary approach to film-making has long been recognised as crucial to British cinema, going back to the late twenties and thirties. The fact that such an interpretation of British cinema underestimated or repressed the existence of less respectable work (such as the romantic/gothic strains of the Gainsborough and Hammer studios) illustrates the hold that the realist tradition has had and the way in which its values came to be an apparently natural mark of quality and seriousness in British cinema. Realism, in this context, meant not only an attention to verisimilitude and plausible motivation but also a value placed on the representation of working-class life and an exploration of the problems caused by social change. The strong aesthetic hold of realism in British cinema transferred to television and as Andrew Higson has commented 'each successive realist movement in British cinema and television has been celebrated both for its commitment to the exploration of contemporary social problems, and for its working out of those problems in relation to "realistic" landscapes and characters.'[16] In television, a climate developed in which the most praised and the most controversial programmes were firmly in this realist tradition – the series of single 'Plays for Today', drama-documentaries like *Law and Order*, fly-on-the-wall series such as Roger Graef's *Police* – powerful material and controversial precisely because of arguments about how accurately they did represent reality. If such programmes have got fewer in recent years, in a political and social climate that has changed considerably, the value placed on 'things as they really are'[17] still remains a strong strand in British critical perceptions.

British soap operas offer a particularly good example of the reworking of the realist aesthetic and of the way in which conventions change and develop in reaction to what has gone before. The first episode of *Coronation Street* was shown in 1960 and Richard Dyer has pointed to its emergence at a particular moment in British cultural history which is exemplified by the publication and popularity of Richard Hoggart's *The Uses of Literacy*. Dyer comments on Hoggart's emphasis on the specificity of working-class culture and the importance he attaches to notions of home and community and women's role in maintaining them; within that culture and community, particular attention is paid in *The Uses of Literacy* to ' "the common sense" of "everyday life" for the working class'.[18] Dyer suggests that *Coronation Street* also 'takes as its mode the interactions of everyday life as realised in common-sense speech and philosophy'.[19] But we should in addition bear in mind that this was also the time of the 'New Wave' in British cinema exemplified by films such as *Room at the Top*, *A Kind of Loving* and *Look Back in Anger* (in turn of course calling on work being done in the theatre and the novel). 1960 was the year of *Saturday Night and Sunday Morning* as well as *Coronation Street* and the serial's concentration on a working-class community, its black and white images of northern streets, its rebellious and outspoken characters and its insistent sense of place are examples of the particular conventions of realism which it shared with the British films of the period.

Coronation Street's appeal to realism (however mediated and changed by other pressures on it) was never really challenged by other British soaps such as *Crossroads*, and it took *Brookside*, over 20 years later, to stake its claim to a realism which it was argued *Coronation Street* had abandoned in a nostalgic appeal to the past. *Brookside* was first shown on Britain's new Channel 4 in 1982 and in publicity interviews before it began the producer, Phil Redmond, specifically attacked *Coronation Street*'s commitment to realism and in particular its emphasis on a working-class community. In an article published in *Woman* magazine, for instance, he criticised other serials for being 'soft and bland' in their approach to 'realistic issues and everyday problems'. Using a typical realist strategy, he calls on the audience to compare their own experience to that offered by *Coronation Street* – 'Did you ever live in a place where the whole street congregates in the same pub every night? It just doesn't happen.' Instead, Redmond argues that 'people will accept and actually want programmes that tell the truth and show society as it really is.'[20] One can feel the conventions of realism in British soap opera shifting as Redmond speaks.

The pre-echo in Redmond's statements of Julia Smith's words quoted earlier – 'We don't make life, we reflect it' – is no accident, for *EastEnders* too, first shown in February 1985, was launched on similar promises and with similar attacks on *Coronation Street* and, this time, on *Brookside* also. According to *Broadcast*, the trade magazine for British television, *EastEnders* 'promises to portray the everyday life of an East End community "warts and all"'. Julia Smith is quoted as believing that 'The Street has created its own environment and got stuck in it' but she also criticises *Brookside*'s use of an actual housing estate as its set. 'Sometimes a studio set can look more realistic than reality. Anyway the *Brookside* approach is one of those ideas which seem great in theory, but don't really work in practice.'[21] But the pre-publicity also made it clear that the new soap would be picking up *Brookside*'s commitment to dealing with 'realistic issues'. As script editor, Tony Holland, put it in one of many newspaper articles which accompanied the launch of *EastEnders*, 'we are not going to duck any social issues. Our stories would deal with all the contemporary problems of London's East End.'[22]

Clearly, the intention of those making a soap does not determine what happens over the years nor how the audience takes pleasure in what is being offered. Nevertheless, it is apparent that the realism which is valued in British soaps is defined through a rejection of each other's conventions as much as through a notion of what is contemporary and important. But if a recognition of the way in which soaps have developed and changed is important in getting behind the claims that soaps merely reflect society, it is also necesary to acknowledge that the commitment to the values of realism remain remarkably consistent in British soaps. The pursuit of realism has been an impetus for change in British soaps but the bedrock of the appeal to realism has remained the same – a value placed on a specific setting, an 'authentic' regional experience and a particular class representation.

In their different ways, all four of the British soaps on which I am focusing work with these concepts. The settings are specific – a street, a motel, a square, a small housing development – and are defined geographically so that the audience builds up a precise sense of place. As importantly, each serial is able to call up and indeed help to create the connotations of a region – least successfully, perhaps, in *Crossroads'* attempts to speak for the Midlands, but crucially in *Coronation Street's* invocation of Manchester and the North, *EastEnders'* referencing of the London's docklands and, most particularly, in *Brookside's* commitment to Liverpool. In all cases, this regional authority gives the soaps a sense of specificity crucial to realism and the ability to work with regional characteristics – cockney quick-wittedness, a scouse eye for the main chance, Northern straight talking and a Midlands aspiration to gentility. In themselves, such characteristics may be clichéd and sweeping but they form part of the way in which British culture absorbs, uses and contributes to regional differences. And finally, the setting and region give each soap the opportunity to present working-class characters, even in the Crossroads Motel where the working-class characters take on the 'servant' roles. The assumption, in British film history, that realism must take as its subject the working class can be traced back to the documentary movement of the 1920s and 1930s and their patronising approach can still be discerned in some of the British soaps, but the commitment to bring to the screen working-class accents, mores, problems and pleasures – still largely absent from much of British television – is an important element in the soaps' claim to realism.

The aesthetic interplay

By now it will be clear that soaps do not offer a coherent aesthetic experience and in particular that they do not work entirely in the realist tradition which is so valued in Britain. Instead, soaps deploy a range of aesthetic elements and offer a mix of generic conventions which confuses or makes them an object of scorn to those who seek to confine them to a particular format. Within a single episode, soaps can move from one set of conventions to another and back again and within an evening's viewing the soaps offer a surprisingly wide range of aesthetic experiences within a common narrative organisation. This shifting between the different traditions contributes to the experience of engagement and distance which is so characteristic of soap viewing. But the values of light entertainment, melodrama and realism do not always fit smoothly together, for while the melodramatic mode might work to pull the audience into the drama, the conventions of light entertainment demand a more detached approach. I will close this chapter, therefore, by demonstrating how an analysis of this shifting between light entertainment, realism and melodrama helps us to understand particular aspects of the aesthetic experience of watching soaps.

Acting style and performance are frequently the subject of critical condemnation or amusement. The classic complaint about soaps is that of bad acting. Thus, commenting on the cliffhanger episode in which Kristen shot JR, Clive James wrote:

> With the possible exception of JR himself, everybody in the cast is working flat out to convey the full range of his or her, usually her, emotional commitment. Sue Ellen, in particular, was a study in passionate outrage. Her mouth practically took off ... It is even possible that Miss Ellie shot him, since she has been showing increasing signs of madness, singing her dialogue instead of saying it.[23]

What is not understood in this kind of criticism, however, is that acting in soaps is required to register in three different ways which are almost inevitably at odds with each other. First of all, in light entertainment terms, the performance is required to be that of a star. Light entertainment looks for an identity between star and character, and in that sense what is valued is not acting but being the character. Larry Hagman *is* JR and his appearances outside *Dallas* on chat shows, for instance, are used to reinforce that claim to identity. Within the programmes, there is a tendency to concentrate on the face as being the main focus of the star's uniqueness and there will be frequent repetition of the star's characteristic feature – Linda Gray's trembling mouth, Noele Gordon's understanding look, Leslie Grant's little boy grin, Joan Collins's mock-innocent gaze. To a certain extent, this emphasis on the face in close-up chimes in with the demands made by the conventions of TV melodrama in which the significance of every gesture needs to be underlined. For the purposes of melodrama, acting is required to be both expressive and mysterious. It needs to express clearly the significance of key words and gestures and to leave sufficient space for the audience to make its own deductions. The emphasis on eyes and mouth, the number of meaningful looks and thoughtful nods, can be explained by these requirements. But the aesthetics of realism demand that acting be 'in character' so that the particularities of each fictional individual are drawn on to give weight to the performance. This mode values an acting style which depends on a distance between performer and character. Unlike the star persona valued by the light entertainment aesthetic, the realist approach demands a fictional character very different in looks and speech from the actor. Thus the actress, Jean Alexander, spruce, smartly dressed and middle class in speech, is in magazine articles set against the character of Hilda Ogden whom she played in *Coronation Street* as nagging, gossipy and down at heel, though capable of moments of dignified pathos. This space between actress and character can be understood as a guarantee of a realist performance but the detailed gestures required by such a style may be at odds with the melodramatic mode in which every gesture has a meaning in terms of the narrative and not just character. A major soap actor may be called on to work in three different modes: that of a star (light entertainment), an emotional representative (melodrama) and a character actor (realism). It is hardly surprising that soap opera acting is sometimes incoherent although the critics who complain of inconsistency are usually unaware of the shifting significance of performance in these programmes.

As this chapter has indicated, a similar tripartite analysis could be made of other aesthetic elements, among them costume, setting, decor and lighting but it might be useful to consider an apparently 'technical' element which is given less attention in television analysis than in film theory. Camera movement and position in soaps are clearly limited by the exigencies of time and money but the three aesthetic elements play their part here as well. Light entertainment, as we have seen, emphasises both spectacle and stars and so camera positioning frequently alternates between long shots establishing the glamorous settings and close-ups of the stars. This is quite clear in *Dallas* and *Dynasty* where the pattern of shots (outside establishing shot, interior long shot to take in setting and clothes, close-up(s) of speaker) is predictable. But the use of a long shot to establish and even explore the setting is not unusual in British soaps. The spectacle of the Liverpool setting is regularly invoked in *Brookside* and *EastEnders* uses camera work to draw attention to its sets – in a 1987 Christmas episode, the camera in a single shot moved through the Square, nudging the shoppers, emphasising the Christmas lights on the market stalls and dwelling on the group of carol singers. In its own way, such a shot is as spectacular, as pleasing to the eye, as any view of Hong Kong which *Dynasty* offers, but in British soaps such shots also have a realist function, serving to underline the specificities of the regional setting and the soap's function of representing one area of Britain to the rest of the country. The long shot can therefore work with both light entertainment and realist values. The close-up has the further advantage of fitting in with the melodramatic mode as well and I would argue that it is the fact that the close-up coincides with the aesthetic demands of all three modes which gives it a dominant role compared with other camera positions in the programmes. The close-up allows, as we have seen, appropriate emphasis on the star but it also offers the audience access to the significant object or gesture, giving them time to draw their own conclusions and fill in meaning. In addition, the close-up can be used to draw attention to realist detail – the photographs on Hilda's mantelpiece or the unwashed dishes in the Corkhill kitchen after Doreen has left both the family home and *Brookside*. Such shots do not progress the narrative but they help to fill in our understanding of the context of what is being presented. Camera-work, when looked at in this tripartite way, becomes not merely a matter of economics or convenience; it can be recognised as integral to the soap aesthetic.

The two examples given here show that the different aesthetic modes at work in soap operas may sometimes be in conflict, as they often are when we analyse acting and performance, and sometimes work together, as they do in terms of camera movement and position. What is important is to move away from the blanket condemnation of the aesthetic experience offered by soaps and the defensive response which refuses to acknowledge the justification of any criticism. The tripartite framework outlined here should enable us to begin to analyse why soaps look as they do and to understand the sometimes contradictory aesthetic pleasures they offer.

3

A Woman's Space

'I'm glad you're with me.'

Pam to Sue Ellen, Dallas

'Men are lucky. They get women. Women just get men.'

Debbie Lancaster, Crossroads

'No one knows women, mate. And if you think you do, you're sadly mistaken.'

Den, EastEnders

The assumption that soaps are for women is widely held and the interest shown in soaps by both feminist critics and the more traditional women's magazines stems from this appeal to a predominantly female audience.[1] This chapter attempts to explore the way in which the programmes offer particular enjoyment to female viewers and to point to the ways in which they differ in this respect from other TV programmes. One of the central arguments of this book is that the prime time soaps I am examining have changed in their attempts to attract a less specifically female-dominated audience. Nevertheless, it is still possible to map out the traditional framework which had been established by programmes like *Coronation Street* and *Crossroads* over many years and to examine the nature of the appeal of more recent soaps like *Dallas* and *Dynasty* to women. This is a complex area in which we need to distinguish between the position offered to the woman viewer by the programmes; the social subject positioned through race, gender and class; and the responses of individual viewers. As Charlotte Brunsdon has argued, a distinction needs to be made 'between the subject positions that a text constructs, and the social subject who may or may not take these

positions up'.[2] A particular view on abortion, for instance, may be
proposed by a soap but it may not be adopted by women in the
audience. The individual woman viewer may reject the positions and
pleasures offered by soaps, as David Morley found in interviewing
women in South London who saw themselves as different from other
women because they did not like or watch soaps.[3] Even those who
accept the invitation may do so for different reasons than those
implied by the programmes, taking pleasure in the spectacle of
Dallas for instance but refusing its emotional demands. Enjoyment
will be affected by the way in which the woman viewer is herself
positioned within the home as mother/wife/daughter, for instance,
and her activities outside it. The teenage girl watching *Dallas* may
enjoy different things from her mother. So in assuming an audience
in which women predominate neither programme-maker nor critic
can assume that women are a consistent or unchanging category.
Nevertheless, the importance of soaps in Western culture as one of
the litmus tests of the 'feminine' still needs to be considered. What is
it about soaps that makes a male viewer assert, 'it's not manly to talk
about soaps'?[4]

The personal sphere

The concerns of soaps have traditionally been based on the commonly perceived split between the public and the personal, between
work and leisure, reason and emotion, action and contemplation.
This tradition not only offers a set of oppositions but consistently
values what are seen to be the more active modes – those of the
public sphere – over those whose terrain is the personal and hence
deemed to be less effective and more passive. The use of such
distinctions are endemic in our culture and are as common for
instance among left-wing trade unionists as among right-wing businessmen, both emphasising work as primary, action as necessary and
cooperation between people (race and gender immaterial) as being
essential for progress and change. This is not to say that both groups
operate in the same way, let alone have the same aims, but that the
vocabulary of the public world springs to their lips because their
aims, however different, are to affect what they perceive as the
public arena. The ultimate pair of oppositions, on which such
differences rest, is masculine and feminine and it is feminists who in
different ways have been questioning the naturalness of such dicho-
tomies. In some cases, the task has been to bring the personal into
the public sphere and thus to repair the split (the introduction of

child care and sexuality issues into trade union activity, for example); in others, it has been to celebrate the specificity of women's pleasures and to re-evaluate them against the grain of male denigration.

In this context, it becomes possible to see why soaps are not merely seen as silly but positively irritating and even unmanly. Soaps overturn the deeply entrenched value structure which is based on the traditional oppositions of masculinity and femininity. Compared with other TV programmes, such as police series or the news, the actions in soaps, while heavily marked, lack physical weight. Bobby's periodic punch-ups with JR hardly compare with the regular confrontations even in *Hill Street Blues* let alone *Miami Vice*. Instead, the essence of soaps is the reflection on personal problems and the emphasis is on talk not on action, on slow development rather than the immediate response, on delayed retribution rather than instant effect. All television relies on the repetition of familiar characters and stories but soaps more than other genres offer a particular type of repetition in which certain emotional situations are tested out through variations in age, character, social milieu and class. Personal relationships are the backbone of soaps. They provide the dramatic moments – marriage, birth, divorce, death – and the more day-to-day exchanges of quarrels, alliances and dilemmas which make up the fabric of the narrative. The very repetition of soap opera plots allows them to offer a paradigm of emotional relationships in which only one element needs to be changed for the effect to be different. Soaps offer a continually shifting kaleidoscope of emotional relationships which allow the audience to test out how particular emotional variations can or should be handled.

On a broad level, soap stories may seem to be repetitive and over familiar. One set of stories, for example, deals with the relationships between men and women, offering a recognisable scenario of courtship, marriage and separation through quarrels, divorce or death. At the micro level, however, the differences become crucial since the testing-out process depends on the repetition of a number of elements but with one significantly changed. The audience is engaged by the question 'What would happen if . . .?' and given the opportunity to try out a set of variants. *Coronation Street* offers a good example of this process in its handling of the courtship/marriage scenario. It invites the audience to consider a number of pairings as if to test out which is the most satisfying and durable. What happens to a marriage, it asks, if the husband is the local liberal conscience of the community and the wife lively, sociable and previously married to a ne'er-do-well (Ken and Deirdre Barlow); if a stolid middle-aged grocer marries a flightly blonde with a dubious past (Alf and Audrey Roberts); if 'one of the lads' marries a woman who is more mature and sensible than he is (Brian and Gail Tilsley); if 'one of the lads' marries an irresponsible but determined young girl with a mind of her own (Kevin and Sally Webster).[5] The same stories yield a rich vein of plots in which the differences in age, character and status are minutely explored. The same variety can be seen in other general plots – those concerned with parent–child relationships for example or with the parameters of community and friendship. This testing-out process is, of course, carried out within the serial by the commentary of the characters, some of whom achieve an almost chorus-like function, underlining the nuances of the changing situation. We have noted in chapter 1 the crucial role of audience discussion about soaps and it should now be clear that such 'gossip' between episodes serves not only the narrative function of engaging the viewer but also provides the means by which the paradigms provided by the programmes can be tested. Viewing soaps with friends or family is often accompanied by a commentary of informed advice to the characters – 'she shouldn't trust him,' 'if he hadn't said that, it would have been alright,' 'how could she forget?' When the popular press asked their agony aunts whether Deirdre Barlow in *Coronation Street* should remain with her husband or leave him for her lover, they were making concrete (and using one of the sources chosen for support by women themselves) the conversations which were taking place in homes and workplaces all over the country.[6] The weighing up of the qualities of the two men against Deirdre's own character, the financial situation, the needs of the child involved – all these factors had to be taken into account and the pleasure for the female viewer in rehearsing the decision-making process without the responsibility for its consequences should not be underestimated.

For it is still women who are deemed to carry the responsibility for emotional relationships in our society – who keep the home, look after the children, write the letters or make the phone calls to absent friends, seek advice on how to solve problems, consult magazines on how to respond 'better' to the demands made on them. It is this engagement with the personal which is central to women's involvement with soaps but it is important to be precise about how that involvement works. It is not just that soap operas have a domestic setting. Much of television takes place either in home settings or leisure venues. Nor is it that social problems are made personal or manageable in soaps. It could be argued that many different types of TV programmes, including police series and the news, use the same mode. Nor is it just the fact that soaps feature strong women in major roles though the pleasures of that are certainly substantial. It is the process which is important, the way in which soaps recognise and value the emotional work which women undertake in the personal sphere. Soaps rehearse to their female audience the process of handling personal relationships – the balancing of each individual's needs, the attention paid to every word and gesture so as to understand its emotional meaning, the recognition of competing demands for attention.

This engagement of the audience in a constant rehearsal of emotional dilemmas has been articulated in a number of ways. Two of the most important contributors to the debate, Tania Modleski and Charlotte Brunsdon, have specifically looked at the structures by which soap operas address their female audience in a way which chimes with the construction outside the programmes of women as the emotional centre of the home and family. Modleski, in her influential study of US daytime soaps, argues that 'the formal properties of daytime television . . . accord closely with the rhythms of women's work in the home.'[7] She describes two different kinds of women's work, to be both 'moral and spiritual guides and household drudges'[8] and sees the daytime soaps as permitting and indeed supporting both roles. For the household drudge, the soap operas, with their slow pace, repetition, dislocated and overlapping story lines and their emphasis on the ordinary rather than the glamorous, provide a narrative which can be understood without the concentration required by prime time television. 'Unlike most workers in the labor force,' Modleski suggests, 'the housewife must beware of concentrating her energies too exclusively on any one task – otherwise, the dinner could burn or the baby could crack its skull.'[9] The soap opera form replicates this fragmented and distracted approach and makes it pleasurable. Modleski argues that the housewife's 'duties are split among a variety of domestic and familial tasks, and her television programs keep her from desiring a focused existence by involving her in the pleasures of a fragmented life'.[10] In doing so, the soap opera 'reflects and cultivates the "proper" psychological disposition of the woman in the home'.[11]

On the moral and emotional front, Modleski ascribes to soaps a similar function of reinforcing the work ascribed to women of nurturing relationships and holding the family together. Again, she adroitly links the formal properties of the genre with its subject matter and proposes that 'soap operas invest exquisite pleasure in the central condition of a woman's life; waiting – whether for her phone to ring, for the baby to take its nap, or for the family to be reunited after the day's final soap opera has left its family still struggling against dissolution.'[12] It is important to Modleski's argument that soaps do not, as they are sometimes accused, present ideal families able to achieve harmony and resolution. Instead, the literally endless tales with their variety of insoluble dilemmas offer reassurance that the woman viewer is not alone in her inability to reconcile and hold together the family unit. What is demanded by the soaps is the tolerance of the good mother who is able to see that there is no right answer and who is understanding and sympathetic to 'both the sinner and the victim'.[13] 'Soap operas convince women that their highest goal is to see their families united and happy, while consoling them for their inability to realise this ideal and bring about familial harmony.'[14] And indeed the goal is unrealisable in more ways than one since Modleski points out that the soap opera does not offer a mirror image of the viewer's own family but 'a kind of *extended* family, the direct opposite of her own isolated nuclear family'.[15] What the housewife experiences is an isolation rooted in her real experience for which soap operas offer a form of consolation.

Modleski does offer the housewife/viewer an outlet for the frustrations and contradictions implicit in her dual role. Here she cites the delight viewers take in despising the soap opera villainess who uses situations such as pregnancy and marriage, which frequently trap women in soaps, to her own selfish ends. The villainess's refusal to appreciate, let alone acquiesce in, the needs of others is in contrast to the passive role of the other characters (and indeed the viewer) and provides 'an outlet for feminine anger'.[16] But because the villainess is a bad figure, Modleski argues that women's frustration is directed 'against the one character who refuses to accept her own powerlessness, who is unashamedly self-seeking'.[17] Soap operas continually acknowledge the existence of women's contradictory impulses – the demise of one villainess leads to the creation of another – but they are, in Modleski's view, rendered harmless since 'woman's anger is directed at woman's anger, and an eternal cycle is created.'[18]

Loving with a Vengeance deals with US daytime soaps which in their scheduling and format are different from the soaps discussed in this book. Nevertheless, there is much here which rings true, particularly in Modleski's account of the way in which soaps encourage the viewer to take into account a number of viewpoints on the same story and provide, over a period of time, explanations (or perhaps excuses) for ill-advised or even wrong actions. It is sometime unclear, however, whether, Modleski is analysing the position of the good mother which soaps encourage their viewers to adopt or is describing the housewife/viewer as a social subject, formed by her own social and economic circumstances. This is, as we have seen, a difficult distinction but in either case the female viewer seems curiously passive and isolated. Despite her argument that soap opera is in the vanguard of all popular narrative art and her appeal to feminists to build on rather than reject the fantasy of community offered by soaps, Modleski's viewer comes close to the model offered by less sympathetic critics. She is distracted, lonely, unable to make judgements or to discriminate; her anger is internalised, directed at her own scarcely expressed desire for greater power. She waits for the nonexistent family to return so that she can perform her role as ideal mother but is denied even 'this extremely flattering illusion of her power'[19] by the genre's insistence on the insolubility of the problems it is the mother's task to solve. Almost despite herself, Modleski seems to share the doubts which feminists and others have expressed that soap operas, like other forms of women's fiction, serve only to keep women in their place. The depressing nature of this place seems to come about not merely because of the low economic status of 'the housewife' but also because her very pleasure in soap opera is based on a masochistic acknowledgement of her powerlessness and the uselessness of her own skills.

Other feminist critics have taken a more positive approach which, while not doubting the oppression imposed on women in and outside the home, has argued that it is important not to underrate women's role in the personal sphere. Charlotte Brunsdon, in her article on *Crossroads*, examines the notion of a gendered audience in an attempt to come to terms with the pleasures offered to the female viewer. Brunsdon argues that the scheduling of the programme in the late afternoon/early evening and the advertising and spin-offs surrounding it – interview material, cookbooks, knitting patterns – are addressed to the feminine consumer, the viewer who is constructed in her gender-based role of wife, mother, housewife, and that these extratextual factors 'suggest that women are the target audience for *Crossroads*'.[20] Drawing attention to the distinction made between public and personal life, Brunsdon defines 'the ideological problematic of soap opera' as that of 'personal life in its everyday realisation through personal relationships' and argues that 'it is within this realm of the domestic, the personal, the private, that feminine competence is recognised.'[21] She acknowledges the incoherence of *Crossroads* in terms of its spatial and temporal organisation, its narrative interruptions and repetitions and its dramatic irresolution but argues that its coherence, for those (feminine) viewers who know how to read it, is articulated through the moral and ideological frameworks which the programme explores; 'Crossroads is in the business not of creating narrative excitement, suspense, delay and resolution, but of constructing moral consensus about the conduct of personal life.'[22] The competent viewer needs to be skilled in three areas – that of generic knowledge (familiarity with soap opera as a genre), that of serial-specific knowledge (knowledge of narrative and character in Crossroads) and that of cultural knowledge of the way in which one's personal life is (or should be) conducted. It is this last competence to which Brunsdon draws particular attention for it is the basis of her argument that Crossroads as a text (rather than through its extratextual factors) implies a gendered audience; 'it is the culturally constructed skills of femininity – sensitivity, perception, intuition and the necessary privileging of the concerns of personal life – which are both called on and practised in the genre.'[23] Crossroads requires skilled readers to make it pleasurable and the competencies necessary for that process are the very ones which are valued in the soaps themselves.

The process of testing out emotional situations which I described earlier clearly owes much to Brunsdon's notion of competence in personal life. Brunsdon does not take up Modleski's suggestion of the viewer as the 'ideal mother' possessed of endless tolerance, although she agrees that Crossroads, like the US daytime soaps, offers a 'range of different opinions and understandings' and 'a consistent holding off of denouement and knowledge'.[24] Nevertheless, the article does imply that the viewer is called on to make judgements about characters even while recognising that events next week might change the basis of that judgement once more. Brunsdon emphasises the importance of stories which centre on lies and deceit when the audience knows more than the characters involved and 'can see clearly what and who is "right"'.[25] She adds that the question determining a soap opera narrative is not 'What will happen next?' but 'What kind of person is this?' – a question which both acknowledges the importance of the individual character and implies a moral/social judgement about that character. I emphasise this, perhaps against the grain of other parts of the article, because it seems to me that it is this acknowledgement of the capacity to judge which enables Brunsdon, unlike Modleski, to value the process she describes. The judgements may not be firm or final; certainly the moral framework is not fixed – two similar actions (the breaking off of an engagement, for example) may require different decisions and the viewer may indeed decide to postpone judgement until a more suitable time, in itself an active decision rather than a passive one.

But until we replace the model of the tolerant viewer accepting everything with that of Brunsdon's competent viewer weighing the emotional dilemmas put before her, we are always going to underestimate the position offered to the female viewer of soap operas.

The question of judgement is the more important because it is tied in with one of the most consistent pleasures offered to women by soaps – that of being on our side. Again this is not just a question of a domestic setting or an emphasis on a particular type of story both of which could apply to situation comedies without the same kind of effect. It is more that soap operas, not always, not continuously, but at key points, offer an understanding from the woman's viewpoint that affects the judgements that the viewer is invited to make. This sense of being 'down among the women' is crucial to the pleasures of recognition which soaps offer women – a slightly secretive, sometimes unspoken understanding developed through the endless analysis of emotional dilemmas which Modleski and Brunsdon describe. This effect is achieved in a number of ways but essential to it is the soap's basic premise that women are understandable and rational, a premise that flies in the face of much TV drama.

Because soaps are rooted in the personal sphere, the actions of the women in them become explicable and often, though not always, correct. In itself this runs counter to much television drama in which women's association with the personal is deemed to be a disadvantage because it clouds their judgement. In soaps, competence in the personal sphere is valued and women are able to handle difficult decisions well because of it. One simple example of this occurred in *Crossroads* when, following the death of Diane, a long-standing and well-loved character, her friends Jill and Adam Chance (married but at the time separated) discuss funeral arrangements with the undertaker. Throughout the interview, Adam urges a commonsense view that Diane would not want too much money spent while Jill tries to insist that they have the best. This exchange would not be unusual in any other TV drama. What is striking, however, is that Jill is not exposed as hysterial or overemotional but as trying appropriately to recognise her own loss and Diane's worth; the viewer is invited to understand Jill's concern and her approach is presented as rational and appropriate.

Such small moments are common in soaps. On a larger scale, consistent recognition is given to the emotional situations which women are deemed to share. At its most obvious, this sense of a common feeling marks major events such as birth, marriage, the death of a child or the development of a romance. When such a moment occurs for a female character, the other women are seen to understand it even while they might not welcome it. Thus, Pam in *Dallas* was sympathetic to Miss Ellie's fears when the 'new' Jock Ewing appeared and encouraged her to talk about her sexual and emotional feelings. Sue Ellen, though very dubious about what would happen, accompanied and supported Pam in her search for Mark in Hong Kong. Similarly, Deirdre Barlow in *Coronation Street* supported her step-daughter's decision to have an abortion and argued with Mike Baldwin that he should be looking to his wife Susan's needs rather than his own desire to have a child. Even when the women are at odds with each other they share a common sense of what is at stake. When Nicola in *Crossroads* tried to explain to her long-lost daughter why she had given her away at birth, Tracy was angry and upset. But she and Nicola were able to conduct a dialogue from which the men were excluded either because of ignorance or from a desire to rush to hasty judgement. In *Dynasty*, Karen, Dana and Alexis had opposing and competing interests in Adam but shared common feelings around maternity when Karen bore Adam's child and Dana went so far as to risk Adam's loss of his son through expressing in court her own sympathy for Karen's right as the natural mother to keep the child.

This sense of common feeling is often more rueful than celebratory, rooted in a shared perception that men can never live up to the demands women make of them. Mavis and Rita, in *Coronation Street*'s corner shop, comment, the one wistfully, the other sardonically, on the behaviour of men while, on one memorable occasion, Sue Ellen, so often the butt of other women's sympathetic glances, commiserated with some satisfaction with Miss Ellie and Jenna on the absence of their men from that morning's breakfast table. (Bobby's night out was later explained of course by his death.) In both cases, the sense of a common situation is strong even when reactions to it differ. Traditionally, soaps value this sense of female solidarity and have worked on the assumption that women have common attitudes and problems, are 'sisters under the skin' as the respectable Annie Walker once acknowledged to the rather less respectable Elsie Tanner in *Coronation Street*. Women in soaps define themselves as different from men and pride themselves on the difference, a position which the programmes endorse. 'Despite everything,' says Angie in *EastEnders*, 'I'm still glad I'm not a man.' 'You've got to remember they're like children,' Lou Beale tells her granddaughter Michelle in the same programme, voicing another common feeling shared by women characters in soaps. In addition, the women frequently console each other at the end of a romance, as Bet Lynch did with Jenny in *Coronation Street*, with a variation on

'There's not one of them worth it.' This expression of an underlying solidarity based on a shared position persists even when the women appear to be on opposite sides. Pam Ewing helped Sue Ellen remove her child from Southfork, emphasising that she understood Sue Ellen's feeling in a way in which the men could not. In return, Sue Ellen commented 'I don't want us to lose our friendship . . . we have to try hard not to get into their fights.' 'Take more than a couple of fellas to split us up,' Rita Fairclough tells Mavis in *Coronation Street* in a similarly explicit acknowledgement of the importance of female friendship.

A further factor in establishing a shared female viewpoint is indeed the range of emotional relationships in which the women characters are involved. It is too often assumed that soaps emphasise male–female relationships at the expense of others. In fact, because the central husband–wife relationship is such hard work for the women characters, they need to be supported by other friendships which are more reliably sustaining. The relationship between mother and daughter, for instance, is central to many soaps, providing an irresistible combination of female solidarity and family intimacy. *Brookside* has movingly presented the love and impatience, passion and reticence, which marked Sheila Grant's engagements with her daughter, Karen, while in *EastEnders* Pauline and Michelle seem to be fighting their way through an oppressive relationship to one which acknowledges what they share. In both *Dallas* and *Dynasty*, Miss Ellie and Krystle offer patient affection and support to a variety of surrogate daughters and receive from them a reciprocal understanding. Equally important, perhaps, is the emphasis placed on female friendship and the time spent showing women talking together. In British soaps, a sample of women friends would include the knockabout banter of the elderly Dot and Ethel (*EastEnders*); the longstanding pair of Mavis and Rita (*Coronation Street*); the camaraderie of the women in Baldwin's clothing factory and particularly the friendly bickering between Ivy and Vera (*Coronation Street*); Diane and Shireen (*EastEnders*) moving out of childhood and struggling with the different futures their families plan for them. In the US prime time soaps, the relationships between Krystle and Sammy Jo, Miss Ellie and Jenna, even Callie and Lucy, all offer examples of the way in which women confide in each other. The programmes continually show women talking to each other, sometimes in moments of high drama, sometimes in a routine way as if it were an everyday occurrence that needed no emphasis. When *EastEnders* devoted a whole episode to Ethel and Dot, reminiscing, quarrelling, spilling secrets, making tea, it was unusual only in that it was drawing specific attention to the fact that female conversation is the back-bone of the traditional soap.

The centrality of women in soaps has the effect of making them the norm by which the programmes are understood. They are not peripheral to the stories; they are not mysterious, enigmatic or threatening as they so often are in thrillers or crime stories. They handle the complex web of relationships which make up a soap opera with a care and intensity which makes the men seem clumsy and uncomprehending. Even when the women are wrong they are transparent and understandable, an unusual characteristic for women in a culture in which they are deemed most desirable when they are most opaque and enigmatic. This is not to say that soaps present women more realistically as feminists sometimes demand of representations of women. Neither Sue Ellen nor Angie Watts would be deemed particularly realistic representations and in some ways their characters are presented as particularly and conventio-nally feminine. Married to men who emotionally abuse them, appa-rently irrational and sometimes devious, volatile, brittle and soft-hearted, Angie and Sue Ellen, it could be argued, represent gender stereotyping of a high degree. Yet it is also important that the audience is not only consistently presented with information and comment on what these women do but is also continually implicated in their actions by being drawn into their logic. The baffled assertion of commonsense in the face of women's emotions still permeates much of TV fiction as it did mainstream film genres like film noir. In soaps, such a lack of understanding is impossible for the male as well as the female viewer because we have been led through every step of the woman character's way.

This shift is accompanied by a move away from the male figure as the agent of the action. TV fiction took over from mainstream film the narrative structure in which 'the man's role' is 'the active one of forwarding the story, making things happen'.[26] Even in *Hill Street Blues*, for example, the stories are initiated by men making things happen or by women having things happen to them. But in soap operas, not only do women take action but the audience is led through that process with them. In *EastEnders*, for instance, the traditional triangle of Den manoeuvering between his wife Angie and his mistress Jan might have given the impression that it was the man who was, if not in control of the situation, at least the active agent. Nothing could be further from the truth because the audience was aware not merely of Angie's plans to fight for her marriage through her lies about her illness, for instance, but also of Jan's determination to push for her own needs. Only the man remained baffled, frustrated and incoherent in the centre of an emotional maelstrom. What is important here is not so much the outcome of the action (Angie's strategems failed in this instance) but the fact that the audience was prevented from sharing Den's bafflement. Whatever judgements are made about the women's behaviour, the reasons for their actions are laid out in detail to the audience and are meticulously worked over as the triangle of relationships shifts. In the same way, the saga of JR's dealings with Sue Ellen did not allow the audience to find her actions incomprehensible. Different viewers might have arguments about how far she could have avoided the saga of drink, injudicious affairs and madness, but the reasons for her behaviour, the desperate attempts to get JR's attention without losing control of her son, were always crystal clear.

It would be overstating the case to assert that, in prime time soaps, the position of men as narratively active, women as passive, is reversed. The action of male characters is crucial and often provokes, as in the examples above, the action taken by the women. Nevertheless, the position of engagement with the women characters which the audience is encouraged to adopt is based on the transparency of the women's behaviour; our understanding is invoked by the process of going through the narrative with them. Surprisingly often in soaps men are caught in a position of baffled impotence. 'Women,' they say to each with resigned incomprehension 'who can understand them?' If this were said in a thriller or a police series, the male characters would be speaking from a position of superiority, asserting the irrationality of feminine behaviour. In soaps, such remarks are made from a position of ignorance, allowing the female viewer the satisfaction of knowing more and understanding more than these enraged and frustrated men. This is one of the central pleasures offered to women by soaps, a recognition based not so much on a realistic representation of women's everyday lives but on what it feels like to have so much invested in the personal sphere, while men are unable to live up to or even be aware of its demands – Den and JR, the apparently powerful, caught in close-up at the end of the episode, floored once again by their inability to keep up with the women's ability to operate in the personal sphere.

The public sphere

While soaps are traditionally associated with the domestic and the personal, account needs to be taken of the way in which they handle issues raised in the public sphere of work and politics. Soaps, in fact,

range more widely in their settings than many other TV genres and
the distinction between public and personal space is crucial to their
structure. Clearly, the US prime time soaps have made a feature of
business and the wheelings and dealings of the oil industry, in
particular, figure strongly in their stories. In the British soaps,
business is likely to be more down-market – a small motel, a one-
man clothing factory or building firm. Most characteristically, British
soaps feature a variety of small businesses – cafés, pubs, shops – in
which one or two individuals make a precarious living and contribute
to the life of the community.

Issues concerned with business and politics do get raised in soaps.
In the US programmes, battles over the control of the business are
central to the plot and the audience is given a plethora of detail of
shares, interest rates, loans and takeover battles. In *Dallas*, the drop
in oil prices led to JR's disastrous foray into terrorism and Donna's
lobbying in Washington. In both *Dallas* and *Dynasty*, some reference is made to the fate of the workers who rely on the decisions of
the Ewings and the Carringtons to keep them in employment.
Dynasty indeed began with the grievances of the small contractors
against Blake Carrington, and the downfall of Ewing Oil was at least
partly due to the desire of the wife of an ex-employee for revenge on
the business operation which had treated her husband so cavalierly.
In British soaps, too, although on a different scale, business and
work have provided stories and settings. Mike Baldwin's clothing
factory in *Coronation Street* was over the years the scene of a number
of strikes and industrial disputes and Vera Duckworth, for one, was
always quick to point to the different lifestyles of the male boss and
his women workers. The Crossroads Motel has been the subject of
takeover bids and was incorporated into an international company
with consequent repercussions for the staff. *Brookside* has shown its
characters at work and used a variety of work locations as a base for
stories about pay, health and safety, youth employment and the
experiences of women at work. *EastEnders* has emphasised the
financial pressures on small businesses such as the building firm, the
café and the hairdressing salon.

Nevertheless, it would be misleading to pretend that soaps deal
with work and business relations in any depth or with particular
political insight. A common complaint is that by concentrating on
the personal sphere of marriage, family and friendship, soaps ignore
or glamorise the public sphere of work, unemployment, trade unions
and business. 'Ugly social issues are *reduced* to a level of private,
family melodrama,' wrote one left-wing critic of the way in which
Coronation Street was tackling unemployment.[27] In itself, this com-

ment seems to exemplify the split between the personal and the public as if ugly social issues do not have deeply felt personal consequences and in some ways it seems unfair to single out soaps in this way since much of TV fiction either ignores or sidesteps such issues. Nevertheless, it is important to look at the process by which soaps colonise the public sphere and claim it for the personal and to assess the consequences of this approach.

The settings of the programmes provide a useful starting point for an analysis of soaps' handling of the public sphere. As we have seen, soaps do feature locations which are connected with business and work, whether it be an office, a factory floor or a corner shop. In British soaps, these locations are used not because of a particular concern with the work done there but because in general they provide a public place in which people can meet and the gossip which fuels the narrative can be exchanged. The launderette, the pub, the office provide public spaces for comment on what has occurred in the private space of the characters' homes. This function helps to determine the nature of the public locations which can be deployed in the programmes.

Soaps find it virtually impossible to use work settings which deny or suppress the emotional needs of individual characters or locations in which conversations cannot take place. Here, the advantage of a corner shop or café is clear over a large factory or office where noise levels of machinery or typewriters are high and routine work prevents conversation. Even in the *Coronation Street* factory, the women characters are more likely to be featured at break times or when they are clocking in or out. Public space also needs to be widely accessible, free-for-all areas where no one can be prevented from joining in a conversation even when their views are not wanted. Characters like Hilda Ogden in *Coronation Street* and Dot Cotton in *EastEnders* are marked by their ability to lurk in public places, popping up every now and then to provide a pointed comment. Such behaviour is generally accepted until it intrudes into the personal space of the characters' homes at which point it becomes unwarranted. Mary Smith, for instance, in *EastEnders*, had to endure or try to avoid the chorus of comments on her failure to care properly for her child when they were made in the pub or launderette but she was able literally to eject those who ventured into her room and the audience was invited to share her outrage at the anonymous letter which was slipped under her door in a clear breach of the public/ personal boundary.

The distinction between public and personal space and the use of the public space as the accepted site for commentary applies even in

Dallas and *Dynasty* where the distinction between the home and the office is much more blurred; Alexis frequently conducts her business affairs from her home and the Ewing wives regularly visit their husbands' offices. Even here though, the establishment of personal space in the home is still important. The office, the club and the hotel are locations where information is exchanged, deals are done and actions subjected to public scrutiny. The home provides a retreat from that world and the entry of business characters into Southfork or the Carrington mansion is always represented as something of a violation. In *Dallas*, it is Miss Ellie in particular who preserves and values that distinction. She it is who complains when business is brought to the dinner table or when JR's colleagues interrupt the family's evening. Conscious of her own role in the family, only a serious crisis takes Miss Ellie to the Ewing office. On one such occasion, she told JR and Bobby that she would no longer defend their methods of running Ewing Oil and her appearance in JR's office underlined the seriousness of her intent. Crossing the same boundaries but this time with characteristic relish, Alexis's arrival in Dexter's site office was enough to get under his guard and led to a sexual encounter which was underscored as passionate by the inappropriateness of the surroundings.

It is clear, then, that while the public and private locations in soaps are well defined, they are not watertight and that the most dramatic moments occur when behaviour appropriate to the private space, be it a love affair or a marital quarrel, occurs in public. This is reinforced by soaps' strong tendency both to bring personal relationships into the work arena and to deal with relationships at work as if they were personal. Soaps are of course marked by the intermingling of family and business relationships. Innumerable husbands and wives work in businesses together, whether it be a pub like Angie and Den in *EastEnders* or an oil company like Pam and Bobby Ewing. Children work with their parents in *Dynasty* and *Crossroads*, siblings do business together in *EastEnders* as in *Dallas*. In *Coronation Street*, Rita Fairclough managed the shop her husband owned and in *Brookside* even Annabelle Collins has had her husband help out on occasions with her small catering business. Even when no family relationship is involved, business relationships are based on friendship rather than on the usual employer/employee arrangements. Rita Fairclough is Mavis's boss but she is also one of her closest friends; Terry and Pat in *Brookside* ran their removal business on the basis of being mates and the business collapsed when their friendship faltered. In their case, as in so many others, relations in the public sphere depended on relations in the private and we need to note the way in which soaps tend to provide characters with emotional reasons for business decisions and link business success with personal motivation. Thus, Alexis's pursuit of Blake Carrington makes her a powerful and successful businesswoman; her success, however, is not based on good business reasons but is rooted in her hatred of her ex-husband and her desire to wreak emotional vengeance. Similarly, though this time with unsuccessful results financially, Cliff Barnes continues to avenge his father by pursuing JR through a series of business battles and at key moments threatens his own business stability by his emotional inability to let JR go. In *EastEnders*, the decline of the Queen Vic and Den's financial crisis was entirely dependent on the crisis in his marriage and the success of all the other small businesses in soaps hinges on the relationships between those running them.

Within the businesses themselves, working relationships are conceived of as an extension of family feelings or friendships. Individual bosses run their institutions in a way that expresses their personal characteristics whether it be JR's devious deals over shares in the company or Mike Baldwin's semi-ironic demands for better productivity. The relationship between boss and worker is frequently presented even in the US prime time soaps as one of direct communication and personal knowledge. With his empire crumbling, Blake Carrington is seen to win over the workers on the potential gas field which might save him through personal charisma. In *Crossroads*, the new motel owner, Bomber Lancaster, speaks personally to all the staff about their future. Even more common in British soaps, however, are the situations where there is no evident boss, where employer/employee relationships are blurred or nonexistent. This is clearly the case in husband and wife partnerships where the business relationship operates as an extension of the marriage. But it is also true of other businesses where the emotional ties are less obvious. The launderette in *EastEnders*, for instance, has no visible owner so the working relationships hinge on the friendships (or otherwise) of the women who work in it – Pauline Fowler, Dot Cotton, Mary Smith – as they try to juggle the demands of this work with their other commitments. Similarly, the café in *Coronation Street* for a long time had an absentee owner and even when Gail Tilsley and Alma became business partners, owning the café, the relationships between those who worked there continued to be based on personal feeling rather than work hierarchies. In *Crossroads*, while in the Motel there clearly were established business relationships, the success of this business apparatus depended on the emotional framework which lay behind it. Over the years, the various directors of the

Motel have always had emotional ties of family or friendship between themselves or with their staff and the programme presented their emotional decisions more often than their business ones. In some sense, the emotional decisions stood for their business decisions and the audience was able to intuit how capable they were of running the Motel through their ability to handle their own personal lives.

The question of external power relations in prime time soaps is nearly always, then, either ignored altogether or translated into personal relationships. This may seem obvious and a further confirmation of the split between the personal and the public sphere and soap's inability to deal with the latter. Certainly, the soaps make little attempt to express the abstractions of modern capitalism and the alienation of workers from their labour in ways acceptable to their left-wing critics. Alvarado, Gutch and Wollen are right to argue that *Dallas* and *Dynasty* 'mystify the actual process of multinational wealth creation'.[28] Yet this treatment of the public sphere of work, business and employment as if it were the private sphere repays further examination rather than being dismissed as unrealistic or exploitative. By adopting this strategy, soaps are attempting to explain the incomprehensible – the economy and business – through what is known and understood by their audience – the intricate wheeling and dealing in the personal sphere. The programmes play to the competencies of their audiences as Brunsdon has described them and encourages them to use those competencies in judging the public as well as the private sphere. Clearly such an approach cannot deal with the impersonality, the repetition and exploitation of work which may be the direct experience of many viewers nor with the way in which effective decisions are institutional rather than individual. Nevertheless, the strategy has more positive consequences than may at first be realised.

For a start, it ensures that women, because of their capabilities in the personal sphere, are also seen to be capable in the business world in a way that is still unusual in TV fiction. Meg Richardson could run the Crossroads Motel successfully precisely because she knew the personal foibles and circumstances of all her staff. Alexis, in a characteristic appropriation of female virtues for wicked ends, successfully understands and plays off the emotional weaknesses of those surrounding her. In businesses which are based on marriage, the woman is likely to be seen as a more equal partner at work because the soap gives her (at least) equal weight in the marriage. Thus, Kathy Beale in *EastEnders* succeeds in her wish to run her own market stall because she refuses to defer to her husband in her marriage. The soaps' need for independent women who can be involved in stories about personal relationships thus has the side effect of presenting an unusually large number of economically self-sufficient women who are out at work. Sometimes this almost works against character type. The quiet, shy Emily Bishop, in *Coronation Street*, has worked consistently in shops, hospitals and even in Baldwin's factory. In other cases, the need for economic independence has fitted in and strengthened the established character. When Gail, in *Coronation Street*, was left by her husband to bring up two small children, she was determined to earn her own living and even when her husband, Brian, returned, Gail continued to work outside the home despite his protestations. In *EastEnders*, Naima's desire to succeed with her corner shop was based on her determination not to be dependent on a man again. Even in the factory set-up, in *Coronation Street*, the women asserted themselves with humour and vigour in their working environment because their leading representatives, Ivy and Vera, were characters in their own right outside the factory. In an important sense, then, women are more active at work in soaps than they are in other kinds of TV drama, precisely because the working situation is presented as an extension of the personal – if work is marriage by other means, soaps seem to say, then women are more likely to be engaged with it.

As well as giving a larger than usual role to women in this way, the soap strategy also invites us to make judgements about work and business outside their own terms. Such an approach cannot begin to tackle the complexities of modern capitalism but it can mean that values other than those of business itself are brought to bear on such issues. The judgements are never, of course, unambiguous. The ruthlessness with which JR runs his oil business, his lack of integrity and his devious plotting, are part of the appeal of his character. But even with JR it is significant that his commitment is to the *family* business and his wheeling and dealing loses its glamour when it puts the family at risk. From its beginning, in fact, *Dallas*'s central tension was between JR's gleeful relish of capitalism and Pam's sustained critique of the way in which her brother-in-law regularly put family relationships at risk by his pursuit of more money and power. On an obviously smaller scale, the factory in *Coronation Street* was the site for a number of stories in which the interests and values of Mike Baldwin and the women workers were seen to be different. Traditionally, in dealing with stories of strikes, disputes and difficulties at work, *Coronation Street* heads for the middle ground – yes, Mike Baldwin did push them too hard – yes, the women were wrong not to see that industrial unrest puts jobs at risk.[29] Nevertheless, there have been moments when Ivy Tilsley's clear statement as a union steward of her opposition to Baldwin has provided him with an effective challenge and it could be argued that many of the scenes in the factory represented Baldwin's failure to turn the women who work for him into the quiet, compliant, hard-working automatons he would like. While stories such as these refer to the importance of increased productivity and higher profits, what they show is that the values of the personal sphere – whether it be Ivy upset over a family drama or Vera's urge to disrupt everything with a laugh – consistently take precedence.

Soaps, then, can take up public issues around work and power but they do so by bringing such matters onto their own terrain. The only soap which has recently tried to extend its own space has been *Brookside*, which gave itself the task not only of taking up social and political questions but of changing the context in which they are normally dealt with in soaps. This led *Brookside* literally into the public terrain – scenes took place not merely in the home or the street but in the factory, the picket line, the trade union meeting, the working men's club. In early episodes, Bobby Grant led a strike at the factory and the scenes on the picket line made it quite clear that this was no small family business in the back streets but a large firm with international connections where decisions were made by directors who certainly had no personal realtionships with their employees. As a trade union official, Bobby was later involved in a dispute over the presence of asbestos in a factory when again commercial factors – the need to fulfil orders – dominated judgements. In both cases, while personal emotion was clearly important to Bobby and his family, the values he brought to bear were political ones of justice, class and solidarity.

It has to be said, however, that *Brookside* has found it difficult to move into the public sphere. The factory setting appeared intermittently even before Bobby's disappearance from the programme and none of the characters now has Bobby's fierce commitment to principle outside the family. Frank Rogers has now undertaken this role but his softer character and his more secure place in the family means that the values he brings to his trade union role are more likely to be based on emotion than politics. Heather Haversham's work as an accountant did involve her visiting large businesses and enabled *Brookside* to take up, as we shall see in chapter 7, issues around sex discrimination and sexual harassment, but her romance with the millionaire Tom and her marriage to heroin addict Nick were in the end more central to the stories built around her. Paul Collins's retirement also removed the basis for stories about his position as a redundant executive and the failure of most of the younger characters to find organised work (a failure rooted in the programme's commitment to realism) meant that for some time there were few new work spaces opening up in the programme; characters such as Damon, Terry and Pat, like their counterparts in the other British soaps, fitted into the more usual small business mode of taxi driving or part-time selling. *Brookside* has retained its interest in the public sphere through, for instance, Rod Corkhill's job as a policeman but it is significant that the changes in *Brookside* have led it to concentrate more on the Close and the people in it so that public issues around work are brought back into the home. It has proved more difficult than might have been expected to break out of the 'natural' soap terrain of the family and the community.

4

Family Matters

'Ever since you moved into this family, you've been trouble.'
JR to Pam, *Dallas*

'You can't even run your own family, let alone Colorado.'
Alexis to Blake, *Dynasty*

'You're one of the world's saints, Mum. I wish I was.'
Michelle to Pauline, *EastEnders*

It will come as no surprise that the basis of soap operas is family life. The rich and powerful in *Dallas* and *Dynasty* and the troubled residents of Brookside Close have one thing in common – they live in a family and their pleasures and dramas take place within that all-embracing structure. The reasons for this fit between the soap opera and the family lie in both the requirements of the form's structure and the nature of its appeal to its audience. We have seen that as a continuous serial the soap opera requires a stable framework which provides for seemingly endless variations in story lines and characters. In addition, its role as women's fiction lays emphasis on the importance of emotional and domestic themes and the value of women's skill in the personal sphere. In both cases a family history, it is tempting to say family melodrama, seems to provide the ideal format, a long-running saga of emotional entanglements with the home as the stable centre. Nevertheless, the way in which the family is articulated in soap operas, the differences between them and particularly between the British soaps and US prime time soaps repays further examination and helps us understand more clearly why the family is so central to soaps.

In referring to family melodramas, I am drawing on the theoretical re-evaluation of 1950s film melodrama which took place in film study in the 1970s and which ofered a reassessment of directors like Minnelli and Sirk.[1] As we saw in chapter 2, these fifties film melodramas do not offer a model for eighties soaps at the level of style. Nevertheless, some of the theoretical work which led to the film genre's re-evaluation offers useful insights and in particular Laura Mulvey's account in her article, 'Notes on Sirk and Melodrama',[2] presents a model which may enable us not merely to mark the different ways in which the family is structured in US and British soaps but to begin to account for that difference.

Mulvey challenged the notion that fifties melodramas allowed a hidden or subversive expression of the problems and contradictions which underpin the construction of the family and the role of men and women within it. She argued instead that 'ideological contradiction is the overt mainspring and specific content of melodrama'[3] and that the source of pleasure in such films lay in the direct and open way in which they presented challenges to the prevailing system. Mulvey questioned the notion that Sirkian melodramas, for instance, were necessarily subversive because the coincidences and complications of their plots, the imposition of their happy endings or their stylistic excesses undermined the coherent construction of bourgeois ideology which seventies film theorists associated with realism.[4] Instead, Mulvey argued that melodrama operated more as a safety valve, an outlet for the inevitable contradictions and inconsistencies which are created by the role of the family in bourgeois society: 'No ideology can even pretend to totality: it must provide an outlet for its own inconsistencies. This is the function of fifties melodrama. It works by touching sensitive areas of sexual repression and frustration; its excitement comes from conflict not between enemies, but between people tied by blood or love.'[5] Thus, Mulvey sees fifties film melodramas as having the function of bringing to the fore what has been repressed in the name of the family and allowing the expression of the needs and desires of its members which are inimical to the family's continuance.

Mulvey's emphasis on the overtness of the genre is useful in thinking about soaps. It fits in with a certain didactic quality that soaps have, the testing-out strategy which allows audiences to speculate on what should be done for the best. And clearly the terrain which she describes is the same, 'the private stamping ground, the family',[6] although the mixed generic nature of soaps means that there will be strong variations in how violently the repressions within the family are given voice. Mulvey goes on to distinguish between two different initial standpoints for melodrama. One is coloured by a female protagonist's dominating point of view which acts as a source of identification. The other examines tensions in the family, and between sex and generations; here, although women play a central part, their point of view is not analysed and does not initiate the drama.[7]

In the woman dominated melodrama, then, the story is told from the woman's viewpoint; our knowledge is gained though her and we are invited to identify with her needs and dissatisfactions. In the male melodrama, it is the male hero who is confronted with the dilemma of how he is to accommodate to the emotional and domestic values of family life. In films such as *Written on the Wind* and *Home from the Hill*, it is masculinity which comes under pressure in a scenario in which destructive male power is softened and tamed and the value of domestic life is reasserted. Mulvey describes the characteristic narrative of such films as presenting 'a positive male figure who rejects rampant virility and opposes the unmitigated power of the father, [and] achieves (at least by means of a "happy end") the reintegration of both sexes in family life'.[8]

This distinction, between male and female melodramas, can be seen to be functioning in the soaps under examination here. While the parallels are not exact, the broad division between melodramas which articulate a woman's viewpoint and those which work on the problems of patriarchy through a focus on one or more male figures provides a useful starting point. In this context, I would argue that *Dallas*, *Dynasty* and the other US prime time soaps tend to be male melodramas whereas the British soaps tend towards the woman's viewpoint. This chapter explores the notion of the patriarchal and matriarchal soaps and the different ways in which they establish and expose family relationships.

The patriarchal soap

It seems at first ironic that a genre which lays some claim to addressing women's issues should, in its patriarchal variant, be so heavily dominated by male businessmen. In both *Dallas* and *Dynasty*, the pivotal character seems to be the white male capitalist whose role as head of the business also gives him status as the head of the family. We saw in chapter 3 how the intermingling of work and family relationships could lead to women taking on a greater role at work than might have been expected because they carry into the public world the skills they use in the personal sphere. With the male characters in US prime time soaps, the position is reversed and the men try to take back into the family the authority which they wield at work, insisting that, because the personal and the public are intertwined, action which is valid in one sphere is equally appropriate in the other. As JR reiterates frequently when asked to explain his actions over a business matter, 'I always try and do what's best for the family,' and Blake Carrington similarly emphasises the unity of family and business when fighting off Alexis's attacks on his character and status. On the surface, both men appear to be extremely powerful capitalist patriarchs, giving orders, making deals and sacrificing other people in the interests of the family's income and continuance. But, as Mulvey has pointed out, rampant male virility poses a threat to domestic order and *Dallas* and *Dynasty* both offer different versions of how such power may be curtailed. Much of the drama (and pleasure) in these programmes comes from the way in which patriarchal power is continually challenged, making it difficult for the male hero to hang on to what he believes is his rightful role as head of the family.

JR is clearly the more dynamic of these male figures. In the early episodes, he was nominally under the control of his father who was the head of the family firm. As the eldest son, JR was given the space to make his forays (always immoral, frequently illegal) which set at risk Ewing Oil and hence the Ewing family but he always had to account to his father for his behaviour. Jock's death removed the central figurehead and, despite the will which forced the two brothers to compete for Ewing Oil, JR assumed possession and has continued to act as if he were head of the company and the father figure for the family. JR is set up in an overt way as aggressive and virile in his business and sexual dealings, the two of course frequently coinciding. He is decisive in his actions, seizing whatever opportunity he can to extend Ewing power. He takes risks; his bankers frequently express the need for caution which he as regularly overrides. He dominated his first wife, Sue Ellen, through a mixture of physical violence and psychological threat and he regularly has affairs with attractive women with whom he often has business connections. He sees himself as following in the footsteps of his own father and is bringing up his own son, John Ross, to take on the dual responsibilities of home and family.

But it is precisely JR's excessive (and stereotypical) masculinity which threatens the domestic values so crucial to a soap and JR's assertion of his own power is continually checked and thwarted in *Dallas*. He believes himself to be in control but more often than not his actions are being watched and predicted by others. JR's enemies frequently play on his masculine strengths – his need for quick action, his attraction to women, his desire for more power – and reveal them as weaknesses by which they can plan his downfall. Thus, his ill-fated pursuit of Angelica, in which he believed he could, as usual, make both the woman and a fast buck, was an elaborate set-up, revealed to the audience from the beginning as a trap. Similarly, JR's desire for quick action over oil prices led him into the deal with the terrorist Calhoun and began the process which led to the break-up of the family firm. His behaviour towards the women in his life – Kristen, Sue Ellen, Kimberley – drives them into forms of revenge which threaten his success at business and his life. Thus, it is JR's proudest assets, his virility and his decisiveness, which are actually the weaknesses which undermine his claim to be acting as the head of the family and in its best interests.

If JR is the over-virile representative of masculinity which has to be curtailed, his brother Bobby and his counterpart Blake Carrington in *Dynasty* are most positive male figures. They tend to be more passive than JR; they do not initiate action but respond when it happens; they get on with women and appear happier in their company; they have a capacity for gentleness and are able to express love and as a result their marriages have been much less stormy and are regularly presented as idyllic; in business, they operate with a sense of honour. Because of this, Bobby and Blake are at home in the family in a way in which JR never is. They have been tamed and domesticated so that they respect and enjoy the domestic virtues of cooperation and harmony. There remains some difficulty, however, in representing the domesticated man positively. A story circulates among *Dallas* fans that written into Patrick Duffy's contract is a requirement that Bobby will be allowed to punch JR every fourth episode. True or not, it neatly exemplifies the difficulty of playing the 'good man' and demonstrates how deeply the qualities of action and aggression are written into the concept of the hero. Because of this it is essential that even these 'good' characters have their moments of excessive virility. Bobby does get to punch JR; he has also competed vigorously with him for control of Ewing Oil and significantly put his marriage at risk by adopting JR's values and methods. Blake Carrington, too, is given to moments of ungovernable rage, most notably over his son Steven's homosexuality but also in his dealings with Alexis.[9] In both cases, it is as if the patriarchal melodrama has succeeded too well in taming the male and the outbursts of excessive action are a way of reasserting patriarchal power.

Dallas and *Dynasty* offer us, then, representations of masculinity both out of control and over-controlled. The ceaseless work of both programmes is to attempt to put the masculine figure into his proper place as head of the family and of the business. The ideal position for the hero in the patriarchal melodrama is a static one, at the apex of the family and the business, uniting both into a single entity in which the separate spaces of home and office are merged. This work is never achieved; the patriarchal hero never reaches the position of absolute power. Domestic harmony is always challenged by a business attack; public power by family dissatisfaction with the means by which it has been achieved. And more often than not behind that challenge is a woman.

Women are central to the patriarchal hero's problems in two ways. Most directly, and this is a more recent development, they are presented as rivals in the business sphere. Alexis in *Dynasty* was the first woman to assert herself so clearly and capably in this way as a business rival to Blake Carrington. She takes on the masculine attributes of the hero and returns them in spades; she is as brutal, as single-minded and daring as he can ever be with, in the programme's terms, the additional advantage of a woman's expertise in handling emotional issues. But Alexis is perhaps not typical of the businesswoman in US prime time soaps who tend to be rather more capable of humane decisions than their male counterparts. Pamela Ewing, though always ambivalent about the business world, was shown as competent and effective, able to separate business demands from family ones when, for example, she resisted her brother Cliff's pleas for more money because he was clearly a bad business risk. By working with Cliff as a partner, though, Pam was certainly challenging JR and the integrity of the Ewing family business. Similarly, her mother, Rebecca Wentworth, was an efficient businesswoman who gave her son the Wentworth empire and hence the means to pursue his vendetta against JR. Even Sue Ellen, in later series of *Dallas*, made a success of a floundering lingerie business and while this was not a direct challenge to Ewing Oil, JR understood her entry into the business sphere to be a bid for independence and hence a threat to his authority.

Nevertheless, it is clear from these examples that the women's challenge to men in the business sphere is fuelled by what is happening elsewhere in the family. Alexis and Blake's business feud over the Carrington empire has its roots in their failed marriage and their relationships with the children. Pamela Ewing's rivalry with JR is caused by her position in the Barnes/Ewing families and not by her skills as a businesswoman. Sue Ellen's move into business is clearly related to the state of her marriage as is made explicit in the scene in which, newly confident of her business success and dressed in her own firm's lingerie, she seduces JR only to reject him at the last minute. It is this second source of challenge through the family relationships which we need to examine more closley if we are to understand the nature of the problem posed by women in patriarchal soaps.

As we have seen, while men appear to control much of the action in *Dallas* and *Dynasty*, their preferred position is a static one, in charge of a unified family and business. Structurally, and unusually, the heart of the programmes is the men's homes. This is the place where the idyll could be achieved if only everything (and particularly the women) would fall into place. Hence, we get the slightly absurd situation at Southfork of two or three adult sons still living under their parents' roof and bringing their own families to the family dining table. Similarly, in *Dynasty*, great emphasis is placed on possession of the family mansion; Alexis takes it over in her hour of triumph and the children, Fallon, Adam, Steven and Amanda, all live there well after they could have established their own homes. It could of course be argued that this is just convenient and economical plotting which allows the characters to meet regularly without straining the audience's credulity too much. But it is important to bear in mind that this emphasis on the family home is not, as we shall see, the rationale for action chosen by British soaps and that such choices have consequences for the kind of stories which are then available. In *Dallas*, this central device means that the sons are fixed however improbably around the family home while the position of the women – their wives, ex-wives, potential wives – is much more fluid. If we look more closely at *Dallas* we can see that this greater fluidity means that women hold a crucial role in generating the movement in and out of the family which is essential for its narrative.

Dallas began with Pamela Barnes's entry into Southfork – her movement, through marriage, from the Barnes into the Ewing family forces into the open the past relations between the two families and throws into question the future of the family in terms of the child she is expecting. It is as if the story opens *in media res* with an event which breaks apart the already established family so that a crack opens up which runs back into the past and forward into the future. At the very start, then, it is the woman's change of place which acts as the initial disruptive agent in the narrative and that pattern has continued ever since. Pam herself has continued to move, out of the Ewing family through divorce and her 'marriage' outside, back in again through her remarraige to Bobby and out again after the car crash. Sue Ellen similarly has moved in and out of the family through marriage and divorce. The women are thus the outsiders, taking on the family name but potentially threatening the family both when they enter it and when they leave.

What is the nature of the threat which marks the women's movement in and out of the family? It is, in part, a question of loyalty. As JR trenchantly puts it, 'Some of the ladies in this house have forgotten which side their bread is buttered.' At the heart of JR's complaint is the refusal of the women in the family to concede that the continuance of the family depends on the unifying of the family and business in the person of the patriarchal hero; there is always a danger that they will retain loyalties elsewhere, particularly to the family they have left. This is clearly the case with Pam who is continually accused by JR of being a traitor to the Ewings because of her affection for her brother, Cliff, and other members of the Barnes family. Even after her remarriage to Bobby when she moved back into the Ewing camp, JR's enemy, Jeremy Wendell, accurately describes Pam as 'a Trojan horse at the Ewing table'. Wendell is right, even though Pam is scrupulous in keeping her Wentworth business affairs and her family life apart. Her very presence, her own family history, challenges the Ewing claim to unity because it is evidence of JR's failure to assert his control over who is to be allowed into the family. If Pam is the most clear example of loyalties divided inside and outside the family, the other women also demonstrate the dilemma. Donna is torn between the values of Washington and those of Southfork, a situation dramatised, for instance, when she works on the oil commission against JR or challenges Miss Ellie's cherished family history in order to establish the truth for a book she is writing. Similarly, Jenna Wade brings to her relationships with Bobby and Ray the complications of her own past including accusations of murder, and Sue Ellen, who lacks almost entirely a family of her own, nevertheless brings her sister Kristen into the Ewing family with near-fatal results.

But if family loyalty is at stake here, so also is the control of the women's sexuality for it is women's desire which brings them into the family and may take them out again. At various points in *Dallas*, the Ewing women have moved out of the family home to pursue their sexual desires elsewhere. Sue Ellen's main way of challenging JR (until her more recent business activity) was through affairs with other men – Cliff Barnes, Dusty, Clayton Farlow, Nicholas Pearce. Sue Ellen's sexual adventures are defined as a threat to the family and her own role as wife and mother in it. Gillian Swanson has argued that the crossing of the line between the domestic and the

business sites is a sign of trouble, 'any venturing out being a source
of conflict, of undermining of solidity'.[10] JR certainly warns Sue
Ellen of the dangers of crossing the line. 'You're going to be in
trouble as long as you put your trust in outsiders,' he warns, 'and
you're a Ewing, remember that.' It is important to note, however,
that Sue Ellen's move out of the home is as destructive to JR as it is
to her and that her behaviour is at least partly endorsed by the
audience's knowledge of JR's cruelty to her. This sympathy can be
extended to the other women who step out of line. Pam's relationship with Mark, for instance, has to be judged in the light of Bobby's
increasingly harsh actions during his competition with JR and Lucy's
wayward behaviour outside the home is explained by her stormy
relationship with JR in it. Thus, while the women's departure from
the family is seen as a cause of trouble it cannot be unproblematically condemned since the reasons for their action can be found in
the male behaviour within the home.

The challenge women pose to the family goes further than this
because it is intimately tied up with the question of paternity. For if
marriage is one way the family gets extended, childbirth is the other.
In a fiction which is centrally concerned with patriarchal power,
childbirth becomes a fraught issue because it is the point at which the
father can be least sure of his own control. Paternity is hard to prove
and 'Who is my father? Who is my child?' have been central
questions in *Dallas*. There is nothing certain about fatherhood and a
change in the father–child tie changes the relations with the other
characters in the fiction. This uncertainty about paternity has been
expressed through a number of key stories in *Dallas*. It appeared in
JR's determination to prove scientifically that he was John Ross's
father and in his fights with Sue Ellen over custody of his son; it
appeared in the revelation that Digger was not after all Pamela's
father and that Ray was in fact Jock's son. Even when paternity itself
is not in doubt, the father's ability to control the upbringing of his
child is. This fear was expressed by Ray when the pregnant Donna
left him and he demanded of his lawyer, 'a father must have some
rights.' When Sue Ellen removed John Ross from Southfork, going
first to Dusty and then starting up again with Cliff Barnes, Miss Ellie
was clear about the nature of JR's concern. 'No wonder there's
trouble . . . She's John Ross's mother and JR doesn't want any man
between himself and his son.' JR himself used these paternal anxieties when he set up Lisa to challenge Bobby for the care and
control of his adopted son, basing his scheme on the fact that Bobby
is not Christopher's real father. Paternity remains a time bomb still
for Bobby as Jenna Wade, after a brief sojourn, moved out of the

Ewing household with Bobby's child. Behind all these situations lies an uncertainty about paternity and a fear that if a woman moves outside marriage for sexual satisfaction she throws the fatherhood of her children into question and threatens the father's control of the family to which she 'belongs'.

The male hero in US prime time soaps is engaged, then, in a continual struggle to keep control over the family, to bar entrance to unsuitable entrants and keep inside the family space those who belong there through birth or marriage. On his failure depends the continuance of the story since his absolute success would pressage the lack of movement which signifies a happy ending. This battle for control also helps to explain the other key story lines, those of property and inheritance. Property is the physical manifestation of the family's success; inheritance is the mechanism of its survival. At stake in such stories is not only the family but the patriarchal values around which it is organised. The father can hand on the control of the family (along with its wealth and property) but the rite of succession is a fraud if the child is not a true Ewing, not his father's son. JR literally spells this out for Sue Ellen when with John Ross's alphabet bricks he makes the words, 'MAMA, DADDY, OIL'.

The inheritance procedure is threatened in two different ways by the woman who transgresses the family boundaries. Firstly she casts doubt on the paternity of any child she conceives and even her return cannot wipe out her action. JR's frantic determination to prove that John Ross was his son was thus the more desperate because failure would mean that the patriarchal role would eventually be assumed by Cliff Barnes's child, an outsider potentially given control of the family by Sue Ellen's unfaithfulness. Secondly, a woman leaving the family may take with her the father's child and expose him to values other than those of his father. Thus, James Beaumont's unexpected appearance as JR's illegitimate son, brought up by his mother, poses problems for the unimpeded passage of the business to the legitimate John Ross. Though lacking the same intensity, Pam's removal of Christopher challenged Bobby's influence over the child, and the children of Jenna and Donna, conceived within the family but born as their mothers moved out of it, are likely to provoke the same kinds of difficulties. Pam's offer to buy Jenna's baby had at least the logic of its own terms. For once acting as a true Ewing, Pam, in her desperation to give Bobby his son, articulated the philosophy of child as property which is at the heart of the patriarchal melodrama.

Viewed from this angle, the complexity of the relationships within the family, the notorious coupling and recoupling which is such a striking feature of the US prime time soaps, begins to make sense.

What is at stake is both the preservation of family boundaries and the correct passing on of the family/business inheritance. Given these two requirements, the semi-incestuous nature of many of the relationships offers a way of keeping women's sexuality, with all its repercussions for paternity and property, literally in the family since, as Terry Lovell has suggested, 'incest is precisely the logic of all attempts to confine sexual desire to home and family.'[11] Thus, we have the marriage, divorce and remarriage of the two central couples, JR and Sue Ellen and Bobby and Pamela, when the women left the family only to be brought back in again. On top of this there are a whole series of relationships in which a love affair is preceded by some other family relationship. JR has an affair with his wife's sister, Sue Ellen with her sister-in-law's brother, later turning down an offer of marriage by her lover's father who later still becomes her mother-in-law's husband. Jamie Ewing marries her cousin-in-law's brother and Ray Krebbs takes under his roof his brother's pregnant ex-fiancée whom he in turn marries. *Dallas*'s continual reworking of these para-incestuous relationships gains particular force from the way in which, as we have seen, sexual issues are consistently tied up with those of possession and inheritance. So far as matters of property are concerned, incest is the answer to the problem of the transgressive woman. While paternity might still be in doubt, at least the family name would be the same and the inheritance would not go to an outsider. But incest is the one solution which is forbidden and the hero's search for stable power continues to be thwarted by the refusal of the women in the family to be pinned down.

In arguing that women are central to the male hero's uneasy grasp on power, I have for the sake of clarity used only examples from *Dallas*. Nevertheless, the same scenario can be traced in the other US prime time soaps. In *Dynasty*, the initial transgressive move is that of Alexis moving out of the family. The different direction of that initial move – Alexis moved out while Pamela moved in – helps to explain why, in *Dynasty*, the struggle is much more clearly between two camps competing for the heart of the family. Alexis's challenge to Blake, her rejection of loyalty and fidelity to him, is translated into a struggle for the wealth of the Carrington family. Alexis, as we have seen, fights with Blake over business dealings but she has also used her sexuality to challenge him through a series of unsuitable affairs including his brother Ben, his wife's first husband Mark, and a business colleague Dexter. The fact that Alexis chooses for her lovers men with whom Blake has a family or business connection underlines the extent to which her affairs take on meaning only in so far as they disturb Blake.

While Alexis's challenge is clearly marked as being that of the 'bad' woman, the villainess, other women characters similarly upset attempts at patriarchal control. Claudia came into the family by her marriage to Steven, bringing with her a history of madness which puts his child, Danny, at risk. Sammy Jo moved out of the family and had a series of relationships which Steven jealously observed. Kirby disturbed the precarious relationship between Jeff and Adam when she agreed to marry Jeff, and the rivalry her entry into the family provoked became overt hostility when she eventually turned to Adam instead. Unlike the Ewing family, the Carrington family has two daughters and both Fallon and Amanda's sexual transgressions have also threatened the family which Blake has tried to build up a round him. Even Krystle, the blonde foil to Alexis's revenge, is not entirely under Blake's control. She has left him several times; the appearance of her first husband, Mark, gave Alexis an ally in one of her many assaults on Blake and Krystle's relationships with other men, particularly in the earlier series, disturbed the equilibrium of her relationship with Blake which is at the heart of the serial's representation of the family.

As in *Dallas*, the trouble generated by the women's transgressive movement is expressed in problems over children, property and inheritance. Alexis and Blake fight over possession of the children as if they were still minors. In the manner of Southfork, Blake has provided a home at various times for all his children and Adam and Steven have held posts in both Carrington and Colby-Co, another example of the way in which business relationships provide a means of working out family dynamics. Alexis has consistently tried to lure her children away from Blake and through a combination of fierce (if calculating) maternal affection and business has succeeded often enough to disrupt the patriarchal harmony. Alexis has refused to allow an unproblematic passage of inheritance and her determination to take the children away both physically and morally has consistently provided the motivating force in her complicated plots. Her determination that, in her words, the children should 'realise that Blake is not the God they think he is' has been a persistent and overt rationale running through her actions. Indeed, Blake's desire to control the children reaches beyond the immediate heirs into the next generation. He has, for instance, tried to secure his grandchild Danny, firstly from the effects of his mother's 'promiscuity' and secondly from his father's homosexuality. We shall examine the handling of Steven's gayness later, but for the moment it is enough to note Blake's emphasis on Danny being safe in the family home.

The relationship between sexuality and property expresses itself, as it does in *Dallas*, in allusions to incest. Mark Finch has noted the para-incestuous nature of the relationship between Blake and Krystle, citing not only their relationship in the series but also the previous role of John Forsythe and Linda Evans as uncle and niece in a US situation comedy, *Bachelor Father*.[12] Over the years, *Dynasty* has provided other examples of such relationships. Like *Dallas*, *Dynasty* has featured remarriages in which control over the woman is broken and re-exerted. Fallon and Jeff, Krystle and Blake, Claudia and Steven and Steven and Sammy Jo are cases in point. In some instances, the more directly incestuous liaisons, like those in *Dallas*, seem to offer a way of trying to maintain male control over the wayward or problematic women who have entered the Carrington family through marriage. Thus the sons of the family (Steven, Adam and their brother-in-law, Jeff) have a history of sharing the women they bring into the family. Claudia, while still married to Steven, began an affair with his brother Adam whom she later married. Adam featured in another triangle, this time with Jeff and his fiancée Kirby. Kirby, whose problematic status has its own roots as the daughter of a family servant, moved from Jeff to Adam, having conceived a child from his para-incestuous rape. Jeff himself, having parted from Fallon for a second time, almost immediately began a relationship with Steven's ex-wife, Sammy Jo, whose love affairs have troubled both Steven and Blake.

But incest has a second function in *Dynasty*, arising from Blake's heavily marked role as the father; unlike JR he has no role as a son and, again unlike JR, Blake had, before the serial started, already lost his wife. Thus, in order to regain his proper position as head of the family he must establish his sexual control over Alexis and the narrative of *Dynasty* is marked by a number of semi-incestuous situations which figure the desired but unattainable partnership of Alexis and Blake. Alexis's affairs with Ben and Mark are both examples of a male figure standing in for Blake himself. Their relationship with Alexis is provoked by Blake's unremitting hostility towards them and he thus forces them into Alexis's camp. The fact that neither can control Alexis or indeed be loved by her underlines the inadequacy of the substitution. Alexis's marriage to Dex has a rather different twist but leads to the same conclusion. He is much younger than her and his affair with her daughter Amanda emphasies that he is of a different generation, more appropriately her son than her husband. Once again, it is plain that he is no substitute for Blake. Ironically, Blake momentarily achieves the patriarch's proper position when, reunited with Alexis, his amnesia allows him to believe that the woman is back in her rightful place again. The moment is shortlived since the 'happy ending' of re-established male control, the successful positioning of the hero at the apex of family and business, would bring the story at last to a 'happy' conclusion.

It may be argued that this account of the patriarchal soap has concentrated too heavily on the figures of Blake and JR and has ignored the women who can be seen as the moral centre of their families – Miss Ellie and Krystle Carrington. Certainly, these figures are crucial to the family set-up in that they act as a constant reminder to the men of the need for integrity, humanity and domestic harmony. In *Dallas*, it is Miss Ellie who acts as a restraint on her son; it is she who persuades JR not to bring up Sue Ellen's past in the divorce court, she who warns her sons against the danger of rivalry, who condemns JR when she finds out about his terrorist activities. It is Miss Ellie indeed who maintains the memory of Jock, the last head of the family, and reminds JR of his significance. 'Your Daddy would have been ashamed,' she tells him after learning of the threat to the family which JR had created through his connection with Calhoun; 'Ewing Oil should have died with your Daddy.' Her lack of movement compared with the other women in *Dallas*, her stable position at Southfork, emphasises that she is the still centre around whom the others revolve. Krystle occupies a similar position in the Carrington household. She is clearly the counterpoint to Alexis in moral stature and attitude. The contrast is presented vividly through appearance and style. When she and Alexis compete for Blake the contrast could not be more marked. Alexis is artificial with white make-up, red nails and lips, black curls, while Krystle is 'natural' with fair hair, blue eyes, free hair. Although she does work for Blake, Krystle is normally seen at home and she welcomes into it anyone who needs comfort and support. She accepts without resentment Blake's children and she is frequently called on to ameliorate his patriarchal harshness and his castigation of himself.

Nevertheless, while Miss Ellie and Krystle are clearly crucial to the programmes, they are not the site of the drama. Their struggle is to hang on to pre-established values and to tame the male hero into accepting the harmony of the home. While their moral superiority is plain they offer only one set of answers. They have no hesitation about knowing the right course of action even when it causes them anguish and pain. But the key dilemmas in US soaps are not theirs but those of the hero who is forced to navigate between the moral righteousness of Miss Ellie and Krystle and the more vigorous pleasures outside the home. Miss Ellie and Krystle lay out the moral position clearly enough and in doing so they provide a check on what Mulvey calls 'rampant virility' by their assertion of a different set of values, but they do not directly challenge the hero's capacity to wield power in the same way as the other women in the family. They accept their place within the home in a way in which Alexis and Sue Ellen do not.

It is the position of the hero which is at stake in US prime time soaps. The women may be the strongest figures but it is significant that their function is to offer the male characters alternatives, to challenge his control and to block his power. The pleasure for women viewers of patriarchal soaps is the demonstration that male power, challenged on the one hand by moral questioning and on the other by the women's refusal to be controlled, can never be fully or unproblematically asserted.

The matriarchal soap

The US prime time soaps offer a particular version of the family in which the battle for control centres on the male hero. The family structure is apparently quite loose and pervasive with dead or previously unknown relatives popping up to claim their stake in the family through demands on property and inheritance rights. But the struggles caused by such demands demonstrate that access to the family is in fact limited. The movement of women, in particular, through marriage and divorce puts the family under stress precisely because it is at these points that the boundaries separating the family and the rest are weakest and require the most insistent patrolling by the male members of the family. The women in the family do have a moral responsibility for maintaining relationships and values within the home, especially when they are put at risk through the family's business interests, but the ultimate responsibility for ensuring the family's survival, particularly in its most concrete form of property and wealth, lies with the central hero, although his capacity to do so is both challenged and undermined by the women. Thus, in US prime time soaps, the ideal family is a relatively closed institution, perceiving itself as a fortress against the rest of the world. As Miss Ellie reiterates, it is 'always the family, against all outsiders' and entry is difficult. 'This family does seem to have rather a strict set of rules,' Dana confides to Krystle before her movement into the Carrington family through her marriage to Adam.

By contrast, the British soaps present a model of the family which is more open, less fraught by problems of power and more heavily dominated by women. British soaps are less concerned with the struggles of the male hero to unite business and family. Instead, they present a narrative in which the mother takes on the burden of being both the moral and practical support to the family. This is not to say that families are not under stress in these programmes but that the way in which they are organised and presented is different and hence the moments of crisis occur at different points. An examination of the construction of the families in British soaps and in particular the role of women in that construction will help to establish the nature of that difference.

Crossroads provides a good starting point for an analysis of this difference, since it is the only one of the British soaps I am studying in which the concrete manifestation of family values through business is strongly present in a way comparable to the US programmes. In the other British soaps, as we have seen, families do work together but the emphasis tends to be on family members jointly trying to earn a living rather than to secure the family company and hence the inheritance. In *Crossroads*, however, the future of the Motel is intertwined with the future of the family. But the Crossroads Motel, certainly in its first 17 years, was rather different from Ewing Oil or the Carrington/Colby nexus. Firstly, while it was clearly a business it was also firmly in the domestic sphere. There were decisions to be made about money, takeovers, board meetings and so forth but the basic concern of the motel was to provide a comfortable service for its customers. The aims of such a business are thus very different from the conventionally masculine world of oil rigs and speculative drilling and the task of management in the motel frequently seemed more like organising a large and disorderly family than a high-powered business. This is not to underestimate the power which the first and longest running owner, Meg Richardson, was seen to wield, for it was part of her attraction as a character that she was able to make difficult management decisions in a forceful way and carry them through despite disagreements. Here indeed is the second point of difference between *Crossroads* and the US prime time soaps, for the family business in the British soap was indisputably controlled by the mother and not the father/son of the family. Even when Meg, controversially, was written out of the programme and control moved to David Hunter, women still played a very active part in the running of the motel and a further shake-up in 1985 brought another woman, Nicola Freeman, back in charge.

This shift in emphasis to matriarchal control of the family business has a number of consequences. The risks to the business and hence to the family are presented as external rather than internal since the woman manager is constructed as caring and, in a nonpolitical sense, conservative. Although she too acts in accordance with her emotions, they are much less likely to put the family at risk than the excesses of the patriarchal hero. Throughout the *Crossroads* saga, the Motel has been under outside threat from takeovers, developers, new roads planned to run through it and even from the designs of Meg's various husbands. But unlike JR who, as we have seen, himself constitutes a threat to Ewing Oil, Meg was consistently persented as the Motel's champion and defender. Even Nicola Freeman, who later took over the business and was initially feared as the representative of big business, found herself defending Crossroads' uniqueness to the big hotel chain which had taken it over. Both women combined the roles kept separate in the US soaps, the head of the family/business and the moral touchstone. By uniting these roles, the programme created a different structure, effectively putting a strong mother in charge. Such an analogy is reinforced by the fact that Meg, from the beginning, had her son and daughter living and later working in the Motel and that Nicola brought her stepson and daughter to work under her. Giving the head of the business moral authority has the effect of defusing the struggles for control within the family so characteristic of the US prime time soaps and of turning them into battles against external agents. This change in focus gave Meg, in particular, much greater authority than her male counterparts and confirmed her dominating position in the programme.

The dual role of the women owners of the Crossroads Motel has consequences for the presentation of the male characters. Robbed of the 'natural' role as business head, the men in *Crossroads* have been presented as largely ineffective not only in their personal lives but also in their working relationships. They have not been treated unsympathetically and indeed characters like David Hunter, Adam Chance and Daniel Freeman have had a shifty charm. It is perhaps significant that David Hunter, the most glamorous of the three, also had a measure of power in the interregnum following Meg's departure but even he appeared to vacillate when faced with major decisions, particularly when he had to assert himself against his fellow directors, including his wife, Barbara, and Meg's daughter, Jill. Adam Chance has, as his name implies, always been something of a 'wide boy' with an eye for the main chance and a selfish propensity to seek options which will benefit himself rather than the Motel. His attempts to achieve real power were always thwarted as much by his own weak charcter as by the actions of others. Daniel Freeman, who presented himself as a challenger to his stepmother, Nicola, was also exposed as lazy and feckless, incapable of making the firm commitment to power essential to the characterisation of JR or Blake Carrington. Thus the men in *Crossroads* have lacked both moral authority and real power; their intrinsic weakness has been structured into the *Crossroads* narrative by the positioning of a woman as the central business figure. As Daniel Freeman ruefully put it, 'There are far too many interfering women in this place. I suspect there always have been.'

If *Crossroads* is unusual among British soaps in its strong emphasis on a single family business, its representation of women as the dominant members of the family is by no means unique. In their models of the nuclear family, the British programmes consistently present a woman as the central prop, sustaining the family through moments of crisis. As with Meg in *Crossroads*, the mother figure is the emotional and practical head of the family combining moral insight with a dogged capacity to keep going whatever vicissitudes occur. The classic example of this figure is Pauline Fowler in *EastEnders* who financially and emotionally supports her family, including at various points her husband, mother, children and grandchild. With her husband, Arthur, only sporadically employed, Pauline has had to take on a number of jobs outside the home to try and keep the family afloat financially. Arthur's depression placed on her the burden of boosting his morale and she was for a long time engaged in a continual struggle to keep the peace between him and her mother, Lou Beale. The drama in the immediate Fowler family, then, is not over who controls the family but focuses on how Pauline can sustain the burden of responsibility. Her position is made the more difficult since, while Pauline's role is made clear to the audience, she sometimes has to appear to acknowledge Arthur as the head of the family in order to preserve his male esteem. Such moments normally end disastrously as when Arthur tries to give Pauline 'a day off' as a birthday treat only to find that the cost has led the family further into debt. In his darkest moments, Arthur knows the truth of the relationship. 'I love you, Pauline, because you are strong,' he told his wife on his return home from a period in hospital.

Similar sentiments have been expressed by other soap husbands. In *Coronation Street*, Ivy Tilsley held her family together when her likeable but weak husband, Bert, was unemployed and ill; Hilda Ogden similarly gave her feckless husband, Stan, fierce and possessive loyalty backed up with regular cash to supplement his unreliable window-cleaning income; Vera Duckworth mockingly supports her husband, Jack, and defends him fiercely against the criticisms of others. In *Crossroads*, Kath Brownlow was the moral arbiter in family disputes between her husband and children and went on to be a practical support to her idealistic second husband; Margaret Grice, similarly, took the role of peacemaker in family disputes and had charge of the family finances, adding to their income herself by taking on the local shop. In all these cases, the family life in the programmes revolved quite clearly around the woman who is seen to provide not merely the moral centre, as Krystle and Miss Ellie do in *Dynasty* and *Dallas*, but also the practical and financial means of day-to-day living.

This structure of the strong woman/weak man can be seen even in those families where the husband appears to be the head of the family. In *Brookside*, for instance, Billy Corkhill clearly saw himself, despite being unemployed, as the head of the family, looking to control his wife Doreen and their children in a way which was both loving and bullying. Part of the drama here centred around Billy's desire to hold on to this power, his concern at his son's challenge to him as the main breadwinner, his jealousy over his wife's movements. This story is comparable to that of the Ewings in its emphasis on the male attempt to control the family but it is presented very differently. Unemployment did not create Billy's problems in controlling his family but revealed what was always the case – that the motivating force in the family was always his wife, Doreen. It was her drive that led them to the Brookside house, her fierce loyalties which kept father and children together and her earnings which provided the necessary safety net when Billy lost his job. In the same programme, the Grant family at first appeared to be led by the father and husband, Bobby, who was vigorous, articulate and employed – a somewhat unusual combination for a man in a British soap. Nevertheless, it was Sheila Grant who was at the emotional centre of the family. While standing up for her own needs, her main concern was still to hold the family together. She enabled her daughter, Karen, to leave the family while still preserving her relationship with her father. She protected her son, Barry, from Bobby's anger and provided her other son, Damon, with consistent support. Even following the trauma of her own rape, it was her strength which enabled Bobby to begin to handle his own grief and rage over the event. Again in *Brookside*, Chrissie Rogers has played a similar role in her family, quite consciously the driving force behind her husband, Frank, and fiercely loyal to and protective of her three children.

What is striking here is how consistently the women in British soaps work to hold the family together. While in the US prime time soaps, wives and mothers like Sue Ellen, Pamela and Alexis pose, sometimes despite themselves, a challenge to family unity, the key women in British soaps are the linchpin on which the family structure depends. The strains of the tasks are not underestimated and indeed are a source of the drama but the role itself is accepted. Pauline's position is commented on by others in the Square; she is offered sympathy and well-meaning words but little practical support. She absorbs the troubles and anger of other members of the family with a resignation that implies that there is no other option. Sheila Grant, who is more forceful than Pauline, nevertheless finds herself in the supportive role, pleading with her husband to think first of his family rather than his work and providing consistent and unstinting help for her children. 'What's a mother for,' she asks her son Damon, 'if you can't come to her with your problems?' It was in keeping with this acceptance of female responsibilities that, when Bobby left, Sheila should find herself taking up Doreen's role in the Corkhill family.

This structural role of selfless support is passed on from one generation to another in British soaps. Indeed, the young women seem almost to be in training to pick up their mothers' burdens. Through the years, British soap audiences have been able to watch the young girls in the programmes develop into strong women on whom, in their turn, the family relies. Thus, in *Crossroads*, Glenda Brownlow married Kevin and began to take on the characteristics of commonsense and a stubborn commitment to family values which her mother, Kath, had displayed. Her marriage to Kevin, who was a 'bit of a lad' and found the family somewhat restricting, foundered a number of times but was sustained through financial crises and problems over having children by Glenda's firm determination that it should continue. A similar scenario has been played out in *Coronation Street* with Gail Tilsley. Gail first featured as a giggly teenager who, with her best friend Suzie, was interested only in boys, dates and having fun. Marion Jordan, in the *Coronation Street* monograph in 1981, characterised her as 'not an adolescent in years but consistently treated as such'.[13] But Gail was always the more serious of the two and it is significant that she continued to develop in the programme while the fun-loving but ultimately selfish Suzie disappeared. Gail, like Glenda, married a lad whose commitment to the family ideal was not as secure as her own but Gail continued to support him financially and emotionally, encouraging him to set up his own business and move away from his dependence on his mother. Even during the trauma of Brian leaving, Gail remained the stable centre for the children in contrast to Brian's unpredictable behaviour which put the family, and in particular his son Nicky, at risk. Brian's death has left Gail with even greater responsibilities as the single parent of two small children.

Even further along this narrative road is Deirdre Barlow, also in
Coronation Street. Like Gail, she was a flirtatious and lively young
woman, caught up in a number of relationships with the lads of the
Street. She, like Gail, married a man who lacked her moral values
and commonsense and this marriage similarly foundered when Ray
left her to bring up a young child on her own. Deirdre married again,
this time to the most reliable man in the serial, Ken Barlow, and
over the years she continued to provide a practical foil to his
idealism. It was she, for instance, who reconciled Ken to the fact of
his daughter's marriage and tried to ensure that Susan's choice of
husband did not cause an irretrievable rift in the family; it was she
also who encouraged him to remortgage their home so that he could
buy and run the local newspaper. When his affair threatened their
marriage, Deirdre was fierce in her demand that he recognise that
her practical commitment had made his career possible.

Brookside and *EastEnders*, although they have fewer years behind
them, also provide examples of young girls growing into the strong,
maternal role. In *Brookside*, Karen Grant, while still looking to her
mother Sheila for support, has herself proved more responsible than
her brothers, Barry and Damon, neither of whom found much
direction in life. Unlike the other young women I have cited, Karen
has not married and created her own family but the construction of
her character has been based on a firmer moral and practical sense
than her brothers. Pauline Fowler's daughter, Michelle, in *EastEnders*, has found moving into the role particularly difficult. Michelle
shares with her mother qualities of commonsense, endurance and a
rueful humour. At the age of 16, Michelle had a baby to look after
and she subsequently married the idealistic and impractical Lofty
who was not the father of her child. Significantly, Lofty was himself
virtually without family and looked to Michelle to provide him with a
secure emotional and financial base. Michelle, however, found the
role irksome – 'I have feelings too . . . [Everyone says] No problems.
Michelle's coping and she's fine . . . I want to make things happen
instead of them happening to me.' The subsequent break-up of her
marriage has released her for the time being from her mother's
burden but the history of British soaps is against her making a long-
term bid to escape.

Clearly, the emphasis on the strong maternal characters in British
soaps and the way in which young women grow into such roles
should not be allowed to overshadow the women who do not fit into
this category. The best example of this is Angie in *EastEnders*, who,
while she aspired to be a good mother and supportive wife, consistently found herself goaded into lashing out against the frustrations

of family life. Lucy Collins in *Brookside*, the unstable contrast to Karen Grant, is unpredictable, irrational and unloving to her parents. Even those who accept the maternal burden are prone to lapses – indeed, the stories about them depend on such falls from grace. Usually, these lapses are brought about by the temptations of romantic love which is clearly set up in opposition to the humdrum harmony of family life. The temporary break-up of Gail Tilsley's marriage was due to her romantic affair with Brian's Australian cousin, Ian, and subsequent doubts about the paternity of her youngest child. Deirdre Barlow also was tempted by romance in her famous affair with Mike Baldwin. In some ways, these stories are not dissimilar to those in the US prime time soaps but the attitude towards them and the outcome is different. In both these cases, the women chose to return to the security of the family, and in Gail's case Brian was established to be the father of the child. These examples, in fact, illustrate that the emotional and practical role undertaken by women in British soaps is a demanding and difficult one and that those undertaking it sometimes need a 'holiday' from it. Nevertheless, the rapidity of their return to the fold and their resumption of the family demands demonstrate how crucial the matriarchal position is to the construction of the family in these programmes.

The dominance of the women extends into the older generation too. In some ways, this is not surprising, since older women have traditionally been seen as a source of knowledge and support. *Dallas*, as we have seen, presents its audience with a clear example of this kind of image in Miss Ellie who is the repository of moral authority in the Ewing household. British soaps, however, use this grandmother figure rather more ambiguously. Perhaps because the 'heroine' of British soaps is the young to middle-aged mother, the grandmother is often seen as being yet another of her problems. This was true, for example, of Lou Beale, whose crotchety contrariness frequently added to her daughter Pauline's difficulties. When Lou died her role was taken on by Mo Butcher, an old East Ender who drives her daughter-in-law, Pat, to distraction. In *Brookside*, similarly, the gossipy, spendthrift Julia was a further problem for her daughter, Doreen, and Annabelle Collins struggled to intervene between her husband, Paul, and her mother, the waspish, eccentric and intermittently deluded Mona.

Nevertheless, these older women can take on considerable resonance and power, for while their daughters' role tends to be *in* the family, the grandmothers assert their authority across the whole community. Freed of some cf their daughters's burdens and often without a husband to exert an even minimal attempt at control, characters like Ena Sharples, Annie Walker and Lou Beale demand that everyone they meet pays them attention, and they offer moral guidance to the whole community as if it were an unruly extended family. The programmes have played with different facets of these characters. They are clearly bossy, self-important and smug in their values. Annie Walker, in charge of the pub in *Coronation Street*, was frequently the victim of her own snobbery and many stories featured her being taken in by a well-spoken, apparently well-connected imposter. Ena Sharples could be brusque and uncompromising, refusing to adjust to the changing times. Lou Beale was similarly bossy and obstinate, self-opinionated and grudging. Unlike their daughters, these characters have the space and energy for some eccentricities and a selfish attachment to their own views which precludes them from the endlessly supportive role of the younger women.

Despite the tough exterior, though, the grandmother figure is constructed around a core of compassion and wisdom which makes her behaviour eccentric rather than culpable. When the crunch comes, she too will provide advice and support and will take on her role as head of the family. It is to Lou Beale that granddaughter Michelle turns when she is anxious and frightened about her prospective marriage and later it is Lou who supports her through the abortion. Kathy and Pete Beale go to Lou for advice when their son, Ian, wants to leave home and live with his girlfriend. Neither Annie Walker nor Ena Sharples had this kind of extended family so they created their own out of the Street and the pub. Behind Ena's sharp tongue lurked a kind heart and she was looked to as a moral touchstone even by those who would have felt more comfortable without her presence. Annie Walker similarly could be genuinely supportive to her motley group of staff and customers, particularly to her stalwart barmaid, Bet Lynch, whose emotional crises brought out Mrs Walker's exasperated but motherly sense of compassion and justice.

The use of the grandmother figure as the head of an extended family and as a guardian of the community's tradition is a further indication of the British soaps' representation of the family as a relatively open institution. The matriarch here takes into her bailiwick (sometimes against their wishes) individuals who are not related by blood or marriage but who come under her care by an accident of geography. The family in British soaps is not an exclusive unit. While being a 'battling Beale' is clearly important to Lou it does not prevent a large number of non-family members being taken under her wing. In the US prime time soaps, membership of the family is problematic; it has to be proved by blood and earned by loyalty to the family's continued survival. 'It's more than just a name, you know. It's a world of its own and not that easy to be a real member,' Adam Carrington tells Lesley, ironically just before his own membership is yet again tested. The family here is a more dynamic unit; the movement in and out of it, particularly by the women, is a source of stress and the challenging of the patriarchal order, though often unsuccessful, creates a tension, even an unease, about the way the family structure operates. In British soaps, on the other hand, while obviously there are quarrels and problems between family members, the family itself is a less complicated structure, available to those who need its support. The quarrels are not about the right to be in the family at all but are a product of the pressures put on it by the external forces of unemployment, financial difficulties and changes in society. The representation of the family in British soaps does not challenge patriarchal authority but bypasses it, handing emotional and practical control to the mother. Given this different balance of power, the family becomes less of a battleground and more of a place of safety where there is some protection from the harshness of the world outside. So crucial is the family to this sense of security that it provides a model for the structures of the wider community which will be explored in the next chapter.

5

The Construction of a Community

'I thank God every night I'm not alone in a flat or stuck in the country.'

Ivy, *Coronation Street*

'We haven't got much round here but we try and help each other out.'

Arthur, *EastEnders*

'If they'd have been my own family, I couldn't have asked them for more.'

Hilda of Sally and Kevin, *Coronation Street*

'I feel a slag.'

Pat, *EastEnders*

The extension of the family into the community does not occur in all the soaps I am discussing. Neither *Dallas* nor *Dynasty* are concerned with notions of community; in their worlds, the family is so central that anyone outside it is liable to be a threat, not a friend or neighbour who shares the same concerns. But for the British soaps, especially *EastEnders* and *Coronation Street*, the extension of familial relationships into the community is very important, enabling a group to be brought together which might otherwise be split by the conflicting interests of age, gender and class. A sense of community has been associated with British serials, and in particular with *Coronation Street*, in both theoretical and popular writing on soaps. As Richard Dyer puts it, 'life in *Coronation Street* . . . is defined as community, interpersonal activity on a day-to-day basis'[1] while Suzi Hush, ex-producer of *Coronation Street*, is quoted in a women's magazine as saying, 'the sense of community is a basic human requirement. It feeds our need for gossip, curiosity, belonging.'[2] *Coronation Street* is, as we shall see, exemplary in this respect but its appeal to a notion of community was reworked in a quite conscious way for the eighties by *EastEnders*. The notion that the life of soaps 'is defined as community' seems a commonsense evaluation of the British soaps' appeal, something of which the viewers themselves are as conscious as the critic. Less attention has been paid to how that togetherness, that sense of belonging, is established, and the various factors in the process repay investigation. This chapter therefore looks at the value placed on the community in British soaps, in particular in *Coronation Street* and *EastEnders*, and at the way in which a sense of community is constructed.

The community ideal

First of all, we need to define what is represented by the term 'community' and the values which are ascribed to it. For although community is an important unifying factor, it often proves elusive. British soaps offer the notion of a harmonious community but the chimera is rarely pinned down. The soap opera format denies a final ending and the community can never therefore be finally and securely established. To do so would indeed be both implausible (and thus threaten the soap's commitment to realism) and dull in narrative terms since so many soap stories have personal disagreements and quarrels as their basis for action. Because of this, a sense of community cannot simply be assumed. It becomes an ideal which has to be worked for and which is, particularly in *EastEnders*, only occasionally achieved.

Nevertheless, the ideals of the community are clearly established as an aspiration. They are based on an ethos of sharing, an acceptance of each other's individual characteristics and a recognition that everyone has a role to play if the community is to continue. The ideal of community which is presented depends on shared values of support for each other and stresses the importance of acting with the interests of the community at heart. As Albert Tatlock put it in a 1961 episode of *Coronation Street*: 'more sharing and less grabbing . . . that's what happens when you bring folks together' or as Arthur Fowler remarked, over 20 years later, in *EastEnders*, 'we haven't got much round here but we try and help each other out.'

But this ideal of shared concern does not demand an impossible perfection from the characters concerned. What is acknowledged, or indeed required, by the soap community is that individuals should be essentially themselves. While for some characters – Emily Bishop, Ken Barlow, Kathy Beale – work on behalf of the community comes naturally, for others it requires considerably more effort. Jack Duckworth, Albert Tatlock, Den Watts have to be encouraged to make their contribution, which is worth all the more because it requires them to reveal sides of their nature not normally on show. On certain ritual occasions, indeed, their reluctant presence is all that is required. It is in the nature of the soaps' ideal community that it can draw into itself all sorts of characters – the grumpy, the cantankerous, the complaining, the eccentric – and that they do not need to be transformed into ideal types for the community itself to be celebrated. The community needs the variety of their personalities and would not be complete without them. As Hilda Ogden said to her husband, Stan, in different ways on many occasions, 'you know what we are to folks round here – a couple of comedians,' but no special occasion in *Coronation Street* was complete without them.

The notion of a shared responsibility to the community through a concern for and an acceptance of the individuals within it sounds considerably more priggish than the programmes themselves. Some concrete examples may help to show how the notion of a common viewpoint shared by those in the community saturates *Coronation Street* and *EastEnders*, for the ideal is often expressed in quite mundane ways. Neighbours regularly drop in on each other to ask a favour or share a problem. On a more organised level, help is offered when a specific difficulty arises. Thus when the curmudgeonly Ena Sharples is ill with back pain, the street grapevine finds out the cause of the problem and gets together to collect money for a new bed. When Arthur Fowler in *EastEnders*, who had been a victim of long-term unemployment, has his first wage packet stolen, his neighbours organise a collection to replace the money he has lost. On an individual basis, unlikely characters offer support to each other. In *Coronation Street*, Curly, thrown out by Alf Roberts for not paying his rent, is offered a bed by the normally selfish Vera Duckworth; the tough working-class Pat has a soft spot for middle-class Colin, the gay character in *EastEnders*, and offers him her monumental shoulder to cry on; Arthur Fowler, himself the object of the community's help, in turn befriends the teenage punk Mary Smith and tries to encourage her to better herself.

Such examples illustrate a number of important features of the community. They depend, firstly, on knowledge of particular individuals and of the specific problems which are being experienced. Community solutions can only be found through the intimate knowledge which the characters have about each other. Secondly, those examples which involve financial giving demonstrate a practical response in which the money itself is less important than the communal support which it represents. Such gifts are not perceived by the donors or the recipients as charity. They are based not on the notion of those who are comfortably off helping those in trouble; they demonstrate instead the concept that members of the community who are all more or less in the same position, all struggling financially one way or another, can help the person who is temporarily most in trouble in the expectation that the support will be reciprocated should the need arise. As Pauline Fowler remarked when she invited the financially stretched Cottons to Christmas dinner, 'It's just from one family to another. It's not pity or charity. It's just what you'd do if things were different.' And finally the examples show that the practical application of concern and support within the community need not be hindered by differences in generation, personality or other factors. The old can help the young; the tarty Pat can commiserate with the fastidious Colin; the Cottons may lack charm and gratitude but they can still share the Fowlers' Christmas dinner.

The community defines its existence particularly in moments of celebration. Again these moments can be quite mundane. The special evenings in the pub – the Lancashire hotpot supper night at The Rover's, for instance, or the Country and Western night at The Queen Vic – are arranged by the landlords as commercial ventures but serve to demonstrate the way in which all generations and types within the community are drawn into its social pleasures. Other gatherings can be equally casual. An underwear party held just before Michelle's wedding provides the women in *EastEnders* with the opportunity to have some fun together, to reminisce about their own weddings and to try and offer some reassurance to Michelle about her doubts over the marriage. Because of the all-embracing nature of the ideal community, most parties in British soaps are intergenerational affairs. Although in *EastEnders* parties are sometimes attended only by young people, such events are normally a sign of trouble and the successful social occasions cross generations and include a range of characters. Thus Sally Webster in *Coronation Street*, who specifically wanted her housewarming party to be confined to the younger generation, found herself entertaining a number of the older Street residents. Significantly, her determination to be exclusive was first breached by the clear signs that Hilda Ogden, with whom she had been lodging before her marriage, expected an invitation. Sally could not resist her mother by proxy and followed up the invitation with the explanation, 'You're practically family.'

The high points of the soap community's celebrations, indeed, occur on traditional family occasions. The community does come together for particular public occasions, most frequently those with a royal flavour – *Coronation Street*, for example, celebrated the Queen's Silver Jubilee with an elaborate historical parade. But the communities are at their most united at births, weddings and funerals – all occasions when the extension of the family into the community is most clearly demonstrated and the community is deemed to share family feelings and participate in family rituals.

In *Coronation Street*, for instance, the weddings have taken on an almost ritual quality in which the elements are repeated and reworked so that whichever couple is involved the wedding story itself has a familiar pattern and the community acts as the family, providing the support (and the ritual disasters) necessary for such an occasion. It is striking, for instance, how rarely there is a father to give away the bride so the task falls to a member of the community (Alf Roberts, Ken Barlow) rather than the family. Preparations are often handled by women friends of the bride rather than the immediate family. Deirdre, on her marriage to Ken, looked as much to Emily Bishop as to her own mother for help and got married from Emily's home; Gail's mother was a positive liability, her inadequacy indeed being part of the plot. The wedding itself is preceded by separate celebrations on a gender basis – the traditional hen night for the women and stag night for the men. The stag night is full of opportunities for stories which threaten the event itself. Hangovers, physical injury and arrests for drunk and disorderly behaviour are all hazards which threaten the appearance of the groom and the best man at the ceremony itself. The women, as is generally the case in British soaps, behave more sensibly and usually manage to avoid falling downstairs on their wedding eve. They are not, however, immune to the practical disasters – flat tyres, lost items – which can delay either party and leave the guests waiting in suspense, although the audience will of course generally know that this is a tease.

The wedding ceremony itself brings together disparate members of the community and different reactions are used to point up the individuality of the characters who have been brought together by the event. In the congregation waiting for Ken and Deirdre to arrive, Stan Ogden comments lugubriously to Hilda that 'churches depress me,' while Mavis confides to Rita, 'I know what I'd be thinking [if I were Deirdre]. Another ten minutes and I've got him.' The service itself focuses on the romance of the couple but there is time also to observe other reactions to the familiar words. At Rita and Len's wedding, a close-up of Bet's face hints at her previous relationship with Len, while at Deirdre and Ken's, the words 'all my worldly goods' are matched by a close-up of the elderly and congenitally grumpy Uncle Albert with whom the couple will be living.

The ritual of the wedding is also used to demonstrate the way in which difficulties within the community can be overcome. The initial stages of the event are often marred by some disagreement or resentment, usually on the part of those members of the community who feel themselves to have been slighted in some way. Hilda and Stan Ogden, for instance, feel hurt at not being invited to the ceremony when Rita and Len get married and decide to boycott the reception as well, loudly proclaiming their grievance to the empty bar of the Rover's. Gail and Suzie are not invited to Ken and Deirdre's wedding despite living in the street. Such problems are usually resolved by the end of the event and these narrative devices serve to point up the way in which the celebrations themselves bring together the community despite the disagreements and grievances that exist. Again the emphasis on unity is not at the expense of individual characters. The reconciliation is achieved by accommodating the sources of disagreement, not obliterating them. Gail and Suzie blithely gate-crash Ken and Deirdre's wedding, flirting with the official photographer and providing a reminder of the youthful pleasures which Deirdre Barlow has long left behind her. Hilda and Stan go to Rita and Len's reception in the end only to find that the free drink has run out. In both cases, characters initially outside the occasion are brought into it almost as it were on their own terms. The community has its inappropriate or awkward characters but their presence is necessary for the assertion of the all-embracing ideal. The strategy is neatly summed up in a moment at Ken and Deirdre's wedding when Uncle Albert, despite the festive atmosphere, is being his usual awkward self. Deirdre kisses him resoundingly on the cheek; 'that's for being you,' she says.

The facility with which *Coronation Street* deploys the wedding both to create and display community feeling is deceptive. Such celebrations need not automatically be presented in this way. At Glenda and Kevin's wedding in *Crossroads*, staff from the motel attend the ceremony and reception but Meg and Jill leave early and Meg complains, good-humouredly but pointedly, that the motel has been left understaffed by the event. *Brookside* has apparently deliberately shown that it is possible to have a wedding that does not turn into a demonstration of community solidarity. The wedding reception of Laura and Jonathan took place in a marquee in Brookside Close but close neighbours, such as the Grants and the Collins, were not invited. Instead, the emphasis was on the rowdy behaviour of the yuppy outsiders who took over the Close and on an ongoing story dealing with the Corkhills' financial problems. There was no equivalent here of *Coronation Street*'s confident assertion of a community celebrating its own continuance and the individual families in the Close were not drawn closer together by the event.

The construction of the community

It is wrong to think, therefore, that because community is given such high value in British soaps it is easily achieved. The moments of harmony in which all are temporarily included have to be worked for and the sense of acceptance of each other on which the community at its best is based is easily threatened. Soaps like *Coronation Street* and *EastEnders* which offer the community as an ideal have to construct the ethos by which it is characterised and in doing so deploy in distinctive ways both the soap's setting and its references to the past. Geography and history thus become important strategies in establishing a notion of community.

The setting of a soap is an important way of creating a minimum of homogeneity among disparate characters. Whether it be a workplace or a region, the setting gives a sense of unified experience which draws on notions of the particular characteristics or attitudes generated by a common work experience or sense of place. We saw in chapter 1 how the creation of a recognisable geographic space is one of the ways in which a soap opera engages its audience in the narrative and in chapter 2 how regional references are used to authenticate the realism to which British serials often aspire. We can now see how these two aspects work together to create a sense of community which is a powerful source of the programmes' pleasure.

Both *Coronation Street* and *EastEnders* have successfully established a unifying sense of place in which the permutations of community relationships can be worked out. Both soaps have at their heart a particular fictional space. The Street and the Square are public spaces; these serials, unlike, for instance, many situation comedies, are not locked into the four walls of the family home. Their geography allows for a large number of characters with a variety of reasons for living in the area and different ways of relating to the community. The setting also provides the boundaries which are necessary if the community is to have a sense of its own separateness, its means of asserting its own identity against outsiders. The Street, the Square provide a geographical identity for characters and a location in which outsiders can be recognised by the fact that they are neither literally nor metaphorically at home. The fictional geography of *Coronation Street* and *EastEnders* is indeed remarkably similar. Both communities are presented as working-class in speech and behaviour; both are part of but not economically central to a major British city (Manchester and London); in both soaps, the characters live mainly in nineteenth-century housing rather than high-rise flats or new housing estates; in both, the pub (The Rover's Return, The Queen Vic) holds a key place as the site for formal celebrations as well as for more casual meetings. Both *Coronation Street* and *EastEnders* use their settings, in other words, to invoke a particular kind of community, one which is urban, self-enclosed and on a human scale.

The particularity of this setting is backed up by references to British regional characteristics which mark out the differences in attitude between the community and the outside world. Again, regional references for both programmes are similar. The North invokes, partly of course because of *Coronation Street* itself, an ethos of down-to-earth good humour and a stoical acceptance of disappointment and tragedy. Marion Jordan describes *Coronation Street*'s view of northern working-class life as one in which 'somewhere out there, remote from the metropolis . . . blunt commonsense and unsentimental affection raise people above the concerns of industrialisation, or unions or politics or consumerism.'[3] In *EastEnders*, a similarly mythical regional construction works to present an updated version of the London cockney with a sharp tongue and fierce local loyalty as its main characteristics.[4] These regional particularities were greatly played up in the publicity which preceded the launch of *EastEnders*, making it clear that regional characteristics underpinned the notion of community which was to be established. The British newspapers quickly latched on to the theme; the *Daily Express* talked of 'swarms of cockney characters' and described Lou Beale as 'the head of the cockney clan' while the *Standard* claimed that the inspiration for the programme came from a real street market and quoted a café owner from there: 'there are good and bad characters, they all mix together and it's typical of the East End.'[5] In addition, in both *Coronation Street* and *EastEnders*, regional generalisations about character and behaviour are reinforced by a self-conscious use of a regional dialect which is both idiomatic and forceful.

What is important to the argument is not the accuracy of such

regional stereotyping or the way in which the programmes themselves are part of the process by which more general regional
stereotypes are established and maintained. The point at issue is not
whether Northerners are more good humoured or East Enders more
quick witted than those living in other parts of Britain. What is
significant is that the soaps have used such assumptions as a means of
presenting the viewer with a community in which difference from
outsiders is asserted not by money or ambition or power but by
qualities which can be shared by virtue of living in the same place.
The community, while it has its boundaries and is marked as hostile,
as we shall see, to the outsiders who breach them, is still relatively
open, available by an accident of geography to those born there and
by patient study to those who move there. The ethos 'comes with the
territory' and the setting is a physical expression of a particular set of
attitudes which mark a common sensibility. To live in the Street or
the Square for long enough is to become not just part of the place
but of the way of life.

Tied up with the setting is the use of the past as a strategy for
defining the community, the sense that it exists not merely in a
particular geographical space but in its own time as well. It is this
history which the young members of the community have to learn
and which is used to whip into line the more recalcitrant members
should it become necessary. The past is built up in both serials by the
connotations of a particular setting, the accretion of the programme's own history over the years and the reference to historical
moments which have an existence outside the programmes.

We have noted that the geographical setting of both *Coronation
Street* and *EastEnders* is old-fashioned. Although the programmes
are set in the continuous present, the houses and flats in which the
characters live are not twentieth-century tower blocks or streamlined
modern houses. Shopping is done in corner shops run by one of the
locals not in a large supermarket. The two key pubs are relentlessly
down-market and Den's attempt to bring The Queen Vic up to date
with modern music and videos was a disaster. Only The Dagmar, run
by Den's rival, the upper-class Wilmot-Brown, had pretensions to an
eighties atmosphere. Its pink and green decor, umbrella-spiked
cocktails and designer lighting made the East End regulars look
umcomfortable and despite Angie's traditionally all-embracing welcome, Wilmot-Brown made it clear that he was expecting to attract a
more discerning clientele from outside the Square. Significantly,
neither The Dagmar nor its successor, the even more yuppy wine
bar, became a permanent feature and, in the main, the settings of
Coronation Street and *EastEnders* refer to an architecture of the past

which, because of its smaller scale and layout, has connotations of a lost neighbourliness and community of interest. Richard Dyer has described this setting as one of the causes of *Coronation Street's* nostalgic cast: 'this was most explicit in the period when the credit sequence was based on a camera zoom from a long shot of a high-rise block of flats to a close-up of a back-to-back street, from the impersonality of modern planned architecture to the human scale of the old working-class street.'[6]

The fictional history of the setting is used to give resonance to the community and to establish a sense of tradition which provides a model for the present. Sometimes such references are used quite casually to conjure up a colourful past which, for the older members of the community, still adds pungency to the present. Sitting in The Queen Vic, Ethel and Lou Beale reminisce about the previous landlord who on his wedding anniversary 'had a barrel of beer on the counter all day. The whole street was legless.' At other times, the past is more deliberately recalled. Arthur Fowler, suffering from a mental breakdown caused by unemployment, takes his wife Pauline on a tour of his personal landmarks in the area and finds them closed down and derelict – the church they were married in; Cato Street, where the yearly fair was held, now 'acquired for redevelopment'; the factory where he worked now closed down. The scene demonstrated how Arthur's attempt to hold on to his place in the community was threatened by the way in which its fabric was crumbling around him.

More commonly though, reference to the past does fulfil the function of making the present more manageable, of providing an example of how an order can be created which will enable the community to continue to survive. One striking example of this, though not of course unique in British television to soaps, is the way in which the experience of the Second World War is used to provide a model for how to behave. Much has been written on how the Second World War provides British culture with images and references which are drawn upon and reworked in different contexts.[7] The process has a particular resonance in British soaps since the notion of the community which is at the heart of the representation of the War is also so central to the experience offered by soaps. The Blitz in particular is referred to as an example of how the community could and should respond in times of trouble. In July 1961, when a gas explosion forced the Coronation Street residents to bed down in the Church Mission Hall, there was a good deal of grumbling, arguments and confusion. But Albert Tatlock reminds the Barlow boys (and the audience) about how such moments should be handled: '[there was] more kindness done to me during the Blitz . . . more sharing and less grabbing.' When the train crashed off the viaduct into the Street in 1967, the rubble and searchlights provided the audience with a visual reference to the wartime searches through bombed houses and, with pointed irony, it is an American character, Alan Howard ('not one of us' as Hilda tells him), who draws the comparison to the Blitz as if to prove that he knows how to handle the situation and can therefore join the community in searching for the injured. A reference to the Blitz is not always triggered by such dramatic incidents though; any occasion when the community buries its differences can be marked by such a reference. As late as 1987, a Street fete held to raise money for a local charity caused Vera Duckworth to remark 'there we all were, all pulling together. Just like the Blitz.' Vera's somewhat marginal position as a troublemaker in the community gave the comment an ironic edge but did not reduce its force.

The Second World War has a particular effectiveness in bringing the past into the present in this way because of its historical status and its connotative power. More commonly, the serial's own past is linked to a general sense of the 'good old days' to provide a perspective on the present. It is in the past that the most perfect expression of the community's values are to be found and, at times, characters mourn this lost past of prosperity and safety when values were more secure and when, in a refrain which is repeated in *Coronation Street* and *EastEnders* with the regularity of a motif, 'We used to look after our own.' In the present, characters fitfully grope to reproduce these values, but the sheer difficulty of the task makes the achieved moments more fleeting. Nevertheless, there are such moments when the bridge between the present and the past is achieved. When Pauline Fowler in *EastEnders*, desperate for money, decides to pawn her wedding ring and other small pieces of jewellery, the pawnbroker comes to see her. During the conversation, it is established that he has known her family well and has been aware of their struggles over the years. Because of this history, he gives her more money than the trinkets are worth and trusts her to pay it back when she can. Hilda Ogden, contemplating a move from Coronation Street and a new marriage, deliberately recalls the early days of her marriage to Stan and the years of struggle together; she gains strength from her memories of this past and reconstructs her future in its light.

Both *Coronation Street* and *EastEnders* thus refer to a lost past of security and order. Nevertheless, it would be wrong to think that this use of the past as something positive in the present is always unproblematic or unambiguous. *EastEnders*, in particular, tries to hold off from an automatic espousal of past values by setting up 'the good old days' as a matter of dispute. The ambiguity of the meaning given to the community's past was clearly laid out in the astonishing first episode of *EastEnders*, which not only moved swiftly between a number of different plots but also established the existence of the community itself. The death of Reg, a long-term resident of the Square but one who is generally agreed to have been 'a nasty old man', provokes a running debate on what constitutes the community and where its roots lie. Lou Beale draws a tight line – 'It's all strangers now' – and specifically excludes the Bengali couple, Saeed and Naima, who actually raised the alarm over Reg. But Lou's attitude is criticised by her daughter, Pauline, who praises Saeed and Naima – 'It's nice to know there's a bit of community feeling left' – and includes them in the community of the Square. At the same time, a semi-philosophical debate is being conducted on the reasons for the decline in fellow feeling. Pete Beale, half-jokingly, ascribes it to political change – 'Community spirit went out the window when the Tories came in. It's uneconomic' – while the older residents, Lou and Ethel, with gloomy relish, blame changes in human nature and the newcomers to the Square. There is even a debate on how good 'the good old days' really were, dangerous stuff for a programme which is basing its appeal on the establishment of a traditional community:

Ethel: We might have had a few fleas in the old days but at least we knew our neighbours.
Den: The old days are gone for good, thank God. You don't see kids running around with snotty noses, rickets or ringworms.
Ethel: Not them old days. Not the bad old days. They're coming back. I'm talking about the good old days when everyone cared for each other. They're not coming back.
Den: They're both the same. Now is where we are.

The first episode of *EastEnders*, then, established both the community and its past as an area of dispute, not a fixed concept, and that ambiguity has remained. It is always easy for the programme to slip into the notion of 'the good old days when everyone cared for each other' and as we have seen this is an important source of strength. But *EastEnders* has also consistently provided moments when the old days are criticised as when Dr Legge reminds the Square of racism in the thirties or when an attachment to the past prevents characters from dealing with the present. There have been times, for instance, when Lou Beale's use of the past as a source of support is criticised as blocking her off from understanding the real problems in her family. When her son, Pete, tries to discuss changes in the running of the market stall, he reports that Lou 'just carried on about the old days'. More seriously, Lou is so determined to observe the family's ritual visit to her Albert's grave that she fails to notice how ill her son-in-law, Arthur, is and indeed makes matters worse by berating him for failing to pay due respect to the dead. Even the Second World War is in *EastEnders* an unreliable guide to behaviour. When Den offers Pauline Fowler a deal on cheap meat (dubiously acquired as so many of Den's goods are), Lou encourages her daughter to accept. Smacking her lips over the shepherd's pie, she draws an analogy with the black market for rationed goods during the war and asserts blithely that everyone was involved. This model of a community based on anti-social behaviour is soon denounced by her granddaughter Michelle, who points out the risks of getting involved in Den's dealings. In a characteristically neat way the episode thus turned upside down British soaps' sanitised recollection of the war as the model of community behaviour while, in the process, dealing a glancing blow at easy assumptions about the attitudes of different generations to law and order issues.

The community as family

The setting and the past therefore provide important ways of identifying the community and bringing it together. But the task of transmitting the community's values and ensuring their survival remains a difficult one which ultimately relies, as does so much in soaps, on the quality of personal relationships. In his account of the affinities between *Coronation Street* and the working-class world conjured up by Richard Hoggart in *The Uses of Literacy*, Dyer parallels Hoggart's 'glowing portrait of the warmth of the working-class mother' with *Coronation Street*'s 'plethora of splendid mums'.[8] This stress on familial relationships in a discussion of the representation of the community is no accident, for *Coronation Street*'s strategy from the beginning has been to equate one set of relationships (the familial) with another (those within a community) and to present a world in which the two could be conflated. The effect is to make stricter the rules by which soaps' complexities can be understood. Not only are all crucial relationships, including those of the public sphere, expressed in personal terms but all personal relationships within a group of people are framed within the terms of reference of the family. The family provides the model by which community relationships in *EastEnders* and *Coronation Street* can be understood and expressed.

The most obvious example is that which Dyer uses, that of the matriarch. We have seen how, in British soaps, the role of the mother is crucial and that one of the central questions of their narratives is the women's ability and willingness to undertake that role. The British soaps' use of the grandmother figure as a sign of the relative openness of the family was discussed in the last chapter. Her role in transmitting the values of the community extends well beyond the boundary of her own family and the firm guidance she offers is backed up by genuine concern for those whom she adopts. But this role is not undertaken only by the formidable 'grandmother' characters such as Lou Beale, Annie Walker or Ena Sharples, who are specifically marked as matriarchial. It is a model also available to older women even if, in the past, they have lacked moral authority and status in the community. Many of the mature women in *Coronation Street* have, one way or another, adopted younger characters in the programme and a number of long-running stories have developed in which the older women try to encourage the younger and more rebellious members of the community to accept traditional standards and patterns of behaviour.

This mothering structure can be discerned in a number of relationships in *Coronation Street*. Rita Fairclough took the more formal route when she became a foster mother and with sympathy and tact tried to adjust the expectations of Sharon and then Jenny to the setting of the street. The less formal route has been through the device of lodgers, whereby the single women of *Coronation Street* provide board, lodging (and moral education) for the younger characters. Thus Elsie Tanner, towards the end of her long *Coronation Street* life, was placed in a number of 'open' family situations in which others turned to her for advice which she felt ill equipped to give. Nevertheless, she did try to guide her lodger, Suzie Birchall, through the vicissitudes of her love life and to restrain the headstrong impulses which Elsie recognised had been the source of her own problems in the community. Emily Bishop is presented as a very different character from Elsie Tanner; shy, frightened of speaking out until roused, a spinster type whose complex marital history is seldom referred to. But she too has mothered a lodger, Curly, trying to encourage his more respectable ambitions and to diminish the 'Jack-the-lad' influence of the disreputable Terry Duckworth. Curly moved out of Emily's care but after a short time found himself lodging once again, this time being knocked into shape by the rather less tender Vera. Hilda Ogden could not be more different again from Elsie and Emily – a widow whose own children have long disappeared and whose love of gossip and intrigue gave her a key role in the Street's Greek chorus. But Hilda, too, has been part of the mothering structure; firstly in leading her lodger, Eddie, away from a life of petty crime and subsequently in ensuring that Kevin, whose own family had moved out of the community, continued to have a family environment of clean sheets, hot food and firm standards. Hilda's role indeed provides an interesting example of the way in which values which are acknowledged to be somewhat old-fashioned are nevertheless maintained by the mother figure. When Sally, Kevin's fiancée, was rejected by her own family and also came to live in the house, Hilda's attempts to ensure that there was no illicit sex under her roof were presented as both comical and rather pointless, a refusal to recognise that times have changed. However, Kevin and Sally's marriage, from Hilda's home and with her practical support, vincidated her stance and ensured that another couple were establishing the kind of family on which *Coronation Street*'s community is based.

This mothering structure which is clear in so many of the *Coronation Street* stories and which plays an important part in the transmission of the community's values has a number of effects on how the community is presented in the serial. It confirms the way in which women dominate the narrative. It gives a value to the older women who do not have a role in their own families but who exercise an influence and a control within the community. The lodger device is indeed convenient in this respect for it allows for a large number of independent women who are therefore themselves available for stories about love and potential marriage but who also perform a matriarchial function in passing on values within the community. The structure may also explain why *Coronation Street* has found the introduction of forceful and fashionable young characters so difficult. If the model for bringing youngers into the community is that of a taming process by the older women, it becomes much more difficult to represent vividly stories of adolescent rebellion and escape.

It is *EastEnders* and *Brookside* which are deemed to have changed the way in which teenagers have been addressed in soaps and that shift will be looked at more closely in chapter 8. But *EastEnders* also presents the community in terms of family relationships, if not quite in the same way as *Coronation Street*. Of course, the Beale/Fowler family is itself much more dominant in terms of size and influence than any one family in *Coronation Street*. Spanning four generations, it provides a model for intergenerational behaviour which applies to those technically outside it. Thus, Lou Beale was a source of advice to her grandchild, Michelle, certainly, but also to Lofty even before he joined the family by marriage and to Sharon who qualified as Michelle's friend. Lou's role as a fount of wisdom is then parodied by Ethel who, with malapropisms flying, tries to draw on the community's past as a source of advice to the young and by Dot who dispenses unheeded words of wisdom, mainly drawn from the Bible. Nevertheless, both Ethel and Dot do provide assistance to others in the Square even if it is in a more sporadic and eccentric manner than their counterparts in *Coronation Street*. Ethel, in particular, kept an anxious eye on Mary and offered soothing words to Sue and Ali in the middle of their public quarrels while Dot took Michelle's part in the abortion debate and tried to give Donna a home during the downward spiral of drug-taking and the alienation from the community which ended in her death. It was significant that when Donna died both her natural mother, Kathy, and her adoptive mother acknowledged Dot's role in offering their daughter the home, however makeshift, which they could not provide. As the serial has developed, Dot's role in the mothering structure has been confirmed; she took under her roof Rod, whose aimless way of life could not be more different from her own but who responded with an irritated and amused affection, and she gave a home to Hazel despite her doubts about the legitimacy of having such a pair under the same roof. In a parallel action, the matriarchial Mo, who took up Lou's role on her death, provided lodgings for the hapless Trevor and attempted to fit him for life in the Square.

Other types of familial relationships can be perceived in the community of the Square. The fierce loyalty between Den Watts and Pete Beale had its roots in their teenage past, a fraternal code which, for instance, demanded that Den unquestioningly came to Pete's assistance when the latter was arrested by the police. The friendship between the women, in particular Pauline Fowler and Angie Watts, was similarly grounded in the past, enabling them to recognise that their lives were as intertwined as if they were related. A more stressful sibling rivalry was presented in the relationship between Angie and Pat in which they got drunk together, reminisced about past escapades and fell out, as always, over Den. In the younger generation, Michelle and Sharon describe their relationship in terms of being sisters. Even the gay Colin used family analogies to express his feelings for Barry as the latter tried to deal with his own emotions about his family. 'Look upon me as your Mum and Dad,' he offers, only half-jokingly, and later, after the pair have split up because of Barry's decision to go straight, Colin tells him that whatever happens, 'I'll be your mate, your friend, even your Dad.'

The transmission of community values is more fraught in *EastEnders* than in *Coronation Street*. Lou Beale's determination to mould the community to her model was criticised before her death and Dot's attempts to help are potentially undermined by her reputation for nosiness and self-delusion. Nevertheless, the notion of the community as a family with loyalties and traditions which do not depend on everyone liking each other is an important factor in understanding how soap communities pass on their values. Family relationships provide the model and the mothering structure the most important vehicle for the transmission of the ideals, however imperfectly expressed, of the community.

Marking the boundaries

The community in soaps, then, is a structure in which the setting and the past provide the framework and the family provides the model for relationships. It depends on notions of mutual support and acceptance and defines itself in terms of its differences from the rest of the world. But the boundaries between 'us' and 'them' are not always clear and many soap stories are concerned with the difficulties of marking them out. One further strategy in creating a sense of community is to exclude those who do not belong and to clarify the difference between those inside the community and those outside it.

On the one hand, the opposition seems clear and differentiates between those who live in the Street or the Square and those who do not, thus employing geographic setting as a key factor. This functions most clearly when the community is threatened from the outside – by developers wanting to pull down houses for instance – or is subject to the scrutiny of officialdom. Outside agencies – the police, social security officers, social workers – are given a hard time in soaps even when the programmes' treatment of them attempts to be sympathetic, because they are inevitably subjecting the community to an outsider's objective gaze. Even when they are well-meaning, such agencies are problematic to the community because they try to rearrange the pattern of life in a way that may be more tidy but is different from that agreed by the residents. Moreover, as we have seen, it is the sharing of problems which often provides the gesture of support within the community and the crucial means of sorting out what is wrong; such mutual support can only take place when all parties are directly involved in the problem. Over-friendliness on the part of officialdom is thus viewed as suspiciously as overt hostility since it cannot be based on genuine communal experience. Michelle's abortion was handled by the clinic staff with just such sympathetic friendliness and she responded with an angry rejection of their claim to understand – 'You act like we're friends. I don't know you. Why all this pretence?'

But the division between the inside and the outside is not always so clear. As David Buckingham has pointed out in writing about *EastEnders*, 'the forces of disruption are as likely to be found within the community as outside it.'[9] Many characters hover on the bound-aries, moving between acceptance and rejection as the situation demands. At times, these insider–outsiders are brought into the community; at others, their presence is marked by an unease as other characters attempt to re-establish the boundaries to exclude them. In examining these characters, however, it becomes clear that they reflect the internal tensions of a community which is not as stable as it first appears. The most prominent of such figures in British soaps can be described as the 'gossip', the 'bastard' and the 'tart'.

The role of the 'gossip' is, as we have seen, crucial to the audience's engagement with a serial and provides both a source of information and a means of speculation for the viewer. In addition, as this chapter has demonstrated, the notion of support for each other based on intimate knowledge of likely problems is fundamen-tal to the British soaps' representation of an ideal community in which practical and emotional needs can be met within the enclosed group. Nevertheless, there is an unease about the price paid for such support and an acknowledgement of the fine line between neigh-bourliness and nosiness. The 'gossip' personifies this unease and though her task of passing on information and ferreting out prob-lems is crucial to the community, she (and it is nearly always a woman) is frequently the butt of mockery and criticism. Although the information she offers is taken up and used, her role is rejected almost as if it draws too much attention to the web of gossip which holds the community together. Thus, Hilda Ogden began her *Coro-nation Street* life as a nosy informant on everyone's doings and, despite mellowing with the years, her capacity to overhear and pass on information was still the subject of critical comment. Her last act on leaving the Street was to pass on to the newly married Alec a piece of old scandal about his wife, Bet's, previous affair with Mike Baldwin. The crudeness of Hilda's original role has been picked up by Vera Duckworth whose 'big mouth' frequently gets her into trouble and whose eagerness to pick up information on other people's troubles is frequently criticised.

In the same way, in *EastEnders*, the avidity with which Dot Cotton seeks out news is the subject of some embarrassment to her more restrained neighbours but the exchange of information which she provides is essential if the community is to give support to its members. The blurred boundaries on which the characters of the 'gossip' operate were clearly seen when Sue left her husband Ali. Dot both notices her absence and speculates with her friend Ethel on its cause, running the gamut of violence on Ali's part and infidelity on Sue's. When Pauline protests, Dot declares that she is just showing a 'neighbourly concern'. Pauline points out that 'you don't know any of the facts,' but Dot and Ethel reassert their commitment to the community values of support and acceptance: 'We only wanted to help . . . We've got to find out what happened otherwise we can't help.'

This is on the face of it true; the community's capacity to respond to problems depends on its ability to find out that something is wrong. The very relish with which Dot and Ethel discuss Sue's disappearance is a sign of their active engagement with the life of their own community. But there is clearly an underside to this neighbourliness which is personified in the 'gossip'. The very transparency of lives within the community, their openness to each other, makes individual members vulnerable. The 'gossip' draws attention to that vulnerability which is an inevitable part of being in the community and her participation in the very process of exchanging information makes her an essential but mistrusted figure.

Other tensions in the community are expressed through another insider–outside figure, the 'bastard'. We have seen how British soaps are dominated by women and particularly by the mother and that men rarely challenge the women's control of the personal sphere. Nevertheless, this weakness of the men remains a source of some unease and the 'bastard' figure represents an attempt, albeit unsuccessful, to wrest back some power for the male. The archetypal figures are Den Watts in *EastEnders* and Mike Baldwin in *Coronation Street*, both of whom transgress the codes of the community by refusing to espouse its female-centred values. Den liked to think of himself as a bit of a bastard, attractive to women whom he prided himself on giving the runaround. He was accused by both his wife and his mistress of being unfeeling and selfish. He dispensed advice to the men of the Square which ran counter to the community's official ethos of care and acceptance. Thus he advised Ali not to make the first move after a quarrel with Sue since it would be 'a sign of weakness'; give presents when 'you're on top' he concluded, 'not under the cosh'. Similarly, Den continually told Lofty to be more assertive with Michelle and criticised other men in the Square for giving in to their wives. This attitude to women was reinforced by other aspects of the characterisation: Den was caught up in a series of shady deals; he cheated the brewery; he sold stolen goods on the side; and he had connections with the local criminal underworld. He trusted no one and did not expect to be trusted himself. He mocked those like Ethel or Pauline who asserted a notion of community centred on the square and indeed, his character was constructed around a series of rejections of the demands the Square made of him for friendship, loyalty and support.

A similar description could apply to Mike Baldwin in *Coronation Street*. Paterson and Stewart describe him 'as an insider of sorts, but still suspect because of his London background, and marked by his exploitation of women'.[10] His character, as is common in soaps, has mellowed over the years and he sometimes joins in the Street's community life as unproblematically as Alf Roberts. Nevertheless, his potential as the 'bastard' figure still remains. His history of casual relationships with women marks him as unfeeling and manipulative. During his marriage to Susan Barlow, he behaved as if he were the boss in his own home as well as in the factory, laying down the law and undermining her attempts to establish her own career. His emphasis on making money as an end in itself and his flashy lifestyle are a marked contrast to the values of the community. Like Den, he gets involved in dubious deals with shady characters and the source of his money is not always entirely clear. Like Den, he too asserts the importance of being free of ties or responsibilities to others in the Street.

The 'bastard' figures thus represent in British soaps an attempt to establish a strong male figure in the face of female dominance. They express an unease about the weakness of most of the male characters and a challenge to the values of the community so strongly held by the women. Nevertheless, although they provide an opposing voice, their challenge is rarely successful. The ethos of the serials is so strong that it seems impossible for the 'bastard' to be fully developed as in *Dallas* and *Dynasty* where, as we saw in chapter 4, they are structured at the heart of the family. Both Den Watts and Mike Baldwin are basically softhearted. When pressed, they do join in with the community even if they sometimes prefer to do so unobserved. Mike Baldwin participated in the Street celebrations such as the party for the Queen's Silver Jubilee and indeed helped to organise the farewell party in The Rover's when Hilda Ogden left.

Den was the harder of the two but he presided with sardonic relish over the locals' celebratory get-togethers in The Queen Vic and could be generous with his money when no one was looking.

In addition, the 'bastard' figure's attempts to assert masculine control are singularly unsuccessful. Den's marriage to Angie was marked by his inability to control her drinking, her moods or her behaviour; when she left, giving him the freedom he apparently wanted, she succeeded in wrecking his finances and his relationship with his mistress, Jan, who refused to join him in serving behind the bar at The Queen Vic. Similarly, Mike Baldwin, though financially more successful than Den, has failed to establish a relationship with a woman on the terms which he wants. His affair with Deirdre collapsed when she decided it was time to end it. He has a son whom he was not allowed to see and later his wife, Susan, left him after she had had an abortion. His attempt to have a subsequent fling with Gloria was foiled by her dignity and commonsense. Despite a lot of noise, neither Den nor Mike succeeds in asserting a different set of values than those of the female-centred community in which they live.

If the insider–outsider figure of the 'bastard' marks the boundary of unacceptable male behaviour, the figure of the 'tart' represented unease about how far female characters should assert their autonomy, particularly in the sphere of sexuality. Soaps give a strong presence and endorsement to their women characters but it is important to note that at some points the reins are pulled in. As we have seen, soaps are centrally concerned with personal relationships and sexuality is clearly at the heart of many of these liaisons. It is not surprising, then, that the community seeks to mark what is acceptable behaviour, since those who go too far threaten the community's own stability. The boundaries to be established are not, however, between those who are chaste and those who are not, since 'respectable' women like Deirdre and Michelle can just as easily be caught up in a love affair. The distinction which the 'tart' figure marks is between those who are taken unawares and those who make themselves available, who are aware of sexual possibilities.

The 'tart' thus marks the boundary for the women characters, a warning for those who are tempted to go too far. Pat in *EastEnders* is clearly such a figure. Her appearance, the dyed blonde hair and solid stature, identify her as suspect. Her vindictiveness towards her ex-husband Pete and particularly to the sympathetically presented Kathy, his second wife, combined with her crude language and bad temper to reinforce the first impression and it was no surprise to find that she was flirting with prostitution. Pat was clearly marked as an outsider and her subsequent move into the community through taking on Angie's role as the landlady of The Queen Vic had to be accompanied by a parallel move into more respectable monogamy with Frank. The 'tart' is not always clearly identifiable as an outsider. Mary Smith was an insider–outsider from the beginning of *EastEnders*, her appearance as a punk marking her as different. But the real ambiguity about her position was expressed when she tried to earn a living for herself and her baby through exploiting her sexuality – first through stripping and then, at Pat's instigation, through prostitution. Both Pat and Mary were brought back into the community at the point when their involvement with prostitution forced the issue. This was done through a *deus ex machina* of plotting – both were assaulted in the street – and by the reaction of the other women which, through friendly and not so friendly support (neighbourliness and nosiness once more combining), brought them back into line. Donna was not so 'lucky'; her act of sleeping with Ali, for money, for a drink, for companionship, backfired badly when he rejected her and she was blamed for breaking up his marriage to Sue.

Coronation Street has not dealt with the issue of sexuality so directly but the same pattern can still be seen. Elsie Tanner was perhaps the most ambiguous 'tart' figure, clearly an insider at the centre of the community but for many years an outsider whose sexuality challenged the mores of the Street. Like Pat and Mary, her appearance marked her out. Often slovenly and untidy, she dressed to draw attention to her figure and the history of her love affairs and marriages provided a basis for much talk. Elsie's demand to have her own private life challenged both the community's unspoken views on sex and the assumption that whatever happens is fair game for gossip. Many stories centred on Elsie's affairs, stressing not only their impact on her but on the rest of the community. Unlike Pat, Elsie's adventures were treated understandingly and the viewer was invited to sympathise with her weakness rather than condemn her waywardness. Nevertheless, the tensions caused by Elsie's behaviour, particularly in the early years, were clearly marked as divisive in the community. Thus, in one typical story, Elsie receives an anonymous letter, warning her about messing about with men. Elsie's violent reaction draws further attention to her capacity for a passionate response which the letter criticises. Her alienation from the community – the pub falls silent as she enters it – is increased by her accusations about the letter's author and by her wrong identification of Annie Walker. The episode ends with a fight in the Street as Elsie discovers the letter's true source in Ena Sharples and physically attacks her. While Ena is clearly in the wrong (she is fulfilling the figure of the 'gossip' in this episode), it is Elsie's sexuality which has opened her up for criticism and caused dissension in the community. Throughout *Coronation Street*, Elsie Tanner's pursuit of her own pleasure, at the cost sometimes of her own happiness, invited the strictures of other Street residents. Her behaviour indicated that the strong woman of British soaps could only go so far before she became a problem to the community rather than its prop.

Too often it is assumed that a sense of community is easily achieved in soaps. This chapter has shown that this is far from the case and that the moments of acceptance and sharing on which the communities of *Coronation Street* and *EastEnders* depend have to be worked for. The establishment of boundaries between the community and the rest of the world, the distinctions based on ethos, setting and the past are not always clear and can be challenged from within the community itself as well as from the outside. The strategies used to create a sense of community are not themselves free of ambiguity; neighbourliness turns into nosiness; the past becomes an escape route rather than a source of strength; insiders become outsiders. Nevertheless, soaps have successfully presented to the viewer a community which, if not perfect, at least seemed indestructible. It took more than Elsie Tanner's wandering eye to break up the world of *Coronation Street*. But the pressures of gender, class, and race were beginning to build up and in their very different ways *Brookside* and *Dynasty* were to take them on in the eighties.

6

Utopian Possibilities

'Things will change. They always do . . . and until they do we just have to keep fighting.'

Bobby, *Dallas*

'This isn't the Pat I knew. When I think of the energy I wasted hating you . . .'

Kathy to Pat, *EastEnders*

Soaps are not, of course, the only fictions deemed to be appropriate for women. In other media and in other times, other formats have also been characterised as women's fiction. While soaps have been contrasted with different forms of television they have not been so readily compared with the other forms of fiction which women have available to them. This chapter therefore examines two other formats which, it is argued, have had a particular appeal for women – the romance and the woman's film – and seeks to use their different approaches to throw into focus the specific appeal offered by soaps. Women's fiction is a broad term and I hope that this approach will contribute to the more specific analysis of its terms which is currently taking place.

Women's fiction is usually and rightly in a sense labelled as 'escapist' or 'fantasy'. It is associated with an allegedly self-indulgent desire to move away from reality and to retreat into another world created by the fiction. It is as if women are taking time out and in doing so are laying both themselves and their source of escape open to criticism. Janice Radway describes the act of romance reading as a means of the reader absenting herself from the demands of her work in the home; 'reading in this sense,' she suggests, 'connotes a free space where they [romance readers] feel liberated from the need to perform duties that they otherwise willingly accept as their own.'[1] Although little work has been done on analysing film audiences for the women's picture of the 1930s and 1940s, it seems likely that the woman's film gave female audiences a socially acceptable reason for getting out of the home and escaping into the unobserved dark of the cinema. The family viewing situation for television makes such literal or metaphorical escape more difficult for soap viewers but there is evidence in Dorothy Hobson's work that women saw the *Crossroads* slot as their own brief moment of relaxation in the maelstrom of the evening's homecomings and Ann Gray and David Morley offer examples of women in the family seeking to watch *Dallas* and *Dynasty* without the trial of male comments and interference.[2]

This creation of another space by the act of enjoying women's fiction is reinforced within the fictions themselves by the organisation of their narratives around utopian possibilities. The most common criticism of fiction aimed at women is paradoxically either that it is too happily escapist or that it is too depressing. On the one hand, the romance is seen as a fantasy, offering a happy ending in which no one could really believe while on the other, the unhappy ending of many woman's films led to the derogatory nicknames of 'weepies' or 'four handkerchief pictures'. In both cases, the absorption of the female reader, bound up in the emotional life of fictional heroines, is the subject of derogatory comment. Soaps too are criticised on both grounds; while *Dallas* and *Dynasty* are seen as escapist because they allow viewers to retreat into a fictional world, to forget their own problems by being absorbed in an hermetic fantasy, *Brookside* and *EastEnders* are felt to be dominated by bickering and quarrelling and to offer an image of life which concentrates excessively on disagreement and unhappiness. Women's fiction thus tends to be seen as excessive both in the unreality of the world it creates and in the emotional response it demands from the reader. The importance of the other worlds which are at the heart of women's fiction is that they offer models of both happiness and grief and the opportunity thereby to rehearse the extremes of emotional feeling; they establish utopias in which emotional needs are imaginatively fulfilled or, more frighteningly, distopias in which the values of women's fiction are undermined and destroyed. If this is recognised it becomes possible to see why 'escapist' may be a proper term for much women's fiction and that its derogatory connotations are ill placed. This chapter begins therefore with an examination of some of the work done on the romance and the woman's film and then looks to a utopian model to provide a comparison with the soaps under discussion.

The romance

The romance is perhaps the genre which springs most readily to mind when the term 'women's fiction' is mentioned. Although challenged by the more modern variations of popular women's fiction – the shopping and sex blockbusters of Conran and Krantz, the family sagas of Catherine Cookson – straightforward romances, often known generically by their publishers' names, still hold sway. Feminist attempts to define the romance have ranged from an analysis of particular books, such as *Rebecca* or *The Thorn Birds*, through examinations of a particular publisher's output, such as Harlequin or Mills and Boon, to work based on readers' responses to the books which they define as romances. While the complexities and nuances of these approaches reveal differences, it is nevertheless possible to build up a working definition of the pleasures of romance reading from this work.

Running through these studies of romance fiction is the thread of fantasy, the stress on the impossibility of what is being offered, the notion of a happy ending which brings the story to a halt because it is impossible to go any further. Romance, it is argued, is firmly based on the establishment of a heterosexual couple; reading romances both allows for pleasure to be taken in this successful fiction and covertly acknowledges that the need for fantasy is based on the unfulfilled desires set up in the construction of women's lives. Less elevated responses to romance reading have always characterised its readers as frustrated spinsters unable to satisfy desires in their own lives. Radway, Modleski and others argue that such needs are endemic to many women in a society in which they are promised more fulfilment, control and satisfaction in the realm of the personal than men are able to concede. The story of the romance is indeed an escape to another world where the ideal relationship can be explored and enjoyed.

At the heart of the romance is the development of the relationship between the hero and heroine. Janice Radway, basing her definition of romance on detailed work with a group of readers, argues that 'the most striking characteristic of the ideal romance [is] its resolute focus on a single developing relationship between heroine and hero.'[3] It is 'the *inevitability* of the deepening of "true love" into an intense conjugal commitment' which is looked for by her readers who dislike too much emphasis on 'the myriad problems and difficulties that must be overcome'.[4] Somewhat tautologically but entirely consistently, they rejected anything with an unhappy ending as not being a romance and a number looked at the ending first to check that they were not being cheated. Alison Light also stresses the importance of the ideal couple and the inevitable ending in which they are united. In her study of how *Rebecca* differs from more formulaic romances, she argues that 'romance fiction makes heterosexuality easy . . . [it] offers us relations impossibly harmonized.'[5] Modleski similarly emphasises the way in which romances offer the possibility of reaching an ideal state in a relationship with a man; writing of formula romances published in the US by Harlequin, she comments, 'according to popular romances, it is possible really to be taken care of and to achieve that state of self-transcendence and self-forgetfulness promised by the ideology of love.'[6]

While the attainment of this happy conclusion has to be understood to be inevitable, the process of how it is achieved is as important as the final moment. The central proposition of romance fiction is that the emotional sphere is to be taken seriously and that both men and women must commit themselves to doing so. For the woman in a romance this is seen as a natural though not always unproblematic progress to full womanhood. Radway points out that in an ideal romance the heroine is portrayed not only as very young and therefore not a mature woman but as something of a rebel and a tomboy. The novels often begin with the heroine's 'initial rejection of feminine ways'[7] exemplified in her refusal to be silent and her defiant attitude to the hero, an attitude which is underlined when, as is common, she makes her first appearance in boy's clothes. Modleski notes 'the large amount of anger expressed by the child/woman, almost to the very end of the story. The heroines rebel against the male authority figure and at times wish to be able to compete with him.'[8]

It is normally made clear, however, that the heroine's behaviour is not caused by defects in her own capacity to love but by the disdainful and somewhat contemptuous attitude of the hero. The heroine can move to the harmony of the happy ending when the hero is able to make a similar move for it is on his capacity to change and to acknowledge love that the progress of the romance relies. Modleski and Radway offer rather different views on the pleasures offered women readers by this process. Radway emphasises a positive shift in male behaviour, 'the magic transformation of his cruelty and indifference into tender care',[9] which is valued by the reader even while its fantasy elements are acknowledged. Modleski, however, argues strongly that 'a great deal of our satisfaction . . . comes . . . from the elements of a revenge fantasy, from our conviction that the woman is bringing the man to his knees and that all the while he is being so hateful, he is internally grovelling, grovelling, grovelling.'[10]

However one reads it, the romance depends on bringing out in the man qualities which are not normally permitted in the male hero so that in the fantasy he is allowed to become both loving and masculine. The reader is normally alerted to the hero's hidden capacity for tenderness early on in the novel and is thus able to watch it develop in ways unappreciated by the heroine. Radway identifies in this process a reinforcement in the story of the triumph of female values, 'the imaginative transformation of masculinity to conform with female standards'.[11] The men in romances, as much as the women, are in the end shown to be driven by love; the public world to which they were so committed turns out to be less important than the caring relationship and in the end the male hero is proved to be competent in the personal sphere, affording women readers the reassurance that, in Radway's words, 'men really do know how to attend to a woman's needs.'[12]

Romances thus remodel the world in a way which gives value to the needs and desires around which femininity is constructed. Romances give pleasure, it is argued, precisely because the satisfactions which they offer contrast so dramatically with the lack of fulfilment in their readers' emotional lives. Alison Light thus concludes that reading romances is as much a symptom of women's needs as an endorsement of the position offered in the books:

> That women read romance fiction is, I think, as much a measure of their deep dissatisfaction with heterosexual options as of any desire to be fully identified with the submissive versions of femininity the texts endorse. Romance imagines peace, security and ease precisely because there is dissension, insecurity and difficulty.[13]

Modleski, too, sees Harlequin romance as a testimony to 'the depths of women's discontent' and argues that it 'deals with women's fears of and confusion about masculine behaviour in a world in which men learn to devalue women.'[14] Radway gives the most comprehensive account of the needs which are, albeit temporarily, fulfilled by romance reading. 'All popular romantic fiction,' she stresses, 'originates in the failure of patriarchal culture to satisfy its female members.'[15] It is the function of the romance in this context to offer a vision which

> reforms those very conditions characterizing the real world that leave so many women and, most probably, the reader herself, longing for affective care, ongoing tenderness and a strong sense of self-worth.

This interpretation of the romance's meaning suggests, then, that the women who seek out ideal novels in order to construct such a vision again and again are reading not out of contentment but out of dissatisfaction, longing and protest.[16]

This emphasis on the capacity to imagine or envision another world is reinforced by the pervasive metaphors of utopia in these analyses of the romance project. Romances both imagine the perfect moment of harmonious mutual love at the end of the narrative and offer the reader the experience of fulfilment through reaching that conclusion. Modleski argues that 'many of the contradictions . . . derive from the attempt to adapt what for women are utopian ideals to existing circumstances.'[17] Radway goes further and comments that 'the romance functions always as a utopian wish-fulfilment fantasy through which women try to imagine themselves as they often are not in day-to-day existence, that is, happy and content.'[18] In this context, 'utopian' seems to be used as a reinforcement for the key psychoanalytic term 'fantasy' referring to unconscious structures rather than an ideal social organisation. Elsewhere, Radway uses 'utopian' rather differently when she concludes that 'the vision called into being at the end of the process of romance reading projects for the reader a utopian state where men are neither cruel nor indifferent, neither preoccupied with the external world nor wary of an intense emotional attachment to a woman.'[19]

Here Radway suggests that romances begin to offer the possibility of a different social order in which feminine values hold sway not just between two people but throughout a society. While presumably this remains a possibility for romance writers, Radway believes that by confining women to 'the arena of domestic, purely personal relations' the romance pulls back from its more radical possibilities; 'it refuses to ask whether female values might be used to "feminize" the public realm or if control over that realm could be shared by women and by men.'[20] In the end, then, it would appear that the romance's version of utopia is firmly placed on the emotional terrain of the central couple. Imagining one man fulfilling a woman's needs is clearly hard enough work for any romance; extending the utopian possibilities further into the organisation of social relationships is too hard a task.

The woman's film

Feminist writing on romance has clearly taken up the challenge of the epithet 'escapist' and has reworked it sympathetically, though not uncritically, to analyse the appeal of the romance. The other world created by women's fiction is not always so harmonious, however, and in the woman's films of the 1930s and 1940s critics have found a rather different appeal being made to a female audience. Rather more than with the romance, there have been problems as to how to define a woman's film and to fit any proposed definition into the broader perspective of melodrama. At one level, the definition requires simply (although the implications are far from simple) the presence of a central woman protagonist. Pam Cook argues that 'the woman's picture is differentiated from the rest of cinema by virtue of its construction of a "female point-of-view" which motivates and dominates the narrative, and its specific address to a female audience.'[21] Maria LaPlace, in her exemplary analysis of the film, *Now Voyager*, refers to the industrial situation which led the Hollywood studio system in the 1930s and 1940s to produce so many woman's films and points out that gender-differentiated surveys conducted by the Hollywood studios concluded that women audiences preferred female stars. LaPlace thus concurs with Cook on the importance of the central female figure in the woman's film and adds other criteria familiar from our study of soap opera: 'the woman's film is distinguished by its female protagonist, female point of view and its narrative which most often revolves around the traditional realms of women's experience: the familial, the domestic, the romantic.'[22] Mary Ann Doane refines her definition more specifically to the assumption of a female audience as the premise on which the films are made, commenting on: 'the nomenclature by means of which certain films of the 40's are situated as "women's pictures" – a label which stipulates that the films are in some sense the "possession" of women and that their terms of address are dictated by the anticipated presence of the female spectator'.[23]

A broad definition based on a female protagonist and an address to a female audience is thus a possibility but it covers a multitude of films and behind its wide front lurks a confusing number of subgenres including the maternal melodrama,[24] the 'gaslight' genre[25] and what LaPlace calls 'the "heroine's text", a story of a woman's personal triumph over adveristy'.[26] The central female protagonist in such films may be the successful career woman (*Imitation of Life*), the grieving, self-sacrificing mother (*Stella Dallas*), the emerging individual (*Now Voyager*) or the self-abnegating woman who demands nothing (*Letter from an Unknown Woman*). We need to recognise that not only does the woman's film, unlike the more orderly romance, allow for a number of narratives, it is also crisscrossed by other genres – melodrama, film noir and horror among them. There is indeed a certain confusion between how far it is necessary to distinguish between a woman's film and melodrama and how precisely individual films of the period can be placed. Christine Gledhill suggests that this uncertainty can be traced to the films themselves: 'confusion – or contest – is suggested by the range of permutations produced in the 30s between patriarchal melodrama and women's fiction, offering such sub-genres as maternal sacrifice, fallen woman and romantic melodramas alongside women's pictures.'[27]

What seems to hold such films together as a group is the underwriting of the importance of domestic values and the acknowledgement of the critical role of women in determining the nature of emotional relationships. In creating a world in which female strengths can be valued, the woman's film, like the romance, sets up the possibility of a different kind of society but unlike the romance it goes on to dramatise the high cost paid by the heroines who seek to make such a world. The conventionally unhappy endings of these films seem to be the counter weight to the equally conventional happy endings of the romance. In one way or another, the different variants of the woman's film mark out the precariousness of the romance's utopia.

Two rather different instances of the genre can be cited here. The first is the cycle of films which Doane calls 'the paranoid woman's film'[28] – films like *Rebecca, Secret Beyond the Door* and *Suspicion* – in which the newly married wife comes to believe that her husband is a (potential) killer who is likely to turn on her. Far from setting women's desire in the utopian world of the romance, this variant of the woman's picture presents a world of shadowy terrors in which the woman's viewpoint is distorted by paranoia and fear. The heroine is isolated and confused, her helplessness reinforced by her inability to make sense of the world in which she finds herself. In such films, women's desire is marked as illness and 'the woman's ability to see is frequently questioned; she may be . . . blinded by desire (*Spellbound*), or lost in a world of shadows and uncertainty (*Rebecca, Suspicion*). Her desire is often presented as a symptom, resulting in mental and physical illness.'[29] Doane points out that in the most paranoid of these women's films, the strict separation of the public and domestic, male and female space is breached; 'the paradigmatic woman's space – the home – is yoked to dread, and a crisis of vision.'[30] The woman's fear that her husband is going to kill her manifests itself in the dark corners, hidden rooms, twisting staircases and blind windows of the home of which she is notionally the mistress. This gothic version of the woman's film allows a happy ending only through the heroine's active acquiescence in suffering, making herself the potential victim in order to allow the 'misreading' of her husband's nature to be revealed, accused of madness herself in trying to cure her husband's madness. In such woman's films, female values struggle to survive and the transformation of the hero, if it is achieved at all, is a fragile and precarious victory.

The other strand of the woman's film offers a more positive heroine even if her strength is not always recognised by the other male characters. In films such as *Imitation of Life*, *Now Voyager*, *Stella Dallas* and *Letter from an Unknown Woman*, the heroines learn how to survive, to bring up children and to express their emotions without the support of the hero. Even in those films where the woman is unable to mould the world to her desires, her capacity to act on her own decisions is critical. The unhappy endings of *Stella Dallas* and *Letter from an Unknown Woman*, for instance, in which the woman loses or gives up her child, still acknowledge the stoical strength of the heroines and their capacity to feel emotion which the men in the films cannot match and which they undervalue because they cannot understand it. The audience is invited to recognise female worth even if in these films it cannot transform the world and the woman can only forlornly gaze into a society which is incapable of responding to her needs. In other films, the heroines are more successful in establishing an order which accommodates and sustains them. In *Now Voyager*, the heroine, Charlotte, transforms the gothic mansion of her mother's house into an ideal world in which 'peace and contentment' are the norm. LaPlace describes it as a domestic utopia and comments that 'the space has been transformed into one of laughter, light, music and gaiety.'[31] In Stahl's *Imitation of Life*, the heroine, her financial security threatened by the death of her husband, establishes a business which enables her to be financially independent and live luxuriously in the home which she has paid for. At the end of both films, the heroines specifically reject the hero's offer of romance and thereby refuse him the role of head of the household. Other relationships, particularly that between mother and daughter, are given value and indeed take precedence over that between the hero and heroine so that both films end with the woman's rejection of a central relationship with the man in favour of a domestic harmony which she controls.

Critical analysis of what the woman's film offers its female audience has been less unified than work on the romance's appeal. Conclusions vary considerably, in part because critics frequently argue a general position on the basis of an analysis of particular films and, as we have seen, the films themselves differ quite considerably in their narrative organisation and themes. Maria LaPlace, in her analysis of the discourses which sustain *Now Voyager*, suggests that the film's use of women's wider culture has created despite itself 'a symbolic system in which women can try to make sense of their lives and even create imaginative spaces for resistance'.[32] Doane, looking specifically at the gothic paranoid sub-group, argues that by trans- muting women's desire into metaphors of illness and paranoia, the woman's film works effectively 'to deny the woman the space of a reading . . . it functions quite precisely to immobilise.'[33] Williams, on the other hand, in her discussion of *Stella Dallas*, questions this assumption that the female audience automatically identifies with the heroine and asserts that 'melodrama does not reconcile its audience to an inevitable suffering. Rather than raging against a fate that the audience has learnt to accept, the female hero often accepts a fate that the audience at least partially questions.'[34] As we shall see, when we consider the way in which these films organise their utopian possibilities, the imagined world of the woman's film is a more complex and difficult one than that offered by the romance.

Soap opera and utopia

Placing prime time soap opera within the complex discourse of women's fiction is problematic. As we have seen, both the romance and the woman's film have their own internal conventions and their relationship with their audience has only begun to be explored. In addition prime time soaps, unlike their daytime equivalents, have never been conceived of as entirely or even predominantly for women in the same way as the romance and the woman's film have, and in the 1980s, as we shall see in the final chapters, the pressures to change have moved them even further from exclusive categorisation as women's fiction.

Nevertheless, the soap operas I have been discussing in this book do have much in common with their equivalents in the other media, enough to make a comparison of their similarities and differences a fruitful task. Even this brief survey has shown areas of common ground between the romance, the woman's film and these prime time soaps. In each genre, the emphasis is on the central woman protagonist(s) whom the reader is invited to support and whose reasons for action are understood by the audience although not necessarily by the male characters. In all three, there is a division between the public and the private sphere, male and female spaces respectively, and the woman's pre-eminence in the narrative is based on her understanding and control of the emotional arena. If she is threatened or defeated, it is because this commitment proves inadequate in the public world and her skills go unrecognised or are discarded. Within the three genres, physical action tends not to be the motivating force in the narrative; instead the emphasis is on the building up and maintenance of relationships in which the verbal expression of feeling or indeed the withholding of such expression is crucial to the resolution.

In addition, I would argue that all three genres seek to enable their readers to imagine an ideal world in which values traditionally associated with women are given space and expression and in which there is some model of the way in which relationships, particularly those between men and women, could be differently organised on women's terms. The emphasis on fantasy and escapism in women's fiction is linked with the way in which it explores these issues through the creation of utopias, in which the values associated with the personal sphere are dominant, or of distopias, in which the consequences of ignoring such values are laid bare. This double-edged escapism is so central to women's fiction that it is worth pursuing further and examining more closely the ideal world which is so tantalisingly offered. In doing so, I want to move away from the psychoanalytical model used almost exclusively by US feminist critics and instead to map the contours of soap opera and subsequently some elements of women's fiction across the utopian framework offered by Richard Dyer in his influential work on the values of entertainment.

Dyer, in his article 'Entertainment and Utopia', provides a model which enables us to look at the function of the urge to escape and to explain why it remains such a persistent characteristic not just of entertainment, as Dyer argues, but more specifically of women's fiction. Dyer proposes that entertainment functions by offering

the image of 'something better' to escape into, or something that we want deeply that our day-to-day lives don't provide. Alternatives, hopes, wishes – these are the stuff of utopia, the sense that things could be better, that something other than what is can be imagined and may be realised.[35]

Dyer stresses that what entertainment offers is not a representation of what an ideal world might be like but what it would feel like; 'the utopianism is contained in the feeling it embodies. It presents, head-on as it were, what utopia would feel like rather than how it would be organised.'[36]

Dyer categorises the experience offered by entertainment into five 'utopian solutions' and suggests that they are related to specific inadequacies in society. Thus the experience of scarcity and the unequal distribution of wealth is set against the utopian satisfaction of abundance and material equality; exhaustion, 'work as a grind, alienated labour, pressures of urban life', is contrasted with the expression of energy in which work and play are united; dreariness and monotony are set against the utopian solution of intensity with its emphasis on excitement and drama in individuals' lives; a feeling of manipulation, an inability to get beneath the surface, is contrasted with the utopian concept of transparency, of 'open, spontaneous, honest communications and relationships'; and, finally, the experi-ence of fragmentation, 'job mobility, rehousing and development ... legislation against collective action', is set against the utopian feeling of belonging to a community which is underpinned by com-munal interests and collective activity.[37] Entertainment thus offers the experience of a different world, one which is escapist precisely because it is based on the inadequacies experienced in day-to-day life. Dyer does not argue that the full possibilities of this search for a utopian solution are exploited in the musicals he analyses but sug-gests that 'this possibility is always latent in them'[38] and that the utopian sensibility represented in entertainment needs to be under-stood if change is to be both achieved and enjoyed.

The utopian possibilities offered by the prime time soaps under discussion here are not uniformly present in all the programmes. The application of Dyer's model demonstrates that soaps offer a spec-trum of pleasure which allows for a different emphasis within indi-vidual programmes and ensures that gaps in, for instance, the British soaps are filled by their US counterparts. Different functions are fulfilled by different programmes and it is only when we look at the range of soaps that we can understand that the utopian promise is offered by the soap opera genre taken as a whole. Table 1 shows the area of overlap as well as the differences and a more detailed examination of how the five categories can be applied will enable us to delineate more accurately the utopian worlds of the soaps.

Energy in British and US prime time soaps is expressed formally through the pace at which the plots are developed and used up and through a narrative structure which allows the overlapping stories to succeed each other with scarcely a pause for breath. *EastEnders* in particular moves with rapidity, cutting from story to story in quick bursts of action. One half-hour episode in March 1988 had 30 scenes, some of which dealt with more than one storyline; in one story a major character, Mags, conceived the idea of leaving the Square at

Table 1 Utopian possibilities in women's fiction

	Energy	Abundance	Intensity	Transparency	Community
British soaps	strong women characters, quick repartee, pace of plot	–	emotions strongly expressed at key moments, Angie/Den, Sheila/Bobby	sincerity of key characters: Deirdre Barlow, Kathy Beale, Sheila Grant, True Love: Deirdre/Ken Chris/Frank	characters offer support, friendship, gossip outside programme
US soaps	strong male characters, business activity, pace of plot	glamorous settings, clothes, luxurious objects food etc.	emotions strongly expressed at key moments, Sue Ellens's madness	sincerity of key characters: Bobby, Pamela, Miss Ellie, Krystle True Love: Blake/Krystle Bobby/Pamela	asserted within family, rarely achieved, relationship with audience
Romance	strong male character	provided at end by hero	story works towards moment when hero speaks of love	story works towards moment when true love is revealed	community not important
Gothic woman's film	strong male character	wealthy male, luxurious trappings, big house	emotion sought by heroine, witheld by hero	sincerity of heroine, opacity of hero	community presented ambiguously
'Heroine's text' woman's film	strong female character as heroine	heroine works for it, for herself or her children	heroine's expression of love for child, work or man	sincerity of heroine, misunderstood by man	woman initially outside community, may fight her way in

the beginning of the episode and effected the move at the end of it. Events in *Dallas* and *Dynasty* have a similar urgency in their story-lines and their capacity to change pace within an episode. Since daytime soaps have been characterised by their slowness of pace it is worth noting the way in which all the prime time soaps discussed here are marked by the capacity to move very quickly in and out of storylines, to effect rapid changes in characters and to develop a situation swiftly through a number of short scenes.

Energy is also expressed through character, and indeed character-isation is important in particularising each of the abstract qualities outlined in Dyer's definitions. The difference in the way in which the US and British programmes characterise energy is quite distinct. In the US prime time soaps, energy is expressed largely through the male characters or through the female characters who are operating in the public sphere. It is marked by an emphasis on the dynamics of business, on the willingness to gamble on a risky hunch and experi-ence swift changes in fortune. Since many of the business operations are deliberately opaque the emphasis is on the activity itself rather than its purpose. JR is the character most readily associated with this kind of energy but Alexis and Blake are also examples of the way in which energy is expressed through the business side. In pointing to these examples, it is noticeable that energy is a concept most readily associated with the 'evil' character, making attractive those like JR and Alexis who cannot be trusted and bringing out the ruthless characteristics in Blake. Energy is thus a characteristic which appeals to the viewer as an expression of how it feels to act vigorously and to affect events but it is also understood that it can be readily mis-directed if it is not allied with one of the other categories.

Energy in the British soaps, however, tends to be associated with women characters and is expressed not through business but through active engagement with the public life of the community. It can be seen most clearly in the strong women characters in *Coronation Street* and *EastEnders* with their quick repartee, capacity for organ-isation and determination not to be overlooked. Bet Lynch, never lost for a word behind the bar at The Rover's, resilient in her private affairs and with a brave face in public, exemplifies this concept in the British soaps. As in the US soaps, it is the activity which is important rather than the actual events but this expression of energy, like that of the US prime time soaps, has a dark underside when it can be experienced as bossiness and self-importance and is resented by the other characters. There seems also to be a difficulty here in relation to how women express energy through activity which we shall return to at the end of this section.

The category of abundance is also handled differently across the programmes, being more readily identifiable in the US soaps than in the British programmes. In the US programmes, poverty is eliminatd by the simple tactic of ignoring it and the audience is invited to enjoy the spectacle of abundance through the emphasis on sensuous luxury. This is particularly the case in *Dynasty* where the costumes and setting seem chosen more for their look and feel than for their appropriateness to the plot. The women's dresses are silk, satin and velvet, fabrics with a sheen which connotes sensuality. The settings overflow with luxurious items, ranging from fresh flowers in every corner to expensive paintings on every wall. Basic necessities are transformed into luxuries by their endless availability. Food and drink appear magically in their most expensive form – champagne flows literally like water or like tea in the British soaps. Hotel suites are used as homes as if a holiday treat were a commonplace means of getting a roof over one's head. Land is bought and sold as if in a supermarket. Transport is summoned up and private jets whisk characters across the United States as if they were crossing town. However unhappy the characters, they have at their disposal the abundant fruits of Western capitalism. It is interesting, indeed, that abundance is impartially available and unlike energy is not made problematic by its association with the 'evil' characters. Both Krystle and Alexis, deliberately contrasted in other respects, enjoy the ease of abundance and the sensuousness of material fulfilment.

It is precisely this endless consumerism which so scandalises the critics of *Dallas* and *Dynasty*, and there is indeed a shocking irony in the way in which *Dallas* is watched worldwide by those who are themselves the victims of the predatory activities of US big business. But to criticise the viewers is to underestimate the phenomenon and the utopian basis of its appeal. What *Dallas* and *Dynasty* offer is the feeling of what it would be like to have all material needs met, to conquer scarcity and enjoy abundance. Critics may call it greed but greed and selfishness have their roots in scarcity, the knowledge that there may not be enough to go round. With a world where everything is on offer, the viewer is safe merely to enjoy, without the fear that anything will run out. Hans Magnus Enzensberger's words apply with particular aptness to the US soaps:

Consumption as spectacle contains the promise that want will disappear. The deceptive, brutal and obscene features of this festival derive from the fact that there can be no question of a real fulfilment of its promise . . . trickery on such a scale is only conceivable if it is based on mass need . . . Consumption as spectacle is – in parody form – the anticipation of a utopian situation.[39]

If abundance is the category most vividly and extravagantly figured in the US prime time soaps, community is by and large the prerogative of the British programmes. Enough has been said in this book to indicate how crucially the sense of a community underpins the British soaps. As we have seen, the experience of community is offered to the audience most explicitly in the rituals which mark major events in *Coronation Street* or *EastEnders*. But it is present in the more everyday exchanges in which the role of each individual in the community is understood and valued. It is the women characters who embody the function of community in the form of the matriarchs who hold the community together. It is clear that the ideal community only functions if women are in control: they bring isolated and disparate individuals into the community/family; they organise its rituals; they transmit its values and spin the web of gossip through which it is continually renewed. In the British soaps, a sense of community remains the ideal to which the characters and the audience are invited to aspire. Unlike abundance, however, which fits into strongly articulated ideas of the individual consumer, a sense of community has become more difficult to express in the 1980s. It runs against the prevailing emphasis on the pursuit of individual success and entrepreneurial enterprise and both *Brookside* and *EastEnders* have questioned the more unproblematic version of community presented in *Coronation Street*. Nevertheless, it may be that one of the most important and hard-fought functions of British soaps in the eighties has been to keep the ideal of the community as a utopian possibility at a time when the tide in political thought was firmly running the other way.

But community is not simply present in the soaps themselves, it is also experienced in the interaction between the programmes and their audience. Soaps offer a common currency to viewers which permits the enjoyment to be shared between those who do not watch the programmes together. This effect of uniting disparate audiences goes well beyond television's capacity to provide the subject of conversation the morning after. The pleasures of soaps are so much bound up with speculation and analysis that they demand that viewers share the experience. The narrative strategies outlined in this book are dependent on the audience's capacity to predict and evaluate the characters' actions so that there is a common participation in the problems being portrayed and the variety of solutions on offer. While soaps are viewed in the home, alone or in the 'family circle', they can be discussed by friends, acquaintances and strangers in a variety of situations – at work, in pubs or bars, at bus stops or on trains. Like conversations about sport which are probably the male equivalent, such conversations demand a shared knowledge of the history of the subject and offer a mutual pleasure in the pooling of information on significant details and the disagreement over questions of interpretation. Unlike sport, discussion of soap operas also involves sharing ideas on personal relationships and emotional dilemmas. There is some evidence that families use soaps as a way of raising awkward issues and easing discussion of them.[40] Such a process can also be seen in conversations at work where soaps provide a common basis for conversation for those who share an intimacy based on proximity rather than choice. In such situations, soaps can be used to establish a common perspective or negotiate difficult situations in a way which would not have been possible had the fictional crises occurred in real life. They enable attitudes to be tested out within the safe haven of a fictional world. Such a process offers the feeling of community, through the experience of shared pleasure, even when viewing soaps like *Dallas* and *Dynasty* in which the concept itself is scarcely represented.

If energy, abundance and community are handled rather differently in the British and US prime time soaps, intensity and transparency are the two categories where the similarities can be most clearly seen. Soaps certainly offer moments of intensity when emotion is expressed, as Dyer puts it, 'directly, fully, unambiguously'.[41] Such moments may occur between characters when feelings of love or indeed anger and hatred are expressed without the characters stopping to think or fearing the consequences. What is valued is this capacity for expression even if the outcome is not always a happy one. Characters who live life full-bloodedly are essential to soaps and provide a source of much of the drama. But intensity is also a feature of the relationship between the audience and these characters so that the full emotional intensity is often expressed directly to the audience when the character is alone. This relationship with the audience is particularly marked in the treatment of women stars such as Sue Ellen in *Dallas*, Elsie Tanner in *Coronation Street* or Angie Watts in *EastEnders*. The mask that they put on for other characters, particularly their husbands, is dropped and the full extent of their grief and anger is revealed. Thus while Sue Ellen and Angie often behave deviously and hide their true feelings from the other characters, they still fulfil the function of intensity by expressing emotion 'authentically' to the audience. Elsie Tanner and Bet Lynch similarly keep a brave face in public but the audience shares with them their private moments of grief and despair. The audience knows these characters more intimately and more directly than the others and this may help to explain why these particular characters become the 'incandescent star performers'[42] of the soaps and are a source of particular interest and pleasure.

Transparency is closely linked to intensity in that it too can be recognised through the way in which emotions are represented in the programmes. In this category, however, it is the nature of the emotion which is at stake rather than the way it is experienced. Transparency emphasises the utopian possibilities of being open and honest in emotions without being hurt and Dyer associates it with the conventions of 'true love'. In soaps, it is associated with the idyllic marriages of, for example, Blake and Krystle and Bobby and Pamela. Despite ups and downs, these marriages are seen as ideal because neither partner lies or deceives the other and they represent a partnership which is based on mutual support and trust. As we shall see, there is a strong element of romance fiction here and examples are easier to find in the US soaps which incline more to fantasy. More modest British examples might be Sally and Kevin and Ken and Deirdre in *Coronation Street* (until the crisis of Ken's departure) or Chrissie and Frank in *Brookside* whose marriages are founded on commonsense, frankness and affection which carries them through day-to-day difficulties and major upsets.

Transparency, like the other categories, is associated with particular characters and creates its own kind of stars who not merely are deemed to be sincere in relation to other characters but can also be trusted by the audience. Bobby Ewing is the clearest example of a male star consistently associated with sincerity. He is JR's opposite and expresses their antithesis in terms of his commitment to the truth: 'JR lives by the two things I hate most – secrecy and lying.' Bobby has sometimes deviated from this commitment, particularly in his battle with JR over control of the company. It was significant that, in this story line, Bobby displayed qualities associated with the category of energy and promptly threatened the utopian relationship between himself and Pam. In the main, it is the women characters who are marked by the ability to see and speak out honestly and consistently. In the US prime time soaps, Pam and Krystle are associated not merely with moral values but also with the capacity to speak out when necessary in defence of the truth. Deirdre Barlow has a similar function in *Coronation Street* and Kathy Beale in *EastEnders* can be trusted by the audience to divine what is right and to hold firmly to that position.

We can see then that within the soap spectrum the whole range of utopian possibilities are on offer but that they differ in the weighting accorded to each of them in the individual programmes. A hierarchy is thus established whereby certain functions are essential to the utopian world delineated by these soaps while others offer more peripheral pleasures. All of the soaps under discussion here are characterised by the intensity and openness with which emotional lives are laid bare and great value is placed on the capacity to express feeling vividly and directly. On the other hand, there is a clear difference in the way in which the US and British soaps articulate the concepts of community and abundance and this split in functions accords with the aesthetic and thematic differences we have identified in earlier chapters. Thus, the emphasis in US soaps on the possibilities of abundance chimes with the values of light entertainment – stars, spectacle, decor – outlined in chapter 2. In their British counterparts, however, a tradition of realism finds it less easy to accommodate the illusion of all material wants fulfilled but is able to draw on an ideology of community which offers an equally utopian promise of individual needs met by a communal response.

A study of the way in which these soap operas present the possibility of an ideal world also reveals that the concepts offered by Dyer for its analysis are not gender neutral. Intensity and transparency, the functions most crucially concerned with the ideal experience of personal emotions, are present and central to all these programmes and are, with the exception of Bobby Ewing (a deliberate contrast to his macho brother), associated with key women characters. Community too in British soaps is linked with women characters who are the most successful in providing the nurturing strength on which a successful community is based. Abundance in US prime time soaps is also refracted through gender; it tends to be provided by the men for the women to enjoy and display. When a woman claims it for herself, as Alexis does so wholeheartedly, it becomes a sign that she is taking on the masculine role. The provision of abundance, as opposed to the sensuous enjoyment of it, is thus linked with the concept of energy, the category least amenable to female co-option. The association of men with the 'capacity to act vigorously'[43] goes deep and the public sphere in which this action is best expressed in soaps is difficult ground for the women characters. Energy, then, is linked with masculine behaviour, either openly through male characters like JR or women like Alexis who take on male values in the business world or less overtly with bossy women in the British soaps who try to impose their own wishes on others rather than enable communal energies to be expressed. Either way, unless it is softened by being linked with one of the other more 'female' categories, energy is likely to be associated with cruelty and lack of emotional integrity.

Utopian sensibility and women's fiction

The utopian possibilities which we have mapped across soap opera can also be revealing when they are applied to the other modes of women's fiction under discussion in this chapter. By undertaking such an exercise, we can examine further the ideal world which underpins the three genres and identify common patterns and, as importantly, different emphases which allow for choice within the broad framework. Table 1 shows in a fairly general way how the utopian categories might be applied to the romance and the woman's film as well as to soaps. An examination of the romance and the woman's film in these terms shows that they share with soaps the hierarchy which gives value to intensity and transparency but which finds the other categories more difficult to place. The romance and the woman's film also share with soap opera the tendency to exemplify certain categories through particular characters and to make gender a key factor in how utopian values can be expressed.

Each genre, however, has its own structures and preoccupations which allow for different nuances to be reworked. The romance, for instance, shares with soaps an association of transparency and intensity with the female protagonists but the narrative structure is predicated on the gradual education of the male hero, a trajectory which allows for a more confident assertion of an imagined world than in the less focused soaps. The utopian possibilities are initially clearly allocated on gender lines with transparency and intensity being the mark of the heroine and energy and abundance being strongly associated with the hero. The story moves inexorably towards the moment when the male hero can enter the female world of emotion, when truth and feeling can come together and be expressed directly and honestly. This is a sentimental education for the hero but it is important to note that the male qualities are not lost but redirected in this movement so that the process of the romance narrative is also to bring the powerful activity of the hero into the woman's arena. The energy which has formerly been on display in the public world is turned like a spotlight on to the heroine and used to enable the romance to be fulfilled. Abundance is another of the hero's gifts to the heroine, a freedom from want and the ability to move in a richer and more diverse world. The only category which remains unfulfilled by the romance is that of the community and its absence underlines how tightly the romance focuses on the couple and its inability to draw on feelings which cannot be tied into its central emphasis on the movement of the couple to a happy ending.

It is this capacity of the romance to reach a conclusion which is a crucial factor in its capacity to present a single relationship in an ideal moment which unites transparency and intensity in a declaration of mutual love. In soaps, by contrast, intensity can involve anger, grief and hatred and is strongly present in relationships that could not be characterised as transparent or open. The conclusion of the romance presents a more perfet relationship than any in soaps but the precariousness of the ideal is underlined by the romance's inability to take the imagination beyond the moment of conclusion, the happy ending.

The woman's film offers a different set of permutations of the utopian categories. The gothic model, exemplified by films like *Rebecca* and *Suspicion*, presents a nightmare extension of romance's utopia in which the heroine, having married the hero, comes to fear for her life at the hands of her husband. In examining these films across the utopian framework, it becomes clear that they function as the dark side of the romance scenario and come close to offering a distopia which the happy ending, even if it occurs, does little to dispel. Here, the transparency and intensity in emotional relationships which the woman seeks are despised and rejected by her husband who, far from being gradually educated like the hero of the romance, becomes increasingly the object of her suspicion. The heroine's desire for a sense of community is threatened by her translation through her marriage to a world in which, despite her efforts to make friends, she can trust no one in the hero's family or community. The male qualities of energy and abundance are exposed as a source of danger. The hero's wealth, his capacity to free the woman from want, is represented by the imposing mansion in which she is trapped, its very luxuries – the winding staircase, the large rooms, the four-poster bed, the heavy curtains – becoming symbols of her oppression. The energy which he embodies appears to be turned against her while her only weapon is a courageous but passive waiting for the critical moment which will confirm or disprove her fears. The exclusive concentration on the couple turns into a trap. If the heroine gets her husband's undivided attention, the aim of the romance heroine, it will, she now thinks, kill her. The ideals which the romance articulated on behalf of its heroine are here turned into their opposite, the utopian vision becoming a suffocating nightmare.

The second example from the woman's film, 'the heroine's text', moves away from this concentration on the couple in the organisation of its narrative. Like the soap opera and the romance, the categories of transparency and intensity are given central attention, although in this case the relationship in which they are most fully expressed is maternal rather than romantic. As in the soap opera, the heroine's capacity to express emotion fully is appreciated by the audience even if the hero fails to recognise the quality of the relationship being offered, and the gradual education which occurs in the romance is blocked either by circumstance or the woman's choice. Energy in this permutation is not so clearly a male category and is often expressed through the woman's desire to change – examples would include Charlotte's transformation to *Now Voyager* and Beatrice Pullman's rise to be head of a successful company in *Imitation of Life*. In the most utopian of these films, the woman is also able to provide the experience of abundance and community. In films such as *Now Voyager* and *Imitation of Life*, the woman is able to provide her own freedom from want, through inheritance or a successful career, and she does so while maintaining her position in the community and the family. In other films, such as *Stella Dallas*, the utopian vision falters and the heroine takes up a position outside the community. Nevertheless, this group of films, despite some differences between them, are important in indicating that utopian possibilities can be hinted at outside the stranglehold of the romantic couple. Although the sacrifice of the central heterosexual relationship is presented as a loss, it does allow the woman both to take up roles in the categories of energy and abundance and to explore the ways in which the feelings embodied in the categories of transparency and intensity can be expressed in relationships with children or female friends.

Women's fiction, as an examination of these genres has shown, far from being simply escapist offers women a range of experiences, allowing the reader to explore what is at stake in the personal sphere which is deemed to be hers. The categories of transparency and intensity are dominant in all three genres because they fit most easily with other aspects of women's fiction, in particular the emphasis on a female viewpoint and the concentration on the domestic and personal sphere. The categories of energy, abundance and community are less consistently present because they are more likely to challenge the exclusive emphasis on the heterosexual couple. The impulse to utopianism is strongest in the romance where what is offered is the experience of balance, harmony and recognition through a sexual relationship. This idealised vision is counterbalanced by the utopia turned nightmare of the gothic film. In some sense, the soap opera stands between the two, offering a recognisable world in which utopian possibilities are expressed in quite practical and down-to-earth ways. The key difference, however, and soap's major contribution to women's fiction, lies in its ability to handle change.

Utopias are generally conceived of as perfect, static worlds in which an ideal has been achieved and there is therefore no need to change. The clinch at the end of the romance has precisely that static quality in which movement would wreck the symmetry of the en-

ding. A conventionally unhappy ending can have a similar resonance, emphasising the exaltation of a powerful emotion by prolong-
ing its expression. In a woman's film like *Stella Dallas*, the maternal
sacrifice is captured and exalted in the moment of the ending,
rendering unimportant what happens next. One of the difficulties in
thinking about utopian sensibility as a force for change is that the
process for getting there, the movement and the upheaval, tends to
be ignored; when change is imagined it is generally conceived of as
being threatening and unpleasant.

Soaps, because of their formal construction and their scheduling
function, do not have the luxury of an ending and have to deal
continually with pressures for change. Their stories have to come to
terms with how utopian virtues, particularly those involving the clear
expression and communication of feeling, can survive and be maintained under the pressure of social problems. This is not to say that
soaps are necessarily progressive in the versions of utopia they offer.
The image of 'something better' which they present is often conservative, based on the family or on a community set in the past which
turns its face against any change which threatens its stability. But if
the structure of the romance leads inexorably to the formal moment
of harmony, the narrative construction of soaps demands change and
disruption to generate new stories. While there is pleasure in the
regular appearance of well-established characters, the format demands also that new characters are provided to add impetus to the
story lines. While the family and the community provide a solid basis
for the programmes, the narrative engages the audience by continually threatening the boundaries of these institutions. The families and communities on which soaps are based have continually to
accommodate new problems and tensions if they are to continue.
Soaps have at least the potential to suggest the utopian possibilities
of movement rather than fixity.

The experience of watching soaps, therefore, is one in which
problems are continually presented, tested and temporary solutions
arrived at. Often the solutions rest on the ability of the characters
and the audience to recognise the need for change and to be able to
accommodate it. Thus, it is quite possible for characters initially
presented as 'bad' to be redeemed and welcomed into the soap
community. Ben Carrington, for so long Blake's rival for Alexis and
the estate, was finally welcomed into his brother's house and expressed remorse. On a more mundane level, Pat, in *EastEnders*,
initially presented as a hard-faced tart, gradually found a place in the
community and took charge of the central meeting point of the
Square, The Queen Vic. Bomber Harris, whose bombshell takeover

shocked *Crossroads*, became a friend of Adam and Jill Chance and part of the community of the motel. Such moves are characteristic of soaps and recognise the way in which the audience's relationship with a character gradually develops over a period of time. Similarly, major events are soon put into the past – serious quarrels such as those between Blake and Steven in *Dynasty* are made up, the departure of one character is compensated for by the arrival of another, divorce is survivable, deaths are forgotten or even reversible. New problems or new versions of old problems are essential to keep soaps moving and, since they are not aiming at a single fixed point of resolution, different solutions can be proposed and tested out. The framework we are offered is one where differences can be accommodated. The audience is offered the opportunity to make a judgement on a situation and then to watch the elements shift until it is necessary to revise that judgement. Soap operas allow us to change our minds, reflect on our attitudes and redefine our values in the light of new evidence.

It would be foolish to argue that the programmes I have been analysing in this book have consistently made the most of the utopian possibilities which I have discerned in them. Although the 1980s have been a boom time for soaps it has also been a difficult period. Hugely popular, the programmes have been marketed to vast audiences and sometimes seem to have been forced into a frenetic treadmill of ever more spectacular plotting in order to maintain their notoriety. It may be that the bubble is about to burst, with *Dallas* faltering in the US ratings, *Dynasty* and *Crossroads* killed off and the departure of the linchpin pairing of Angie and Den from *EastEnders*. If the soap opera is due for a period of retrenchment, it is worth marking that, potentially, the soap opera format, precisely because of its escapism, offered a utopian vision in which change was not only possible but enjoyable, in which no character was entirely bad and no action entirely irreversible. It offered the possibility of solutions to emotional problems which translated the key utopian categories of women's fiction – intensity and transparency – into the practical competences of women's experience and offered a means of testing out how they could be lived in the day-to-day world. Such a judgement sounds almost intolerably sloppy, as perversely optimistic as the programmes themselves sometimes are. But in reflecting on a period, when public rhetoric took on a harsh and intolerant note, an eagerness to condemn and a refusal to deviate from a fixed position, we might be grateful that at least one form of popular culture in the eighties gave its audience the experience of accommodating and responding to the possibilities of change.

7

Sex, Race and Class: the Pressures for Change

'When I see a woman like you, it gives me hope.'
Lesley to Alexis, *Dynasty*

'I'm just a working girl. I don't want to be an issue.'
Shirley, *Coronation Street*

'Our Damon's dead because she closed Liverpool down.'
Bobby Grant, *Brookside*

'Why can't I hold your hand in the street if I want to? Who does
it hurt? Who does it deprave?'
Chris to Gordon, *Brookside*

The argument that soaps have a capacity to present change positively
may seem to fly in the face of common conceptions of soap opera.
Indeed, I have argued in earlier chapters that it is possible to see in
the range of soaps under scrutiny a consistent set of values based on
personal relationships, on women's responsibility for the maintenance of these relationships and the applicability of the family model
to structures as dissimilar as an US oil company and an East End
square. Because of this consistency, it is tempting to think of soap
operas as a place of safety, a refuge from the apparently more
demanding police serials and thrillers and the more serious news and
documentaries. Tied up with the notion of soaps as 'a refuge, a safe
haven'[1] is the sense of a stable world established by a soap which,
though full of events at the level of plots, is essentially consistent in
the values it espouses. This view has been specifically expressed in

131

relation to US daytime soaps. Mary Cassata, in an article entitled 'The More Things Change, the More They Are the Same', writes that 'in classic soap opera, it is the interaction of the soap opera characters within a stable social framework which we have come to count upon all these years that has made us feel comfortable and secure.'[2] Writing of the US daytime soap, *The Guiding Light*, Robert C. Allen similarly remarks on its sense of continuity and comments that 'the soap opera community is a self-perpetuating, self-preserving system little affected by the turbulence experienced by its individual members or the fate of any one character.'[3] Dennis Porter, analysing the way in which time is organised in the daytime soaps, refers specifically to the way in which the passage of time seems to have little or no effect in the soap world: 'Nothing grows or ripens in soap time and nothing is corroded or scattered . . . There is no future and no past but an eternal featureless present in which every day looks like the last or the one to come.'[4]

These critics are referring to US daytime soaps but the views they express can be found among critics of the prime time soaps under discussion here. Peter Buckman, for instance, includes the prime time programmes in his definition of soap opera and argues that soaps are pleasurable because they do not surprise the audience or try to change attitudes. Instead, soaps offer a reassurance that the world is not changing as quickly as it seems. Soap 'deals with the victory of old-fashioned and traditional certainties over evanescent fashions that assail them'.[5] He goes on to list a number of archetypal characters which he argues will be found in any soap – 'the decent husband', 'the good woman', 'the villain', 'the bitch' – and suggests that their stories draw on fundamental human traits. 'The soaps are heirs to a dramatic tradition of morality drama,' he asserts 'whose plots and characters are timeless, no matter how the actors are bedecked.'[6] Such an analysis suggests that even when tensions about social change are clearly at play in the programmes they are best understood as part of a static formulation in which eternal or ahistorical values are presented in a series of never-ending variations which always have the same outcome. Soap characters, Buckman says, 'are not there to surprise you, quite the contrary. Their purpose is to reassure.'[7] Anthony Easthope, writing in a rather different vein, also suggests that the characters in *Dynasty* have an archetypal quality which means they represent fixed positions which are not amenable to change. Commenting on the contrast between Krystle and Alexis, he notes that 'the meaning of each stereotype, the "good girl" and the "bitch", is repeated and repeated with little change through a long series of events.'[8]

Clearly, soap operas do offer audiences a stability which is somewhat rare on television. A casual viewer switching on at 7.30 pm on a Wednesday will find *Coronation Street* going on after nearly 30 years, regulars like Ken Barlow and Emily Bishop still suffering from the same problems and responding in the same way; Ien Ang's correspondents valued the way in which regular characters provided familiar pleasures in *Dallas*.[9] This establishment of soaps as a safe place is not just a matter of repetition and scheduling. Soaps do, as we have seen, offer a coherent set of values, based on the importance of personal relationships and consistent espousing of the woman's viewpoint. Their capacity to reimmerse the viewer in their particular world makes them an easily identifiable landmark amid the changing fashions of TV programming.

This emphasis on the stability of soaps may however disguise the extent to which soaps are under pressure to respond to change. Mary Cassata, again referring to US daytime programmes, argues that 'soaps will pursue social concerns only to the point which the audience will allow'[10] but this chapter seeks to demonstrate that the pleasures offered to the audience by the prime time programmes cannot be understood so homogeneously. The soaps that I am discussing, both in their format and in their interaction with each other, have been actively caught up in the process of representing social change. In this context, it is important not to think of individual soaps in isolation but to consider the range of programmes from which the viewer selects. Within that spectrum, the way in which soaps pick up and represent particular social pressures will vary and, while some may indeed be slower to do so than others, the appeal of certain programmes is at least partly based on their ability to confront the viewer with changing social issues.

This issue is necessarily a complex one since it brings up the whole vexed question of whether television operates as an agent for or as a mirror of social change. We have seen how Julia Smith and Phil Redmond have argued that their programmes reflect the present state of society while their critics assert that they play a more active role in providing a model for change. In the more general area of media studies, debates have tended to polarise, on the one hand, around empirical 'evidence' about, for instance, the effects of television violence and, on the other, fairly abstract accounts of the relationship between ideology and reality.[11] It is not my intention to rehearse such debates but to work with a model which suggests that soaps respond to social pressure around, for example, the women's movement, but are also part of the process by which change is thought about and acted on. In other words, soaps constitute a particular discourse through which change in a society is spoken and the way in which this process occurs sets up a range of invitations to the audience. How far social concerns can be pursued in soaps involves a myriad of factors, including overt censorship and professional conventions within television about what is possible. But we do also need to bear in mind that the position of the viewer is not fixed by the programme and that the sex, class, age and race of the viewer affects the response made to the programmes. The representation of change is a challenge to soaps, since the whole soap audience does not necessarily seek or get identical pleasures centred on stability and reassurance; the way in which new issues are handled may in itself be a source of pleasure to particular groups in the audience. This chapter seeks to examine the way in which this challenge has centred on the representation of issues of class, race and sexuality and argues that this project has both extended the range of material available and changed the boundaries of the soap territory.

A number of factors contributed to and fed off the renewed interest in soaps in the early 1980s and provided the impetus for change. The launching of a new national channel on British television, Channel 4, gave an opportunity to Phil Redmond who had been experimenting with a different audience for soaps, particularly in the successful school serial *Grange Hill*. Redmond had a track record of using social issues to generate a greater sense of realism and such an approach tied in with the new Channel's overt commitment to appeal to groups not represented on the other three channels. Channel 4 made a long-term commitment to *Brookside* which enabled it to survive a rocky start and set up a challenge to its staider rivals. At the other end of the spectrum, the US prime time soaps were demonstrating that it was possible to get away with a greater degree of explicitness on sexual issues and a speedier and more dramatic approach to plotting. *EastEnders* took on the *Brookside* commitment to realism through the dramatisation of social issues and combined it with a US-style paciness. In their various ways, the new serials were thus looking to be marked as different from the existing soaps and issues around sexuality, race and class gave them material which would both stand out as different but could be dealt with through the narrative and aesthetic experience already established by soaps. If there were groups in society who were not represented in soaps in the late 1970s, it is also true that soaps with their rapid consumption of material and their continual demand for story lines were particularly receptive to new material. How that

material was used and how different issues were accommodated is
the subject of this chapter.

The career woman

Soaps, as we have seen, have traditionally been based on the close
study of personal relationships and a particular endorsement of the
women's viewpoint within those relationships. In that sense, soaps
were potentially well able to deal with notions of the independent
woman which developed out of the women's movement and
appeared in a number of fictional forms in the late 1970s.[12] Programmes such as *Coronation Street* had had a long tradition of strong-
minded, tough women who could hold their own with any of the men
and audiences were used to seeing women play a dominating role,
both as characters in the programme and, in the case of actresses like
Pat Phoenix and Noele Gordon, as stars outside them. Nevertheless,
it is possible to identify a new figure in the early 1980s who both
extended the traditional representation of women in soaps and
challenged the basis of home and community which had provided the
female characters in soaps with their strength. Characters like Alexis
in *Dynasty*, Deirdre in *Coronation Street* and Heather in *Brookside*
provided a different kind of experience for the audience than the
matriarchs conventionally associated with soaps.

The key to the representation of the career women in the programmes is economic independence, which makes self-assertion in
other areas, including sexuality, possible if not inevitable. Women
had always worked in soaps, either in the home or in mundane
everyday jobs which drew no attention to their own ambitions. As
women's work became an issue elsewhere, economic independence
and pleasure in a career began to feature in the soaps. In the US
prime time programmes, the key figure in this development was
probably Alexis whose economic self-sufficiency is spectacularly
displayed in her lavish lifestyle. In a fantastic way, Alexis is the
ultimate paradigm of the independent woman as seen by US prime
time soaps. She is seen to 'earn' her money in a series of incomprehensible wheelings and dealings which mark her as superior to the
men in her field. On her own terms, she has struggled hard to get
where she is and she sees herself as continually deceived and let
down in business by men who challenge her right to power. She has
male business partners but does not rely on them and can jettison
them when they get out of line. Alexis does regularly fail to get her

own way but such narrative failures are less important than her structural position in *Dynasty* as Blake's equal in business. More often than not, Alexis initiates the action to which Blake has to respond; she is positive where he is reactive and, while he normally wins the crucial encounter, her ability to wrong-foot him is based on her own skills at the kind of business manoeuvring which was previously deemed to be a masculine prerogative. Her failures are thus less important in this context than the image of her sitting at her desk, her padded shoulders proclaiming to the world her power to act in the public sphere.

It is, of course, possible to ridicule this fantasy as well as enjoy it and Joan Collins's performance, as Mark Finch points out, carries in it a strong element of parody.[13] It seems ludicrous to talk of Alexis as a 'career woman' – career seems too small a word for the internatio- nal intrigue which Alexis's 'work' entails. Nevertheless, it is impor- tant to recognise that, however excessive its representation, the character of Alexis does offer women the pleasure of watching a central female character operating in the business world with relish and (a certain) style. However much one disapproves of her actions, the sheer energy of the role is engaging and the laughter is created as much by amazement as ridicule. The path taken by *Dynasty* with Alexis was picked up, though with less bravura, by *Dallas*, which began to give women characters roles which gave them economic power as the basis for their independence. The most extreme of these figures, and the most like Alexis, was Angelica, who embroiled JR in international scandal through a combination of irresistible business offers and sexual invitation. More charcteristic of *Dallas*, though, has been the economic independence of Rebecca Went- worth or the pursuit of a 'career' by Pam, Donna and latterly, Sue Ellen. We have seen in earlier chapters how women brought perso- nal values into the public sphere of work. Here it is necessary only to note how the later series of *Dallas* have been concerned to present women like Pam and Sue Ellen moving confidently from running boutiques and aerobic classes to the world of high finance.

The British soaps have characteristically followed a more subdued line, inhibited or sustained, according to one's preference, by their commitment to plausibility and realism. They were, of course, able to build on the tradition of strong, independent women which had been established through Meg Richardson as the motel owner in *Crossroads* and Annie Walker, Ena Sharples and a host of women characters in *Coronation Street*. Nevertheless, there has been a change in approach and the notion of the independent career woman has been taken up as an issue in the soaps and rather uneasily grafted on to the earlier images. *Coronation Street* provides the best demonstration of this uneven process. On the one hand, young Sally Webster is the classic example of the continuation of the line of *Coronation Street* women. A relatively new character, she operates in the old style. Independently minded, cheerfully determined to get her own way, she quite clearly runs the household and makes decisions which her husband, Kevin, catches up on an episode later. She works outside the home in Alf's Roberts's shop, a job which allows her to make an economic contribution to the pair's finances but which does not take her out of the community or bring her into conflict with the Street's view of how women should behave. Sally's independence is based on her own personality and her relationship with her husband. It neither needs nor raises the question of a career and economic independence.

But, while Sally treads the ground mapped out by her predecessors – Elsie, Rita, Gail – the programme is beginning to use other women characters rather differently. Susan Baldwin, for instance, insisted at the time of her marriage that she did not want children immediately but was looking for work which would give her the opportunity to develop as a person in her own right. Although she never succeeded in her ambition, before being despatched from the programme, her desire to use work for personal fulfilment marked her as different from the other women in the Street – 'stuck up' as Vera Duckworth succinctly put it. Susan, however, was a relative newcomer to the programme; although as Ken Barlow's daughter she had been in it since birth, her appearances have been sporadic and her development as a character has been more off screen than on. More interesting, perhaps, have been the changes in Deirdre Barlow, a long-standing character who over the years developed into one of Coronation Street's traditionally tough women, rearing a small child on her own and bringing her own quick independent mind into the marriage to Ken. More recently, however, Deirde has become the character on whom rather different issues have been pegged and through whom the clash of domestic and career responsibilities have been expressed. The symbolic move was made when Deirdre left the normal women's work in the Street – the job in Alf Roberts's shop which Sally Webster appropriately took over – and became involved in local politics as a councillor. Although this was not a move to full economic independence, it clearly took her out of the Street and gave her a 'managerial' role in the public world.

Chapter 4 showed the way in which the mother figure in British soaps traditionally takes on economic responsibilities along with the other burdens of the family. Although the demands on her are great, they have a unity of purpose because they are seen to be in the interest of the family as a whole. Deirdre's move out of the family into a political career began to raise the notion of competing and possibly irreconcilable demands. As is usual with soaps, the way in which the dilemma was presented seemed to support the woman's viewpoint. Her husband Ken's complaints that in attending to her council business she was neglecting him and her child seemed petty and vindictive, given that he had originally persuaded her to stand for office. Nevertheless, the demands made on Deirdre are seen to be a result of choices she has made, not just a natural part of woman's lot. The dilemma crystallised when her daughter, Tracy, was taken to hospital with appendicitis while Deirdre was trying to handle a crisis over eviction and homelessness for one of her constituents. The competing demands force Ken and Deirdre into confrontation in which Ken's complaint is initially expressed at the level of the reduced level of service he is receiving: 'You've been selling us short, Tracy and me.' At the end of the scene, however, it is clear that it is the change in Deirdre's role which is causing the problem, not the simple allocation of her time:

Ken: You're being a councillor – it's fine with me – just so long as
          you're the woman you used to be for me and Tracy . . .
Deirdre: I'm still me, Ken. We all change.
Ken: Don't change too much.

This exchange neatly exemplifies what is at stake for the *Coronation Street* career woman. The charge is not so much neglect as a change in focus which could lead the woman to abandon her sustaining role in the family and the community for a more personally fulfilling role elsewhere. Deirdre's very tentativeness – 'I'm still me . . . We all change' – illustrates how difficult it is for the programme to move from its own traditions of independent women in the Street to career woman outside it.

   Brookside, beginning in 1982, did not have the problem of redirecting already well-established characters. Heather Haversham, the archetypal career woman in British soaps, was one of the programme's first and most important characters. Although she was married, she was clearly to be used in stories outside the home and as a trainee accountant she was ready primed as a representative of women trying to break into the masculine world of finance and business. As the serial developed, the character of Heather grew into a cross between the fantasy career woman of *Dynasty* and the more down to earth model of the British soaps. Glamorous, forceful and dynamic, Heather passed her exams and became a professional business woman, her commitment to her work sustaining her through a broken marriage and a series of problematic romantic relationships. Like Alexis, she had a relish for her work and took plesure in deflating the egos and expectations of the men who surrounded her. While clearly not in the same financial league as Alexis, her clothes and lifestyle were markedly different from those of the other women in the Close and served the same purpose of displaying the career woman's economic independence. But, while Heather tried to use her career to assert her power and to control her own life, her achievement of independence through work was always more tentative. While Alexis used her own personality to assert control in the business world, *Brookside*'s commitment to realism meant that Heather was much less successful than Alexis in confronting and changing the environment in which she found herself. Thus, Heather's experience of pursuing her career was presented as a series of work-related problems, including sexual harassment, discrimination, ignorance and abuse which meant that she was continually challenging a male-dominated world but failing to change its prevailing attitudes. While Alexis, despite her defeats, carried an aura of invincibulity, Heather, despite her victories, seemed to be subject to a series of ordeals which turned her career path into something of an assault course.

In a sense, the characters of Deirdre and Heather sum up, with their different experiences, the way in which British soaps have tended, despite their basic sympathy and endorsement of women's viewpoint, to see the career woman as a problem issue. Heather and Deirdre's involvement in work as a means of asserting economic independence (limited in Deirdre's case) and individual satisfaction has been used as a peg on which to hang a series of contemporary issues. Dilemmas such as child care, the attitude of the husband, sexual harassment and discrimination are inserted into the stories as if to demonstrate the sheer weight of the problems the career woman must face. While accepting the woman's right to a career, the British soaps quite markedly stress the pains not the pleasures, the defeat not the victory, the tiredness not the elation. The idea of the career woman offers a challenge to the British soaps' traditional way of representing women's characters because it proposes a model in which women act rather than react; a model in which it is necessary for a woman to be self-assertive rather than continually absorbing the pain and punishment on behalf of other members of the family or the community. Given this background, it is perhaps not surprising that Deirdre's and Heather's move to an independent role outside the community has been more circumscribed than might have been expected from a form which has given women considerable space. It remains to be seen how far such characters wll be able to break out of the long-established format.

Blacks in soaps

If soaps were well placed to recognise that the career woman had to be accommodated into their story lines, they were singularly slow to recognise that black women or black families would be an asset to programmes which make some claim to reflect life and which consume stories at a rate which should make new sources of material always attractive. Instead, blacks have tended to be ignored in soaps and, when pressed, the makers of the British programmes explained the absence on the grounds of realism (in Salford? in Liverpool?) or of practical difficulties, such as the limited number of families which can be physically accommodated in *Brookside*.[14] In the last few years, however, there has been a very gradual move of black characters into soaps but the experience does not seem to have been a happy one. An analysis of the strategies adopted will allow us to see why the soaps have themselves caused black characters problems and why an increase in the number of blacks in soaps does not in itself automatically remedy the situation.

Three basic strategies have been adopted by soaps in handling black characters – the exotic, the singleton and the incorporation strategy. None are unique to soap operas but each has particular ramifications when it is deployed in soaps. The exotic is deployed when one-off characters are used as outsiders to add drama to a situation. In such cases, the fact of being black is hardly referred to but is part of the heightened drama which surrounds the event. *Coronation Street* which hardly uses black characters at all has adopted this strategy on occasions most notably for Bet Lynch's son and Ray Langton's lover. In both cases the stories were highly dramatic. In Bet's case, the plot centred on the major revelation that she had had a son when she was very young whom she had been forced to give up and who returned years later only to die shortly afterwards, as a soldier in Northern Ireland; in the other example, Ray Langton was having an affair which became more than a casual relationship. Both stories were major plot hinges, leading in the one case to Bet's attempted suicide, in the other to the break-up of Ray and Deirdre's marriage and Ray's departure from the serial. Both son and lover were presented as innocent, unaware of the trouble and grief they caused, but in the Street's terms they were both outsiders, trouble-makers, and their difference was marked by their being black. Although hardly mentioned in the dialogue, the extra dimension of their blackness gave additional significance to their function as disruptive agents in the narrative.

The exotic strategy is thus marked by the short-term use of a black character to make more dramatic their troublesome effect on the community. It is significant that their disruptive quality is not ascribed to being black, since to do so would be to call into question the community's own notion of itself as caring and supportive. A character cannot be spoken of as troublesome simply because s/he is black even though it is this concept of blackness as threatening and disruptive which is actually being used. When the issue of discrimination on the basis of ethnic origin or more literally colour is raised, it is done through the more amenable strategy of the singleton. The singleton strategy is based on the use of one black character or family in a soap who normally functions in the same way as other characters but whose blackness is picked up and used for stories about black issues. Characters like Dominique in *Dynasty*, Kate in *Brookside* or Mac in *Crossroads* normally feature in the same kind of stories as their white counterpoint. Dominique, for instance, has participated in stories of inheritance, family rivalry and romance typical of the US prime time soaps, while Kate was an ordinary nurse, sharing a house in Brookside Close with two friends and Mac was a car mechanic at the Crossroads garage with the same financial and marital problems as his white workmates. All three appeared to have much in common with their white counterparts and seemed to be operating as characters who just happened to be black. But, looked at more closely, there are clear differences in the way in which they and the white characters were used, differences which demonstrate that the singleton strategy both marginalises black characters and forces them into a position of prominence through emphasising their unique status.

Dominique in *Dynasty*, for instance, was given a career well outside the Colby-Carrington money-making nexus. As a singer, she fitted neatly into the notion of blacks as talented entertainers and, although she became a loyal supporter of Blake, her stories tended to deal with her own career on the fringes of the central thread of the programme, the fight between Alexis and Blake. As the only black character, she was, however, required to carry the burden of stories about racial prejudices and harassment and to explain to white characters the difficulties she experienced because she was black.

Although she had affairs with white men, it was safer to find her a black man and eventually she drifted out of the programme.

Mac in *Crossroads* exemplified a slightly different version of the singleton's role. Given British soaps' lack of regular black characters, *Crossroads'* use of Mac was something of a landmark. He was not so heavily marginalised as Dominique and much was made of the 'ordinary' way in which he cared for his wife, Tina, and the baby, and the grief he felt when his marriage broke up. Nevertheless, like Dominique, Mac tended to be on the fringe of main plotlines concerning the garage, content to be a mechanic while others jostled for positions of greater power. At the same time, stories about Mac's dealings with white characters tended, on examination, to be about them – their liberalism, their thoughtlessness – rather than him. In these stories, Mac was a cipher for something strange but tolerated in the community, a black hole which absorbed the attitudes of others towards him. Thus in one long-running story, Arthur Brownlow consistently expressed his annoyance at Mac's lifestyle in a racist manner which Arthur's wife Kath and daughter Glenda found embarrassing and distressing. The point of the story was not Mac but the reaction of the white characters to him and a series of incidents allowed Arthur's intolerance to be out-voted by the rest of the family and thus for the community to demostrate its continuing acceptance of the black character in their midst. In such a situation, the black character as an individual disappears under the responsibility of carrying the 'race' issue and is used largely to demonstrate the notional tolerance of the largely white community.

The classic example of a singleton, however, was Kate in *Brookside* who was a black nurse living with Pat and Sandra, all three of whom, when they moved into the Close, worked at the local hospital. For much of the time, Kate was part of the routine of the house, caught up in her work and the day-to-day life of its occupants. Little attention was paid to her private life and unlike Sandra she was not involved in stories dealing with her work as a nurse. In the main, she was a foil to the more dramatic lives of her friends and comforted Sandra and made tea for Pat during their various crises. The focus only swung to Kate when the issue of black people in Britain was due to be raised. She and Sandra had vigorous arguments over different discriminations experienced by women and black people with Kate asserting her view that Sandra's concern was over-theatrical and that she worried too much about images rather than substance. One example of such exchanges occurred over Pat's short-lived kissogram business which employed 'naughty nurses' to deliver messages. While Sandra complained that such stereotyping degraded them both as women and as nurses, Kate, drawing on her own harsh circumstances as a black woman, maintained that economic necessity had to be recognised as the final motivating force for women's actions. It was typical that on such occasions Kate would comment on the action rather than be part of the narrative herself. Even when she was actively involved in a plot, she tended to be called on to represent the black viewpoint. In one such story, when Pat was singing in a Liverpool club, Kate and her friends were refused entry, thus enabling her to point out that discrimination on the basis of colour still existed and that her white friends had not even noticed its operation. As in *Crossroads*, such plots tended to focus on white reaction and allowed Pat and Sandra to express a variety of emotions from anger to guilt at Kate's revelation. Given Kate's marginal position, it was somehow appropriate that she should be the one of the three to die in the siege even though the death was based on contingencies other than her ethnic origin.

Programme-makers and writers protest that this marginalisation and overburdening of the black character is not due to design or malice and this is probably true, although individual protestations evade consideration of institutional racism and its effect on programmes. But the treatment of these black characters is not accidental for it is the inevitable consequence of having only one black figure to do the work of a range of characters in the programme. The single black character is in a comparable position to the 'career woman' figure in that s/he is always likely to be overtaken by the issues which her presence provokes. But the career woman is generally saved from becoming a walking pretext on which issues are pegged because her move from the personal to the public is so central to a soap's narrative and is presaged on action as well as discussion. Moreover, the women's issues essential to a soap are carried by a range of characters and are not all dependent on one figure. The single black character has no such support and, as we have seen, tends to be presented as marginal to the main story lines. Thus, while the soaps aim to present black characters as if being black was of little importance, the structural position of the single black figure means that his/her function too readily becomes that of representing and explaining difference to the audience of whites both inside and outside the soap. Put in such a position, the black character tends to become passive, at best reacting to others' racism, at worst a victim of it.

The third strategy, that of incorporation, is most readily demonstrated by *EastEnders*, the only major soap under discussion here to have a range of black characters. The strategy of incorporation depends on the recognition that the black characters will experience the narrative dilemmas of the soap differently from their white counterparts but asserts that basically the soap community is as open to them as it is to other characters. While black characters may have different problems, the programme's central strategy of forging a community based on geographical space and incorporating the foibles and weakness of a range of characters within it can still be applied to them. Black characters have their specific problems but the solution to those problems lies in their incorporation into a community, thus allowing black/white differences to be transformed into the insider/outsider distinction on which soaps are based. The incorporation strategy is based on the notion that black characters are not just representative but are or will become part of the community. The advantage of this approach is that it does acknowledge that no one character can be solely responsible for 'being black' in the programme. What it means to be black is represented in a number of different ways and less emphasis is placed on white reaction. It is more likely that black characters will be narratively active and that they will be involved in a range of plots, rather than being marginalised to provide a commentary on race relations.

When *EastEnders* began in 1985 it seemed possible that its use of black characters could be a breakthrough not only in soaps but on British television generally.[15] It benefited from having a larger than usual number of black characters in a variety of positions in the commuity and coming from a range of ethnic traditions – Bengali, Turkish, West Indian. Their marital difficulties and economic struggles were set against similar problems being experienced by the rest of the characters in the Square. On the other hand, difference was acknowledged and it was suggested that it could be built on to the benefit of the community. Two incidents illustrated this. One was the action taken by the black characters to move out of the role of victim and to rout the racist Nick from the Square, one of the few occasions on British television when a group of blacks has been seen to make a decision to attack a white racist and to carry out the initiative successfully. The other was the death of Hassan, Sue and Ali's young son, when Turkish traditions of expressing grief were presented alongside those of the old East Ender, Lou Beale, and deemed to be as appropriate.

As the programme has developed, it has continued to use its range of black characters to try to subvert certain stereotypes and to move black characters out of their more usual positions. Thus Kelvin, the black teenager, was academically successful, going off to study computing at university, leaving his white friend, Ian, still stuck in the Square. The ill-fated character of Hannah was also an attempt to avoid stereotyping by having a black woman who was middle class, ambitious and something of a snob. Such an approach has its risks since it attempts to shift the audience out of the comfortable position slack stereotyping offers and it may lead to the black characters being presented as less likeable. This is what seems to have happened with Hannah, in that the presentation of the character, in avoiding the cliché of the warm, friendly, West Indian mother, seemed to be overly cold and demanding. The presentation of the 'wide boy', Darren, took similar risks; he was the black equivalent of Den and his presence seemed to indicate a determination not to make all the black characters positive representations and to assert the possibility of having 'bad' black characters without their presence traducing black people generally. So confident is *EastEnders* in its approach that it is able to make jokes about the more careful approach of other programmes. When Dr Singh was featured in a fictional TV documentary being made in the square (a self-reflexive device in itself) he was asked 'Why are you wearing a blue turban . . . is it significant?' 'It just coordinated with the shirt' is the reply.

EastEnders is still outstanding in the generally white world of British television but the hopes originally expressed have, I think, been disappointed. As the programme has developed, its handling of black characters has caused controversy and sometimes bitterness. A number of black actors have left, including the whole of the Carpenter family, amid rumours of general discontent among black members of the cast. Thus Oscar James, the actor who played Tony Carpenter in the programme, was quoted as saying, 'They just don't know how to portray black people and consequently the characters were totally unrepresentative of reality,'[16] while Shreela Ghosh, who played Naima, complained that 'I keep playing scenes week in, week out which have no substance, and I don't think they've successfully merged Naima into the series.'[17]

Certainly, on screen, the black characters seem to have been marginalised, their stories being given less time than those of other characters and fitting less coherently into the overall pattern of the serials. New black characters, such as Dr Singh, have been given a background role and do not have solid stories of their own which would enable them to develop as substantial soap opera characters. Original characters have become more rather than less stereotyped. The treatment of Naima is particularly indicative of this process. She was established as a strong personality from the first episode, a British-born Bengali trying to sort out the problems in her marriage to Saeed. Once the marriage broke up, however, her character became insecure and vacillating. An apparent attempt to address the question of her cultural identity led to her becoming merely a confused character who swung between her British and Bengali backgrounds without any sense of her own already established identity as a character. Issues were speaking, not her. She became trapped in the programme in the traditional role of an Asian shop-keeper, continually worrying about how to make her business more successful. She was not involved in the major concerns of the Square and became a commentator, rather in the manner of Kate in *Brook-side*, on the actions of others. In the end, she was written out in a way which completely destroyed the strong-minded woman she had been at the start, hanging on the arm of her fiancé and proclaiming: 'Where he goes, I go.'

The problems in the programme which led to such a sorry ending for Naima and other black characters were there in the early episo-des and are rooted in the strategy which was adopted to handle them. Oscar James, in the quotation above, ascribes it to lack of knowledge leading to lack of realism but while this may be a factor, it is at least as arguable that the white characters are just as 'unrepresentative of reality'. *EastEnders*, though it deals regularly with social issues, has never adopted the naturalistic mode of *Brook-side*, preferring to force drama out rather than to pay strict attention to surface detail. The problem seems to lie with the strategy of incorporation which establishes the white working-class family as the norm and defines other characters by the way in which they relate to that norm.

This incorporation strategy has two contradictory consequences. Firstly it does not allow differences to be expressed strongly or firmly enough. It tends to assume that the problems the soap addresses, whether they are about personal relationships or social issues, are fundamentally the same although individuals handle them diffe-rently. It therefore finds it impossible, as David Buckingham has pointed out, to recognise racism as more than an illiberal and ugly attitude which is adopted by those outside the community itself.[18] Racism, lived through every aspect of life as opposed to emerging as a social or personal problem on occasions, has not been addressed in *EastEnders* because to do so would be to emphasise too much the differences between black and white characters and threaten the notion of the community coming together through the common experience of problems. There is a tendency therefore to concen-trate on what the black characters have in common with other members of the community – difficulties between parents and children, financial worries, unemployment – without exploring the possibility of there being different reasons for similar problems.

Secondly, though, the incorporation strategy does not in the end achieve its goal because the black characters can never claim full insider status in the community. As *EastEnders* has developed it is quite clear that the black characters cannot enter the charmed circle of the Beale/Fowler family because they do not conform to its white, working-class norm. We have seen how the sense of community in British soaps is created out of a complex sense of geographical space, class identity and quasi-family relationships. At the head of the community is the Beale/Fowler family which provides the key characters in the serial and those who are not literally members are at ease within it. Ethel drops in for a chat while Dot barges in, ignoring the lack of welcome; Angie storms in and asks for Pauline's help; Frank talks to Arthur about the difficulty of raising daughters. The values of loyalty, solidarity and resilience are exemplified by the Beale/Fowler nexus and they provide an unwitting model for others in the Square.

Black characters find it difficult to enter into this family/community. Then tend to wait for an invitation which may or may not come. Darren's sister, Carmel, was respected but her status was largely based on her role as a health visitor and her relationship with white characters seemed to be founded more on her professional function than on friendship. She had no friend to turn to when her marriage disintegrated into violence and although Kathy Beale offered her help Carmel was unable to use her in the way in which the white women characters look to each other for support. Even apparently communal gestures do not always work for black characters. When Naima lodged with Lou Beale and her family it appeared to be an example of the way in which East Enders could help each other, regardless of race or colour. But as it was presented, it was further evidence of the marginalisation of Naima who was always awkward and ill-at-ease among the comings and goings of the household. The logic of the incorporation strategy is neatly summed up by Naima's position as a lodger; she is given a place to live, assured of a welcome but hovers on the fringes of life in the house. The underestimation of difference, the refusal to acknowledge it or speak it, means that the black characters remain outsiders because the model of community still offered by *EastEnders* is based on traditional loyalties. While it seeks to accommodate change, it tries to do so on the basis of suppressing difference rather than acknowledging and welcoming what it offers.

Class

We have seen that concepts of class and a particular class position have been very important to British soaps in building up a sense of community; the implications of the nostalgic recourse to a particular idea of solidarity and community have been discussed in chapter 5. But the way in which class is handled repays further examination since the idea of class as a mechanism for expressing difference as opposed to unity has been an important element for change in a number of eighties soaps and has been a source of stories in programmes which appear to be at the opposite ends of the soap spectrum, *Dynasty* and *Brookside*.

In some ways, the use of class as a dividing line rather than a unifying factor is an extension of what was implicit in *Coronation Street* from its beginning. *Coronation Street*'s concentration on working-class characters, recognisable as such by accent, clothes and lifestyle even if a number of their jobs lent towards the petit-bourgeois, meant that a middle-class figure was instantly recognisable as an outsider. 'Stuck up', 'toffee nosed', 'lah-dee-dah' were terms of derision attached to such characters, reflecting a class difference which helped to delineate 'us' and 'them' and made it clear whose side 'we' were on. Sometimes, the middle-class characters were no real threat and were treated humorously. Annie Walker, who was very much part of the community although she affected a difference between herself and the rest, was always vulnerable to the charms of middle-class figures who claimed to be long-lost cousins or tried, in the most delicate way possible, to sell her something. Such figures could be rudely dispatched by a bit of straight talking but others – property developers, social workers, housing officials – have posed more serious threats and their incursions have, as we saw in chapter 5, caused the community to pull together more strongly as if made more conscious of what holds it together.

Even in *Coronation Street*, though, there are class gradations within the community which allow the audience to make judgements about individual characters or to understand particular alliances. Over the years, accents have grown less broad, characters have changed jobs and houses have been done up. The factory has been demolished and replaced by a new estate, complete with Laura Ashley chintz at the windows and 'heritage' front doors. Ken Barlow, though his allegiance in the last analysis lies with the Street, has achieved the middle-class role to which he aspired as a student. His friendship with Emily Bishop, another character who seems to have become more middle class, is based not just on long association but on shared values which are not those of their neighbours. Hilda Ogden, although immortalised by her rollers, became a much less broad figure, her gentility almost overwhelming what the programme had previously characterised as her lower-class loudness and vulgarity. Deirdre Barlow has similarly becomes less down-to-earth and outspoken as she has moved from typist/shop assistant to become a local government councillor. As these characters have moved up in the world, others have taken up their role – Vera Duckworth taking up Hilda's mantle, Sally Webster becoming a young Deidre. Such characters are sometimes looked down on by others in the Street, but they are as important in marking off the bottom of the class represented as Ken Barlow and Emily Bishop are in marking out the top. The programme thus continues to present a range of class positions while maintaining the programme's consistent claim of seeming to be about the working class.

EastEnders has adopted a very similar strategy to that of *Coronation Street*, using class mainly to define the community but acknowledging some differences within it. As is usual with *EastEnders*, though, the differences are presented more dramatically and class has been an important element of conflict in the Square. As in *Coronation Street*, middle-class style and, more crucially in the 1980s, money, are a mark of the outsider. In *EastEnders*, the Square's residents sometimes talk as if they were a working-class enclave, in danger of being swamped by middle-class, or more colloquially 'yuppy', elements. The outsiders are invoked, almost ritually, by Mo or Ethel in their evocations of the good old days or by Sharon and Cindy when they talk about the difficulty of buying a flat or establishing a firm basis for their small businesses. Lou Beale, interviewed for the fictional TV documentary programme, complains of 'too many yuppies . . . too much money', a comment which is endorsed by others in the Square including a graffiti artist who sprays Wilmot-Brown's house with 'Yuppies Out'. The Dagmar indeed became the centre for the invaders, upwardly mobile characters who patronised both Angie, during her period as a barmaid there, and the local charity night which significantly they see as a financial rather than a community venture. Given this scenario of the threatened middle-class invasion outlined above, it is not surprising that some middle-class characters are never allowed in to the community. Wilmot-Brown, for instance, was clearly on the margins, occasionally kind to Angie and to Arthur, but in general suspicious of the other residents; there were indeed a number of regulars – Dot,

Ethel and Arthur amongst them – whom he preferred not to see in his pub, believing that they lowered the tone for the more up-market clientele he was aiming at. Such lack of solidarity clearly marked Wilmot-Brown as an outsider even before his rape of Kathy put him beyond the pale of the community.

But if *EastEnders*, like *Coronation Street*, uses class differences to establish the community's sense of itself, it also undertakes a more complicated exercise of differentiating between middle-class outsiders and those who might be allowed into the charmed circle. From the start, *EastEnders* differed from *Coronation Street* in that it deliberately introduced characters who were clearly marked as middle class – Debbie Wilkins and Dr Legge, for instance, in the early episodes – but who wanted to play a role in the community. Such characters are always viewed with some suspicion and have to establish their credentials over a period of time. Dr Legge stands outside the main life of the Square, his personal life very rarely coming under the usual scrutiny of a soap and being given very few stories of his own. But tolerance and respect for him are based not only on his profession but also on the fact that he, along with Lou, is the historian of the 'good old days', custodian of the community's own history. Other middle-class characters are saved by their relationships with others who are more readily acceptable – Colin with Barry, for instance, or Debbie with her fiancé, Andy, who as a Scot was deemed to be a proxy-Cockney. But they also have to show that they can join in the community and share its difficulties. Colin, for instance, has been sympathetic with Pauline and helpful to Tony; more importantly, he has got drunk with Pat and has been harangued, along with everyone else, by Dot. His heart is in the right place even if his lifestyle is different.

EastEnders' middle-class characters, like Colin and Wilmot-Brown, are important, therefore, because they help to establish the community's identity, to mark out the extent of its tolerance and its ability to recognise a threat. The difference betwen Colin and Wilmot-Brown lies in their attitude to the community. The Square's cautious acceptance of the former and rejection of the latter helps to demonstrate the legitimacy of a community which is prepared to breach class division when the middle-class outsider is willing to endorse its values. When it comes to the crunch, the community is more important than the rigid class divisions.

If both *Coronation Street* and *EastEnders* use class to help construct a community, *Brookside* approaches the problem from the opposite angle, deeply suspicious of any notion of community which pretends to override class antagonisms. *Brookside* was launched by the new Channel 4 as a serial that would be different from *Crossroads* and particularly *Coronation Street* and the publicity before its first episode emphasised that *Brookside* would challenge *Coronation Street*'s commitment to creating a fictional world which felt comfortable and secure. It is not unusual for a new programme to be launched on the back of its potential rivals but the terms in which the criticism was made are important in anticipating the way in which *Brookside* would develop. As we have seen, realism and plausibility were the watchwords for *Brookside* and Phil Redmond, the producer of the new serial, used publicity interviews to criticise the other soaps for the implausibility of their sets and habits: 'You know how an actor in a studio can't slam a door without the wall falling down; how the geography of mocked up houses is all wrong . . . Ours are all real working houses . . . how many back-to-back houses do you see now?'[19] Redmond was actually criticising one of the fundamental conventions of soaps, the construction of a community in a particular locale which allows lives to be shared so that everyone can participate, if they behave appropriately, in the experience of the community. Redmond was right; it was implausible in the naturalistic terms that *Brookside* adopted. But it worked, as we have seen, to construct both a narrative form and a fictional community and in abandoning it, *Brookside* took a greater leap into the dark than perhaps Redmond knew.

Brookside, then, began like *Coronation Street* with a number of characters living in the same place but the families of the early *Brookside* were specifically set apart from each other. What divided them was class – 'the Harrods, the Habitats and the Hooligans' as TV critic Nancy Banks-Smith described the first families, neatly picking up on the naturalistic attention to lifestyles and the potential for disruption between them. Whereas *Coronation Street* offered a number of characters who shared a broadly similar class position and who, while they argued among themselves, united at times of celebration and grief, *Brookside* began with three main families who seemed to be quite specifically set up as representatives of different class positions and relationships between them were antagonistic and hostile. The Collins family represented the upper-middle classes falling on hard times, the Huntingdons were middle class and on the way up, yuppies before their time, and the Grants were working class, again on their way up but determined not to forget how hard the struggle had been. This very different conception of class and community shaped everything that happened in *Brookside*. There was no common meeting point or shared institution because the families had nothing in common to share. Stories ran parallel to each other and there was little communication between the fixed positions. Although there were common themes to some of the stories – unemployment and redundancy were a factor in the Collins' life as well as the Grants' – they were approached from different ends of the spectrum. Bobby Grant represented the position of a worker and a committed trade unionist; Paul Collins had the instincts of a conservative employer, even though he had suffered from Conservative economic policies. The middle-class characters had a position of their own and there was no question of them being adopted by a working-class community in the model later espoused by *EastEnders*. Furthermore, the soap opera convention that everyone is entitled to a point of view was skewed somewhat by the programme's firm commitment to and sympathy for the Grants' position. For the first time in British soap the viewer was offered a position for understanding a soap which was based on class and not gender.

The pre-eminence of class as the framework for *Brookside* also had consequences for the 'feel' of the programme. *Brookside* used soaps' capacity to mull over problems and to take into account the nuances of a position in a way that had not been seen before by giving class issues the same weight as personal dilemmas. In one episode, for example, Bobby's decision to become a full-time trade union officer, potentially the slippery road to becoming a paid bureaucrat rather than an honourable activist, was subjected to the same careful scrutiny by his friends and workmates that would be given in other soaps to a decision to get married. Later on, Bobby blamed a personal tragedy, the death of his son in a street attack, on political and class factors, on the unemployment which sent Damon out of Liverpool in search of a work, and linked his death to those of soldiers in the Falklands who also died, as Bobby believed, because of government policies.

This was new ground for soaps and offered the genuine pleasure to its audience of seeing their own social and political dilemmas, ignored elsewhere, reworked into a long-running fiction. But the structure of the serial also meant that the antagonism between families was not merely conducted at the level of grand themes of unemployment and economic policies; it was also manifest in the arguments over the garden fence which replaced the casual exchange of gossip characteristic of *Coronation Street*. Roger Huntingdon, for instance, concerned about the property values of his own house, tried to bully one neighbour into taking down an unsightly shed and accused another of burgling his house. It was all too easy, in such situations, for representation of class difference to disintegrate into slanging matches and there was, in the interaction between the characters, a general sense of bickering and bad temper. In rejecting the notion of a community, *Brookside* had also thrown out the utopian pleasures of communal warmth and solidarity. Implausible and unrealistic they might have been but they provided a relief from the disagreements and difficulties which are the staple of soap narratives. Without this sense of community, *Brookside* sometimes felt like a battleground with class differences providing the lines of engagement.

It is possible to argue that *Brookside* has lost the purity and clarity of the first year and that the battle lines have become more blurred. To do so is to misunderstand the nature of long-running drama which cannot stay in one place without becoming atrophied. It is certainly true that the original characters have changed – Bobby Grant did become a trade union official, always vulnerable to the criticism that he sold out; Paul Collins retired and his position as a representative of the employers has become less focused. New characters such as the nurses Sandra and Kate came in whose class position was less clear, perhaps because they were single women with no husband to help define their socio-economic grouping. A pillar box was set up in the Close to give the residents the 'natural' reason for stopping to chat which the pubs provided in other serials. Crises, like the siege of one of the houses in the Close, engendered a somewhat half-hearted community response and parties have marked Christmas, New Year and birthdays as the traditional soap times of celebration.

In the main, though, Brookside has remained true to its refusal to collapse class difference into a celebration of communal values. It has maintained its system of using class as determining how charac-ters are to be understood and as the original families moved away from their positions, other have been brought in to replace them. As the Grants edged in lifestyle if not in allegiance to the middle-class, the Jacksons and then the Corkhills replaced them as the working-class family. The original middle-class couple were split up by divorce but their structural position was filled firstly by Heather's romantic liaisons culminating in her marriage to Nick and then by Jonathan in his pairings firstly with Laura and subsequently with Cheryl which in their combination of career woman feminist and sceptical male ambition have almost exactly replicated the original Heather and Roger. In addition, fractions of the original positions have been taken up and explored. The original working-class posi-tion held by Bobby Grant has been considerably deepened by the development of the newer families. Both the Jackson and the Corkhill families were, on entry to the serial, headed by a skilled worker (a fireman and an engineer) but both were used to show the slipperiness of the upwardly mobile slide and how readily misfortune or bad judgement can lead into a spiral of debts, unemployment crime and even imprisonment. A new layer has also been added by the development of the 'lads' (Barry, Pat, Terry) drifting between unemployment, the black economy and petty crime while Michelle and later Tracy Corkhill took up the girls' equivalent of beautician courses and Youth Training Schemes in hairdressing.

Class positions have thus become more complex in *Brookside* but there has been no real sign of the lines being breached in the interest of mutual support. Families still conduct their own lives very separately, actively discouraging participation from the neighbours. Sheila Grant occasionally offers a sympathetic word but there has been a clear separation between the Grants and the other working-class families and, until the dramatic development of Sheila's affair with Billy, contact between them was rare. The Grants did little to help the Corkhills, for instance, during the crises brought on by Billy's unemployment and Bobby went so far as to express concern that Doreen should not look on Sheila as a soft touch when it came to using the telephone or borrowing sugar. Bobby's stance was not particularly criticised in the programme; it merely expressed in a hard but fair way *Brookside*'s basic philosophy that major problems are caused by factors beyond personal control and that to pretend that community spirit can cover up differences or ameliorate social or economic problems is, to use the terms which have sustained *Brookside*'s project from the start, unrealistic and implausible.

The British soaps, thus, in their different ways, use class difference as a means of defining and explaining relationships within and outside the soap's community. To the British viewer, used to reading the signifiers of class in this way, the US soaps seem to offer a very different approach. The interaction of community and class in *Coronation Street* or *EastEnders* invites the audience to share a common experience, while *Dallas* and *Dynasty* invite us to observe with amusement, amazement or wonder the behaviour of a nouveau riche upper class. Critics have commented that class does not provide a basis for judgement in the same way in the US prime time soaps and have argued that actions are understood in terms of the family or the individual rather than class. Following up Feuer's argument that in these programmes 'the economics of multinational corporations' are dealt with not in terms of class but 'of the familial conflicts which control the destinies of these companies',[20] Alvarado, Gutch and Wollen suggest that 'wealth creation is narrativised as the outcome of the actions of individuals rather than classes.'[21] Thus it is argued that *Dallas* and *Dynasty* deal only with the world of the rich; that capitalism is presented as essentially benign, unproblematically the best way of operating, with the only argument being between the good capitalists (Bobby Ewing, Blake Carrington) and the bad ones (JR, Adam Carrington); and that the workers who create the wealth on which the empires are built go literally and metaphorically unrepresented in the programmes. To make a somewhat unlikely analogy, *Dallas* and *Dynasty* are seen to work, in their treatment of class, in the same way as *Coronation Street*, representing a single class position and concentrating on personal disagreements within it rather than on relationships across classes.

It is interesting, however, to consider what might have been, for *Dynasty*, in particular, began with a rather different project which made more explicit and more problematic the class position on which the series is based. Blake was far from being the benign capitalist he later became and was specifically criticised for his ruthless pursuit of wealth, most forcefully by his son Steven. On the day of Blake and Krystle's wedding, Steven argues with his father over the politics of oil and US energy policies. 'I think you sold this country out,' he accuses and when Blake retorts by pointing out that his son lives off the profits, Steven replies 'At least I don't steal and I don't rob from the people of this country.' It could be argued that this exchange is another example of family relationships extending into the arena of work and politics in the same way as, for instance, Pam's critique of JR is rooted in family dynamics. Steven clearly has other reasons for disagreeing with his father and the conversation, taking place as it does before the wedding and moving into an argument about Steven's sexuality, inextricably links Blake's role as head of the Carrington Company with that of head of the Carrington family. Nevertheless, in this first series, it is not merely Steven who sees Blake as ruthless in pursuit of class interests and the programme goes on to establish the layers of class and their interrelationships as clearly as *Brookside* sought to do. Thus, the servants 'under the stairs' of the Carrington house know their place but are actively engaged in gossip about their employers (unlike the silent Theresa in *Dallas*). They have a subservient but intimate relationship to the Carringtons exemplified by Joseph who follows his master's commands but is highly attuned to the emotional atmosphere in the household. Moving up the social strata, we find the workers employed in the oil field, living rough and doing hard manual work. Heading this group are Walter and Matthew who are fighting Blake's manoeuvres to get their oil field. On the distaff side of this group are Krystle and Claudia, both in appropriately female white-collar jobs, the former a secretary, the latter working in a bookshop. At the top, of course, are the Carringtons and the even richer Colbys, themselves divided into tycoon father figures and the second generation of spenders such as Fallon and Jeff. Much more clearly, then, than in *Dallas* are class differences laid out and particular characters seem to be as representative of a class as of a family position.

In *Dynasty*, however, unlike *Brookside*, it is the movement between these groups which is the mainspring of the early plots. Central, of course, is Krystle's marriage to Blake and her own doubts about making the move are not the conventional pre-wedding fears usual in soaps but are specifically articulated through a class rather than a romantic discourse. She is conscious of the difficulty of moving from the role of middle-class secretary to that of upper-class wife. Her unease at handling servants is frequently drawn to viewers' attention; preparing for the wedding, she is clearly unused to their attentions and after the marriage cannot find the appropriate manner to deal with Joseph who tells her bluntly: 'I belong here, you don't.' Cecil Colby quite clearly advises her against her husband's exploitative tendencies, reinforcing for the audience Steven's earlier criticisms even though he expresses them rather differently: 'Your husband is a dangerous hunter because he's led the pride for so long.' Krystle herself fights against the notion that she is another of Blake's acquisitions: 'I'm not somebody's prize; I'm not a handful of oil leases; I'm not somebody's mineral reserves.' Blake's rape of her, later in the series, confirms that he does indeed see her as an object for his own use and over whom he extends the demands of ownership.

Krystle's comparison of herself to Blake's other interests links the narrative of the marriage to the struggle between Blake and Walter over the Lankershon oil rights. The wedding is counterpointed by the story of the 'accident' at the oil rig which is edited into shots of the ceremony itself and Walter appears at the reception to accuse Blake of sabotage. This narrative, too, is concerned with movement between classes: Walter and Matthew aspire to move upwards in the same way as the Colbys and the Carringtons have, while Steven is moving in the opposite direction into 'the enemy camp' by working for Walter and Matthew and falling in love with Claudia. Krystle's entry into 'he Carrington class and Steven's desperate attempts to leave it both serve to underline the ferocity and ruthlessness of Blake's approach. He goes beyond the wheeling and dealings of JR by, for instance, sabotaging equipment, setting the guard dogs on Walter at the wedding and by permitting him to be beaten up. While

Blake himself does not get his hands dirty, he is deeply implicated in the physically threatening behaviour of his henchmen.

In its early days, then, *Dynasty* both gave screen space to those living outside the Carrington circle and represented the relationship between the class groups as violent and exploitative even when based on marriage. Blake's parody of Steven's position – admitting himself 'a capitalist exploiter of the working classes' – rebounds on him as the viewer is invited to accept that Steven is speaking not merely as a frightened son to an angry father but as a representative of those who are in economic as well as emotional relationships with Blake. As the series developed over the years, the edge of this critique has been severely blunted, with Steven's move into the Carrington Company, the increasingly idyllic presentation of the Blake/Krystle marriage, the virtual disappearance of the working-class characters and the shift away from physical threats to more abstract struggles within the tight clique of the rich and powerful. But the early episodes of *Dynasty* did show that the dynamics of class could be incorporated into a US soap and that attention to class differences is not a purely British prerogative.

Gays and lesbians

I have argued that one of the features of the prime time soaps under discussion in this book is a willingness to take on issues which had previously been considered unsuitable for soap viewers. In this context, stories about lesbian and gay relationships could be considered particularly suitable for co-option since, while they offered a frisson of difference, the terrain was the familiar one of personal and emotional relationships. Unlike class, the notion of using gay relationships as a basis for stories did not threaten the traditional basis for soaps, merely extended it to cover a wider area. The new eighties soaps seemed willing to take up the challenge. *Dynasty* led the way by putting Steven Carrington's emotional and sexual dilemmas right into the heart of the family serial and, although neither *EastEnders* nor *Brookside* included gays or lesbians among their initial residents, both later introduced gay characters through whom they have tried to deal with specifically gay issues while at the same time involving them in the day-to-day life of the serial. The working through of this new material has not, however, been unproblematic although, given the marked unwillingness of television to address gay and lesbian issues generally, soaps may still be able to argue that they are ahead of other kinds of TV fiction.

It is necessary to begin with a qualification, however, for while gay men, for a time, became a standard ingredient in the modern soap, lesbians are still largely unrepresented. *Brookside* had a rather unfortunate attempt at handling a lesbian relationship with Nick's ex-wife, who worked in a somewhat disorganised co-op which Heather was required to audit. The stereotype of inefficient, lesbian, left-wing activists brought criticism from viewers on Channel 4's *Right to Reply* programme and the soaps have largely steered clear of lesbian characters since then. It may be this underrepresentation merely accords with the refusal to acknowledge lesbians generally and the attempt to render them invisible throughout British culture. There may, however, be more particular reasons for their absence from soaps, since, in a sense, soaps, with their emphasis on the central position of women and on the importance of female friendships, would seem to provide ideal ground for issues around lesbianism. But it may indeed be because of the crucial role of women in soaps that the representation of lesbian relationships is so difficult. In the more traditional soaps, female friendship provides an important, stable element, forging strong bonds between Mavis and Rita, in *Coronation Street*, for example, Jill Chance and Diane in *Crossroads* or even Pam and Sue Ellen in *Dallas*. This sense of shared experience is, as we have seen, crucial to soaps, creating a context in which female friendship underpins the audience's understanding of the characters. The entry of a lesbian couple into this shared female world would be genuinely subversive, implying that lesbians are not separate from, indeed had things in common with, other women. The sexualisation of female friendship, however, through the presentation of a lesbian couple, could reverberate through the soap, calling into question the basis of the relationship between other women in the programme. In addition, in the more recent soaps, the representation of the strong, career woman as a lesbian could remove her entirely from the family nexus on which soaps are based. Heterosexuality keeps Alexis in the family, ensuring that she jealously pursues Blake and seeks alliances against him with her children. In the British soaps, the woman's role as emotional support for the family would be put in question if she sought sexual satisfaction outside her current or future family. Ironically, the very strength of women in soaps mitigates against the introduction of lesbians into their narratives and so far it has scarcely been tried.

Where soaps have taken up the issues of sexual orientation, it has been almost entirely through male characters. Mark Finch, in his analysis of *Dynasty*, has argued that for a gay male audience two potentially contradictory discourses are available in the programme: 'the textual articulations of camp, and of the modern gay movement – or liberal gay discourse'.[22] Finch suggests that the liberal discourse which argues for tolerance and the acceptance of an individual's sexuality is of less importance to the gay audience than the pleasure that can be taken in *Dynasty*'s self-conscious excess. This excess can be read within a camp discourse as disrupting narrative coherence with the recognition that gayness is not going to be accommodated within the confines of liberal tolerance and that 'gayness keeps returning as potential disruption to the bourgeois family.'[23]

This tension between acceptance and disruption, the desire to be understood and the urge to challenge, runs through the representation of gay characters in prime time soaps. In *Brookside* and *EastEnders*, it is the liberal gay discourse which dominates. Both programmes are marked by a commitment to take up 'problem issues' and homosexuality tends to be seen in that light. Both tend to be didactic, to use gay characters to explain their position and, as in the black singleton strategy, to undertake the impossible task of representing gay experience as if it were homogenous and univocal.

In *Brookside*, Gordon, who came out as a gay while still at school, was a member of the Collins family and hence a familiar character. A long absence in France and a change of actor on his return rather undermined this familiarity and the new Gordon was probably as much a shock to the audience as to his parents. In the main, the stories about Gordon have tended to centre around his relationship with his lover, Chris, and his family's difficulty in accepting the situation. Others in the Close have little opportunity to comment, given the lack of inter-family relationships in *Brookside*, and so it is in the family rather than in the community that the issue has to be worked through. The focus, in fact, has been largely on Paul Collins who has alternated between pained tolerance, frustrated anger and guarded support for his son. Other reactions have included his mother Annabelle's warmer response and the grandmother Mona's refusal to be shocked, positively relishing Chris's flirtatious, slightly *risqué* approach to her. Within the family, Chris and Gordon have been seen to argue capably for their right to their own sexuality and their refusal to have Paul's view imposed on them. They continually confront him with the way in which his illiberal attitudes lead to discrimination and injustice in society at large. Chris, for instance, points to the unfairness of the building society refusing them a mortgage unless they have an HIV test, while the gay-basing incident, in which Chris and Gordon are themselves arrested after they had been set on in the street, is used to demonstrate the way in which a gay man's attempt to defend himself can be used against him in court. Sometimes, the arguments seem to be pushed rather far – 'If Christ was walking the earth, he'd do the same thing,' is Gordon's response when Paul is horrified to discover that Chris has lent his flat to a friend who has AIDS. Nevertheless, an assertion of a gay liberal position is clearly made within the programme and at moments of crisis Paul responds to the arguments and goes to the help of his son.

Brookside appears to offer the straight audience a positive representation of gay men but it tends to be at the level of intellect rather than desire. The didactic mode of Chris and Gordon towards Paul – their function is to explain to him what it means to be gay – underpins also their relationship with the audience and because their characters tend to be understood only in terms of their sexuality they lack the resonance of some of the other *Brookside* residents, including Paul Collins whose struggles to accept and indeed like his son have given him a complexity which Gordon lacks. We are given little sense of their engagement with politics, with work or college life or with other friends. Chris was little more than a cipher for Gordon's affections and, as so often with *Brookside*, Gordon's most important relationships are within the family as he struggles to find his own space within his parents' troubled marriage. A certain 'thinness' about them is underlined somewhat ironically by the programme's inability to deal with what is meant to be their most important characteristic – their sexuality. Given the censorship that surrounds the representation of gays on British television, this is hardly surprising but the difficulties in finding a way of putting over the physical relationship between them means that the sexual vitality and commitment on which their characterisation is posited is markedly absent.[24]

Similar problems affect the representation of gay men in *EastEnders*. Unlike Gordon, Colin was specifically understood to be a gay character from the start and the audience knew that Debbie's attempts to date him were misguided. The appearance of his lover, Barry, put an end to such 'teasing' and they set up as a gay couple comparable to that in *Brookside*. However, the representation of the gay couple in *EastEnders* has been more broadly based than that of *Brookside*, partly because of the nature of the characters themselves and partly because the interaction between individuals and the community which is so essential to *Eastenders* means that, like everyone else, the gay characters are presented as having relationships outside the immediate family.

The character of Colin is certainly within the liberal gay discourse to which Finch refers. He is middle class, earns a reasonably good living as a designer and his flat is furnished in the greys and blacks of the aspiring young professional. He campaigned for the Labour Party during the election and is concerned about conservation and 'green' issues. He is deemed to be sensitive and caring and is a source of advice to a range of characters in the Square. Often his ability to help is based on his class position. Arthur Fowler, for instance, comes to him for advice on taking out a loan. Sometimes, however, his experience as a gay man is perceived to have shaped the advice he can give; his awareness of the constrictions of conventional male behaviour can be a source of strength which is drawn attention to and endorsed as, for example, when Graham's wife has a miscarriage and Colin tries to comfort him, telling him: 'You are allowed to show your feelings.'

If Colin fits into a particular type of gay representation, his lover, Barry, does not. Barry is a local East Ender whose family, with the exception of his brother Graham, do not know that he is gay. Barry eschews the specifically gay scenes which Colin enjoys – the drag night at The Dagmar for instance – and prefers a more conventional night on the town with his mates or with Donna, the barmaid at The Queen Vic. The relationship between Colin and Barry has been more tense and uneven than that between Chris and Gordon. They have had disagreements over minor domestic arrangements (Barry's untidiness) and major emotional problems (Barry's fear of 'coming out' to his family and particularly his father). The difference in their class position also gives an edge to their sexual/emotional relationship. Although Barry admires and respects Colin, he despairs of his naivety and his lack of street knowledge. Barry, in fact, shares the class position of many of the other characters and acts as a bridge between Colin and the rest of the community.

Because, as we have seen, *EastEnders'* structure is based on the notion of a community in a way that *Brookside's* is not, Colin and Barry are required to have relationships beyond their immediate circle. Both drink at The Queen Vic and are included in the various communal celebrations; both receive friendly support from the Beale/Fowler family, Colin mainly from Pauline and Barry from Kathy. Colin has got drunkenly maudlin with Pat and fallen out with the outsider Wilmot-Brown while Barry has helped Sue and Ali at the café and babysat for Pauline Fowler. Often their relationships within the community serve to emphasise the differences between them. On a comic level, Barry and Colin are on different sides in the pub football competition; more seriously, Barry joins enthusiastically in The Queen Vic's charity night while Colin argues that the

National Health Service should be able to provide proper health care services without falling back on the vagaries of charitable giving. The strategy of emphasising class-based differences has the effect of reducing the importance of sexuality in defining their characters. While Gordon and Chris are alike because they are gay, even being gay cannot make Colin and Barry share the same attitudes.

Nevertheless, although the gay men in *EastEnders* are more broadly characterised than those in *Brookside*, their function remains mainly didactic – that of alerting the heterosexual audience to the problem faced by gays and to plead for tolerance within society. Colin and Barry offer, as David Buckingham has pointed out, a positive image of homosexuality which is reinforced by the emphasis on the tolerance displayed by the other characters.[25] Their love affair is presented as having the same tensions, problems and anxieties as any other romance in the Square and is accepted as such by the community. The difference between their relationship and others emerges only as a focus for prejudice on the part of those whose opinions carry little weight. Accepted by Lou Beale and Pauline Fowler, Colin has little to fear from Dot's Old Testament threats about AIDS or Charlie Cotton's derogatory comments about 'poofs'. Only Pete Beale of the main characters is allowed to express intolerant remarks and his position is undermined by his blustering espousal of an excessively masculine position. Pete's jokes, like much else he does, are unfocused and not followed through. Barry is placed in a more difficult situation vis-à-vis his father, who is fiercely intolerant of homosexuality, but we learn of his views second hand and Barry is strongly supported by his brother, Graham, who makes the gay liberal plea for openness and tolerance: 'You can't hide it any longer . . . You have to stand up for what you are if that's what you want to be.'

Characteristically for *EastEnders*, the most serious threats to Colin and Barry come from outside the community. When Colin is on jury service, he refuses to be 'nobbled' by the 'friends' of those on trial and he is consequently harassed by representatives of the 'underworld' who threaten to expose his sexuality and specifically his relationship with Barry. On the other side of the law, the police, who come to investigate a burglary at the flat which Colin shares with Barry, turn prurient and accusatory when they discover he is gay and become more interested in Barry's age than in what has been stolen. Significantly, this incident has a didactic function and is used both to give the audience information about, for instance, the age of consent for homosexuals and to demonstrate community tolerance of the gay couple through Pauline's dogged support for Colin.

It may seem churlish to cavil at the positive images of and attitudes to gays which *Brookside* and *EastEnders* present and their refusal to lend credence to homophobic attitudes so strong in our society. British soaps have to face a double gauntlet of censorship and prejudice. On the one hand, Mary Whitehouse, for the National Viewers' and Listeners' Association, included the representation of homosexuality in her attack on *EastEnders* for undermining family life; on the other, despite the care taken, the couple were reported by teachers to be objects of derision in school playgrounds. When Barry and Colin split up, with Barry somewhat implausibly declaring his intention of going straight, there was the impression that the issue had got too much for a programme with a huge family audience. British soaps clearly see themselves as conducting a fine balancing act and should be commended for at least attempting to represent gay relationships which scarcely feature elsewhere in television drama. Nevertheless, it is striking that the gay relationships lack the full-blooded drama of, for instance, those between Angie and Den or Billy Corkhill and Sheila Grant and that the extremes of passion, whether it be love or hatred, are hardly allowed to be expressed. In both programmes, therefore, it is not the gay relationship itself which is disruptive but the intolerant response to it expressed by characters (Paul Collins, Dot Cotton) whose opinions on a range of subjects are already suspect and whose views are themselves seen as deviant from the generally tolerant response which is presented as the norm.

It is possible to argue that *Dynasty* has treated Steven's gayness with the same liberal tolerance as that shown by British soaps. Although some characters refuse to adopt it, the 'correct' reponse of acceptance is made clear to the audience and Steven himself, at least in the early episodes, is characterised in the same way as Colin – sensitive, caring, concerned about the environment, interested in the arts. Nevertheless, *Dynasty*'s generic conventions and narrative patterns place Steven in a different position from that of the other gay characters examined here and its melodramatic mode allows for a more intense expression of the feelings involved.

In *Dynasty* as in *Brookside*, the most central relationship for the gay man is not with his lover but with his father. But while *Brookside* asserts that reason can win out, *Dynasty* takes up the dynamics of the issue in a highly dramatic fashion and in doing so emphasises feeling rather than logic. I have argued that one of the characteristics of US soaps is their concern with the precariousness of patriarchal power and their emphasis on the fight of the leading male characters to assert their control. In some senses, Steven's role can be compared with that of the women in such soaps, the issues of gayness being simply another of the sexual and emotional problems which threaten Blake's power. Narratively, Steven's relationship with the patriarch is comparable to that of Sue Ellen with JR in *Dallas*; his challenge to the patriarch, like hers, is not about business and power but a capacity for emotional sensitivity and response. This narrative position is backed up by Steven's refusal or inability to behave 'like a man'. He is praised by the women for his caring nature – Sammy Jo, for instance, assures him that: 'You're the kindest, gentlest man I've ever known.' But the programme is more ambiguous about his lack of physical prowess. In the earlier episodes, he had to call on Matthew to rescue Walter from Blake's clutches and Matthew also protects Steven himself when one of his workmates taunts him as a 'pervert'.

Steven thus disturbs the equilibrium of the family by fighting with his father and moving outside the safe circle of the home; he similarly disturbs the notion of inheritance by engaging in gay relationships which will produce no child and later by bringing up his son outside family and particularly his father's control. It could be argued that the strength of the challenge is undermined by the internal doubts that Steven has about his own sexuality. His lover, Ted, accuses him of being 'in limbo, emotional limbo' and he is presented as being ambivalent about being gay. On the one hand, he defends his position to the other men, Jeff and Matthew as well as Blake: 'I'm not ashamed of it' he says to Matthew when he explains his relationship with Ted. Later on he tells Sammy Jo: 'Part of me is never going to change . . . I can't change who I am.' But at the same time, homosexuality is presented as being a force that drives him rather than a source of satisfaction. There is some incoherence, as Mark Finch indicates, about the reasons for Steven's sexual orientation – neglect by his father, the excessive attentions of his mother, a desire to rebel, 'left-wing' leanings – but what emerges clearly is the sense that he is driven by forces which he cannot control. In the exchange with his father before Blake's wedding, Steven is uncertain and confused: 'Straighten myself out? I'm not sure I know what that means. I'm not sure I could if I wanted to. And I'm not sure I want to.' When he tells Claudia that he has spent the night with Ted, he protests: 'It wasn't something I wanted to happen . . . I'm fighting too . . . It's not that easy for me.' Much later on in the series, when Steven's sexuality is given less prominence, he is still confused and divided by conflicting desires, attempting a reconciliation with Sammy Jo which in the end fails to satisfy him and distresses her.

Steven's internal doubts and indeed his relationships with Sammy

Jo and Claudia can be explained by the programme's own ambiva-
lence towards a gay character, the attempt 'to extinguish his "gay
voice" ' as Mark Finch puts it.[26] Nevertheless, Steven's uncertainties
and incoherences at least release him from the trap of didacticism
which constrains his British counterparts. The gay characters in
Brookside and *EastEnders* explain their needs to others but Steven
explores his for himself in a way which is more characteristic of soap
story telling and which helps to give his emotional problems the
same complexity and weight as those of the other characters. In a
genre which is so firmly on the side of its women characters, Steven's
association with the female position in the narrative and his capacity
to talk through contradictory emotions, help him to avoid being a
single issue character.

In addition, Steven's strong sense of being driven does allow the
expression of some notion of desire which is absent from the British
soaps. Ironically, though, the recognition of gay desire in *Dynasty*
finds its strongest expression in the words and actions of characters
who are outraged by Steven's behaviour: 'you should have seen
them, touching each other, almost kissing' is how a workmate
drunkenly describes a meeting he has overseen between Steven and
Ted. It is Blake, of course, who is an excess of vituperation most
graphically describes the physical element which can scarcely be
shown on screen. His first indication to Steven that he knows of his
son's sexuality comes in an outburst of physical revulsion: 'How can
anyone respect the opinion of a man who'd put his hands on the
body of another man?' Unlike Fallon who fondly embraces half her
father's football team at the wedding reception, Steven is not allowed to express desire in his father's house and it is Ted's appearance
at the Carrington mansion which precipitates Blake's violence: 'In
my house. I'll kill them', he mutters and the point-of-view shots as
he ascends the stairs to find the couple underlines the drama. The
fairly innocuous fairwell embrace between Ted and Steven is thus
perceived through Blake's eyes as indeed an expression of desire
which is subversive of patriarchal expectation: 'get your hands off
my son' is both a literal and metaphorical expression of Blake's fear
of homosexuality and sense of ownership over his son. It is perhaps
an indication of the fundamental way in which gay desire is suppres-
sed that it finds its most powerful expression in horrified denuncia-
tions and that it can be signified most strongly only through the force
with which it is rejected.

In this chapter, I have argued that prime time soaps have attempted
to articulate social change through issues of race, class and sexuality.

It has not been an easy task, however, and different soaps vary in how they deal with what are often perceived to be awkward issues. The various approaches outlined here grow out of the generic and formal conventions which each programme uses in handling the totality of its material. The family melodrama format of *Dynasty*, for instance, allows for a bolder handling of gay desire which is not available to *Brookside*; the communities of *Coronation Street* and *EatsEnders*, constituted through different class and regional constructions, accommodate or fail to accommodate black characters in different ways. Nevertheless, there remains a basic contradiction for soaps in handling such issues. On the one hand, they make good stories along the emotional lines marked out as a soap territory; emphasis on difference – between black and white, working class and yuppy, gay and heterosexual – provides the impetus for disruption on which soap narratives thrive. At the same time, though, if the differences are marked too dramatically, too distinctly, the soap's prevailing ethos that everyone shares the common experience, the same pains and pleasures, becomes untenable. These issues are therefore not just awkward for soaps because they run the risk of alienating some members of the audience or upsetting the establishment. They are also inclined to upset the soaps' classic fallback position that what unites us is more important than what divides us. 'Everyone's the same really,' is a soap cliché that can be drawn on when other solutions have failed, but the issues around gender, class and race explored in this chapter raise awkward problems which cannot be so easily accommodated.

8

Women's Fiction No More?

'Don't listen to the "all men are the same" crap . . . 'Cos we're not.'

Rod, *Brookside*

'It's like not being heard. It's like I don't exist.'

Sheila, *Brookside*

'The tables have turned . . . I'm going to have everything that was yours, so sleep on, little sister, sleep on.'

Katherine to Pam, *Dallas*

The changes outlined in the last chapter have stretched the boundaries of the soap genre and have shifted it away from the traditional concerns of women's fiction examined earlier. In this final chapter, I intend to explore further the effect that this shift has had on the role of women in these prime time soaps and to suggest that, although these programmes do still offer traditional soap pleasures to women, the emphasis has significantly altered. Although I have not argued that the pleasures of identification and involvement in these programmes are available only to women, I have proposed that they do address women in a particular way, that women are the skilled readers by whom the programmes are best understood and that, unusually for much mainstream television, the programmes are orientated towards them in terms of the range of characters offered, the type of stories dealt with and the way in which women characters operate as the norm through whom appropriate judgements can be made. But what has also been clear is that the prime time soaps are also seeking to widen their appeal. Changes in soaps in the 1980s and, in particular the introduction of new sets of issues outlined in chapter 7, have shifted the soaps' areas of concern and the traditional appeal to women has been revised to take in other members of the family group. This opening up of the address of soaps can be identified in changes in story lines and characterisation and in the presentation of different points of view which involve a shift away from women and give a greater prominence to men, adolescents and children. This chapter seeks to examine further the ways in which soaps have sought to extend their audience by what Jane Root calls their 'de-feminisation'[1] and to ask whether this process has not been at a considerable cost to the woman viewer.

Men in soaps

The new space given to men in prime time soaps can be seen in their story lines and in the way in which they look to more masculine genres for their narrative references. While personal relationships are still at the heart of the programmes, they have been supplemented by plot lines which deal more regularly with the public sphere and emphasise the male grip on themes of business and work. In *Dynasty* and *Dallas*, for instance, we have noted the emphasis on high-powered business affairs and the kind of deals which are impressive precisely because only the hero can understand their complexity. Despite the advent of Alexis, this world of oil and high finance is still seen very much as a male sphere and when, for instance, Sue Ellen in *Dallas* tried to expand her lingerie business, she did so with the very firm guidance of her finance adviser, Nicholas Pearce. With Pearce's death and Pam's departure, JR and Bobby have tended to dominate the business manoeuvrings in *Dallas*; Callie and April accompanied them on the trip to Europe, for instance, but had no role in its business side. In addition, there has been a move to stories which emphasise adventure and action. In *Dynasty*, for example, there was the story of Alexis's ill-fated husband, Sean, a double-crossing mercenary who was involved in a sabotage expedition; in the final series, the Nazi hidden art plot smacked more of Len Deighton than Mills and Boon. *Dallas*, similarly, has regularly featured action stories such as JR's and Jack's encounter with terrorists in Martinique or Calhoun's pursuit of JR which ended with the kidnapping of John Ross and a gun battle. *Dallas* specifically uses generic references to the Western in such stories. The confrontation between Calhoun and JR had all the connotations of a Western-style shoot-out as JR and Calhoun tracked each other through a deserted railway yard, ducking behind coaches as the bullets zinged past, until the narrative was resolved by the arrival of the cavalry in the shape of Ray and Bobby. Similar references were drawn on in the 'ranch war' on Ewing land when a fight over oil rights was conducted on the range with the participants on horseback as well as in helicopters.

The British soaps have also adopted story lines which allow them to move outside the domestic and personal. In *EastEnders* narratives have been built around what are generally deemed to be male interests such as the soccer match between the two rival pubs. The selection of the teams, preparation for the match and the game itself were used to exemplify the rivalry between Den and Wilmot-Brown and the differences in their attitudes were exemplified in a game of football; the use of a male sport as a metaphor in soap opera seemed particularly ironic. In the main, though, *EastEnders* has turned to crime/police series as the source for its more masculine stories rather than sporting occasions or the US Westerns. In *EastEnders*, Den was regularly involved, through the pub, in petty crime. His initial dabbling in stolen goods led to a major story which had him carrying unspecified goods illegally out of the country. The treatment of this story included scenes and characters which seemed to have strayed in from a crime series – the seizure of Den and the waiting in the hideout, the interrogation and the threats of the East End hoods, the nervous walk through customs. After Angie's departure, Den's connections with the criminal world were given more emphasis and he was accused of arson in a long-running story which featured Den's criminal connections, the police investigation of the fire at The Dagmar and the vicissitudes of his life in jail. Other characters have also featured in stories of this kind – most notably, Darren, the black 'wide boy' of the Square, and Frank, who is both a second-hand car salesman and Den's successor as landlord of The Queen Vic. The generic references to crime series apparent in the plots and milieu of these stories are reinforced by *EastEnders*' deployment of cockney characters and ethos, making connections between the soaps and prime time British crime programmes like *The Sweeney*, *Minder* and *The Bill*.

But it is *Brookside* which has most clearly foregrounded what are deemed to be male preoccupations with stories which move well outside the traditional soap opera material. *Brookside* has developed story lines which depend on action and resolution rather than the more soap-orientated narrative strategies of commentary and repetition. One example of such a story would be the extended drama of the seige when Sandra, Kate and Pat were held hostage in their house in the Close. Part of the story drew attention to the effect of such an extraordinary event on their relationships but the extended narrative line and the abandoning of serial time for a slower timescale pulled the siege out of the day-by-day drama of the serial. The presence of the police, the emphasis on their procedures and the final shooting of Kate shifted the focus from the minutiae of personal relationships to the broader sweep of TV drama with its emphasis on action and resolution. Like *EastEnders*, *Brookside* has also turned to the crime genres for its more male-orientated stories. Thus, there have been a number of plots in which the lads, Barry Grant, Terry and Pat, have got involved in a series of brushes with the Liverpool underworld, led by a gangster-type figure, Tommy McArdle. These stories are marked by considerable violence and threats – in one, Terry and Barry were badly injured when they got on the wrong side of McArdle – but also offer a way out of desperate financial situations and a fantasy of the escape to the good life through crime. One of *Brookside*'s location trips exemplified this when Pat and Terry lay around on white beaches on Barbados, chatted up 'the birds' and sipped long drinks under the somewhat unlikely pretext of looking after McArdle's mother (who herself was, of course, part of the scam). In a rather more serious vein, Billy Corkhill, driven to the edge by unemployment and poverty, agreed to get involved in a raid on a supermarket only to find himself caught up in a nightmare of identification parades, secret phone calls and threats to his daughter.

   Brookside has looked to the conventions and rhythms of the crime genre when it has moved outside the usual soap terrain by taking up such stories. The location moves from the Close to the streets of Liverpool; the narrative from the internal drama of personal relationships to the overt action of car chase, threats and physical violence; the overall hermeneutic from the long-term changes in feelings and characters to the short-term enigmas of 'Will he get caught, will he get hurt?' In some cases, the soap genre works with that of the police series/thriller to powerful effect. The story of Billy Corkhill's descent into crime was marked by conventions of series such as *The Sweeney*, *Fox* or *Out*.[2] Billy and his partners were characterised as small-time crooks, nervous, shouting at each other and panic-stricken when the gun went off. The street location, the close-up camera-work, the police procedure of questioning and identification followed a format familiar from crime series. In this instance, however, the criminal narrative tied in with the family narrative more traditional to soaps: Billy's son, Rod, was potentially involved in the inquiry through his work as a policeman; the threat made by the crooks on his daughter, Tracy, was the more poignant when she herself suspected her father's lies and evasions; and his wife's ultimatum to leave him if he was unable or unwilling to disentangle himself meant that a traditional soap dilemma (to leave or stay in a marriage) was inextricably tied in with the crime narrative.

But there are times when the link to the Close is barely made and the story is more of a one-off providing some drama but demanding of the audience few of the soap skills of concern and judgement. One example of this type of narrative would be Barry Grant's involvement with art thefts which attempted to cover up its lack of emotional significance by invoking a plethora of crime series connotations. Seduced by a glamour girl in a posh car who turns out to be a gangster's moll, Barry finds himself blackmailed into helping with the art thefts by her lover, Sizzler, who, with his pale, gaunt face, black clothes and stammer, fits every hackneyed criteria for the part. In the end, the story fell into farce with secret meetings in the woods and the exchange of the wrong parcels as if even the excessive characterisation of Sizzler could not disguise the failure of this story of crime and intrigue to fit into *Brookside*'s soap world.

This change in narrative organisation, and a reorientation towards the more masculine genres, has been accompanied by an extension in the range of masculine characters. It is not necessary to over-emphasise this since the prime time soaps have been particularly careful to continue the traditional role of strong women in soaps. Nevertheless, while recognising that, as we saw in chapter 4, women are still the main source of strength, the weight given to male protagonists and the space given to their characterisation represents a marked shift in the balance of *EastEnders* and *Brookside*. In *EastEnders*, Arthur Fowler may be presented as weak and some-what unstable but the regular viewer is invited to understand the reasons for his situation. The financial and emotional pressures of unemployment have been clearly laid out and the effect on his pride at not being able to pay for his daughter's wedding, for instance, has been elaborated in some detail. Similarly, while the audience was invited to sympathise with Michelle's discontent at being tied into a marriage at such a young age, it was also informed of her husband Lofty's past, his unhappy childhood, his rejection by the army and the death of his much-loved aunt. In the debate that followed Michelle's decision to have an abortion, Lofty's point of view was given considerable space and was presented with a sympathy which was not afforded Mike Baldwin in similar circumstances in the more traditional *Coronation Street.*

David Buckingham has argued that, in *EastEnders*, 'traditional definitions of masculinity have been called into question' by the undermining of the male role as the head of the household.[3] In the process, however, there has been a shift of focus to an examination of the male characters' personal and emotional life and a tendency to present even the weak males as sympathetic characters who are to be understood, rather than dismissed with the conventional soap phrase, 'They're all the same, men.' *Brookside* goes further than this and has created, as Jane Root has pointed out 'powerful, complex male characters . . . very different from the gentlemanly heart-throbs of *Crossroads*'.[4]

This was particularly marked in the early years of *Brookside* when its attempt to incorporate issues of work and trade unionism led to an emphasis on the male characters who operated in the public sphere. The presentation of Bobby Grant, in this period, was extremely powerful, taking up a complex set of problems and exploring the relationship between a trade union, its members and its full-time officials and articulating them with a degree of urgency rare in British television and unique in soaps. Bobby's relationships with his family were also explored in a moving way which allowed the audience access to a depth of masculine feeling which in *Coronation Street* tended to be expressed with a shrug and a sigh. Other male characters are given similar space. In the Corkhill family, as much emphasis was placed on Billy's relationship with his daughter, Tracy, and his response to unemployment as on his wife's increasingly desperate attempt to keep the family together. When Doreen left, it was Billy's anguish which was shown and his clumsy attempts to comfort Tracy gave him a central role in the family. Outside the family, male characters are given similar attention and all male households have been a characteristic of *Brookside*. Pat and Terry lived somewhat uneasily together for a considerable length of time and when that arrangement broke up Jonathan offered Terry temporary accommodation in his home. The pensioners Harry Cross and Ralph Hardwick established a regime based on surface bickering and mutual understanding with Harry obstinately fending off the women who find Ralph attractive. Such domestic arrangements mean that *Brookside* allows its audience access to masculine conversation in a way that is unusual in soaps and allows male characters to discuss their problems with each other and on occasion to acknowledge the importance of their own friendships. The comparison with the traditional *Coronation Street* set-up of female interactions – Ena, Martha and Minnie in the snug, Rita and Mavis in the shop, the women in the factory, Annie, Bet and Betty behind the bar – is striking.

The greater emphasis given to men in terms of story lines, characterisation and generic references, has placed, as a consequence, greater emphasis on action and a quick response and less on the meditative pleasures of analysing emotional problems. In the US prime time soaps, there was a marked shift from the leisurely pace of the daytime programmes with more emphasis on swift movement and physical action; in the words of one critic they played 'too fast and loose with the predictableness of soap opera conventions'.[5] In the new British soaps, *Brookside* and *EastEnders*, there was similarly greater emphasis on action as the extended range of male characters and the force and weight given to them combined with the changing conventions in realism identified in chapter 2. Issues such as drugs, unemployment, rape and prostitution were to the forefront and the programmes took on a harsher tone. Arguments became more violent, rows seemed louder and physical force was no longer a rare phenomenon. *Brookside* was forced by audience response to tone down its language but found that its audience was engaged rather than put off by the bitter confrontations between Bobby Grant and his son, Barry, or the highly charged arguments in the Corkhill family.

In this context, the first episode of *EastEnders* can be seen to have had a self-conscious significance. The first shot of Den's boot breaking down Reg's door provided an indication that the supposedly cosy world of soaps was being broken into and turned upside down. The first characters presented to the audience were a group of men and the episode continued rapidly to establish a number of stories including a possible murder and a fight in the pub between the racist Nick Cotton and the Turkish Ali. The episode finished with Den physically removing both men from the bar and the final shot of a hand crashing through the glass of the pub door in defiant protest. Nothing could have signalled more clearly that while *EastEnders* was, as we have seen, working within established soap conventions, it had every intention of challenging the assumption that soaps were a secure and safe place for women viewers.

The development of the teenager

The space and scope for male characters has been matched by a new attention to teenagers. Children and young people featured very rarely in traditional soaps like *Coronation Street* and *Crossroads*. Babies were born but they tended to disappear as did, for instance, the Barlow twins in *Coronation Street* who were narratively dispatched to Scotland. When young people did appear they were already taking up the model provided by their elders. Meg's children, Jill and Sandy, followed their mother in playing an active role in running the *Crossroads* Motel; the teenagers, Gail and Suzie, aped the glamorous middle-aged women of *Coronation Street* – Elsie, Rita, Bet – in their eagerness to enter the adult world. In part, the absence of young people were a sign of the age of the programmes. In the early days of *Coronation Street*, the young Lucille Hewitt, Dennis Tanner and Ken Barlow had provided an outlet for the programme to express its version of teenage views and a focus for stories of adolescent angst. In the early 1980s, those days were long gone and, by contrast, *Brookside*'s introduction of characters who were still at school seemed a genuine innovation. The characters of Damon and Karen Grant allowed the programme to explore different attitudes to and experience of school and, over the years, to follow Damon through unproductive Youth Training Schemes into unemployment and Karen to becoming the first of her family to get to university. Against this was set the experience of Lucy and Gordon Collins, children from a much more privileged background struggling to adjust to their father's move down in the world.

Aging has been a problem for *Brookside* too in its handling of young characters. Five years in the life of a teenage character can change them and their situation out of recognition whereas five years in the life of Elsie Tanner or Annie Walker was hardly noticeable. Damon Grant, for instance, was almost kept too young in order to maintain what was a key character position for the programme. But, in the main, *Brookside* has successfully replaced its children and young people in a way which allowed the programme to continue to claim 'a marked concentration upon the problems and concerns of the Close's younger residents who contribute so much vitality and authenticity to the show.'[6] The introduction of Tracy and Rod Corkhill increased the number of teenage characters and care was taken to replace the representatives of the younger age groups as the original characters moved on. The schoolboy Jackson twins thus came into the programme as the Grants left school and the Rogers family with its three young teenagers moved into the Close when the Grant children disappeared and Tracy and Rod Corkhill were moving towards adulthood.

EastEnders too has paid particular attention to a range of adolescent characters. Although school and its difficulties has featured much less than in *Brookside*, *EastEnders* has from the beginning, through the central characters of Sharon, Michelle, Kelvin and Ian, presented its audience with a set of variations on how to handle the movement from child to adult. Michelle's experience of 'growing up fast' as a pregnant 16-year old was contrasted, for instance, with Sharon's attempt to shake off her feeling of being father's 'little princess'. The attitudes of Kelvin and Ian were similarly contrasted. Kelvin was academically bright and his decision to continue his education at university was paralleled by Ian's more tentative and less well-organised approach to establishing his own business when he left college. *EastEnders* has also attempted to incorporate the more casual leisure interests of young people through a long-running story line in which the core group of young people attempted to set up a band. The story of the band was of course another pretext for examining relationships between members of the group along the lines of any other soap narrative and it also had outside commercial interests (a record was released of a song regularly featured in the programme). Nevertheless, the inclusion of a story line based on what is deemed to be a major interest of young people also indicates the intention to incorporate adolescent concerns into the programme even if one suspects that the intended audience found it, as David Buckingham did, 'anonymous and completely anodyne'.[7] Like *Brookside*, *EastEnders* has had to replace the original young characters as they became more mature. Darren's son, Junior, came to live with his aunt, Carmel, and the stories in which he featured tried to link his mischievous behaviour to the desire to emulate his admired but absent father. Pat's marriage to Frank brought his two teenage children to replace Sharon at the pub and to provide a contrast with the school-age children in the Karim family. *EastEnders* has been less consistent than *Brookside* in giving its young characters major story lines but they have nevertheless maintained an active presence in the Square.

Brookside and *EastEnders* not only give space to their young characters but they also encourage the audience to endorse their point of view. They are not of course the only source of correct judgement but they are given that role with sufficient consistency to make them characters who have to be taken seriously. Thus, in *Brookside*, Rod and Tracy Corkhill argued with their parents that they should be told more about the financial crisis which was hitting the family and be allowed to offer support to their parents, emotionally, and in Rod's case, financially. The programme explored the parents' refusal to share their problems – Doreen's over-protectiveness, Billy's fear of being undermined as the head of the household – and invited sympathy for them, but the children's viewpoint that their parents were wrong in denying them knowledge was consistently endorsed. Even more clear was the weighting towards the younger characters in the story of Damon Grant and Debbie. The relationship between the two was opposed by their parents on the grounds that Debbie was too young but the programme itself treated the teenage romance with absolute seriousness; it was the parents who seemed to be behaving like ill-tempered children while Damon and Debbie recognised and worked through the difficulties with patience and some humour. As Damon pointed out when Debbie came to tea with the Grants, she may only be 16 but she is the 'most adult person here'. When the final bust-up with Debbie's father occurs and the Grants refuse to take her in, the pair decide to leave and Damon's final comments show how clearly the programme has presented his viewpoint: 'We tried to do it your way but it was a con,' he tells his parents. 'We have to sort it out for ourselves.' Damon's death was used to hammer home the point that the Grants were wrong not to take the relationship as seriously as the young couple themselves did.

EastEnders, too, has not merely allowed its young characters to express their own attitudes but has endorsed their views as a correct response. Sometimes this has been done somewhat obliquely as with Mark whose flight from the Fowler family was initially presented as thoughtless and heartless but is now seen as a legitimate if extreme response to the stifling nature of the Beale/Fowler nexus. More consistently, children have been seen as capable of observing and commenting accurately on their parents' relationships. Thus Kelvin kept a mordant eye on Tony and Hannah Carpenter's attempts to live together again and was capable of criticising both Tony's hasty rushes to judgement and Hannah's snobbery about the Square. Sharon was also used to comment on the fights between Den and Angie and her decision not to get involved in their arguments is seen to be sensible. In an ironic inversion of the normal soap dilemma (how do parents let their children go?), Sharon decides that she cannot reconstruct their relationship and tells Michelle: 'I've learnt a lesson. You're stuck with your parents . . . I've got to let them go now.' The examples of both Kelvin and Sharon illustrate that the authority given to teenagers in the programme is based on their experience of living with the problems of their parents. Caught between arguing adults, the adolescent has a curiously detached view which is offered to the audience as a relatively objective position.

The extension of the range of soap characters by *Brookside* and

EastEnders has had its effect on *Crossroads* and *Coronation Street*. While the treatment of the male characters has changed little in these more traditional programmes, the attempt to appeal to a young audience by representing teenage characters as a specific group within the community has been emulated in the older programmes. *Crossroads* made a nod in the direction by introducing Jason and Beverley Grice, both of whom were still at school and at odds with their parents. Little was made of Jason who, being in his early teens, hardly fitted into story lines which centred on the Motel. Beverley and her girlfriend, Sara, were given more central roles but the effect was to fit their characters into the Motel structure (Beverley took on a temporary job as a chambermaid, Sara used the sports centre) rather than to change and expand the range of stories to accommodate teenage characters.

This process has been even more marked in *Coronation Street* which has tried to establish a group of young characters who are part of the community but have a separate identity within it. Thus, Curly, Terry Duckworth, Kevin and Sally formed a core 'teenage' group which other characters, such as Andrea and Jenny, joined as appropriate. Story lines began to feature youth unemployment, further education, first love and teenage pregnancy. If *EastEnders* has had its less successful moments (with, for example, the band), *Coronation Street*'s foray onto a specifically teenage world has generally been disastrous with the characters only taking on resonance when, like Sally after marriage, they move into the adult world. The inadequate representation of a younger age group arises because the young characters, rather than being given their own interests and specific problems, are required to ape the adults. *Coronation Street*'s young characters are older than those in *Brookside* and *EastEnders* and even when Andrea and Jenny were both at school, no stories were set there and it featured little in their lives except to make exam results a source of anxiety. The younger characters meet in the pub just as the older ones do and are integrated into the life of the community by the mothering structure identified in chapter 5. Even the moments of teenage rebellion lack pungency and force. On the one hand, they are fanciful as, for example, Jenny's romance with a well-to-do Frenchman Patrice; on the other, they show young people following in the footsteps of the adults, literally in the case of Terry Duckworth who got into trouble for having a farcical affair with a married woman whom his father had already been bedding.

Coronation Street's failure to build up a credible group of young characters is shown most clearly in the programme's refusal to acknowledge them as a source of truth in the manner of *Brookside* and *EastEnders*. Its fundamental commitment is to its women characters who, as we saw in chapter 3, provide the audience with the means of understanding what is happening and the values by which to make judgements. While Jenny may be correct in her appeals to her father to be less strict about her boyfriends, it is Rita who provides the careful assessment of what is appropriate; while Terry Duckworth's laddish behaviour may have provided some entertaining escapades, he can never be given moral weight; even the idealistic Curly in the end relies on the advice of Emily Bishop. Thus the young characters inevitably remain perpheral to the programmes until, like Sally, they begin to take on a woman's responsibilities which bring with them the capacity to judge. An example of the contrast between this approach and that of *Brookside* can be seen in a comparison of the romance between Damon and Debbie described above and that between Jenny and Patrice. On the surface, both were stories of young love in which the parents opposed the relationship because the girl was deemed too young and still had her education to pursue. *Coronation Street*, however, proposed the adult viewpoint of the affair as the correct one. While Jenny was clearly sincere in her feelings, the relationship was presented as a foolish one which could not be sustained. Whereas Damon and Debbie in *Brookside* were sensible and down-to-earth, Patrice and Jenny's affair was couched in terms of high romance and ill-thought-through commitments expressed in extravagant terms. The break-up when it came was no surprise and merely confirmed what Rita and the other women in the programme had always predicted.

It would be unwise simply to assume that the presence of young characters, the development of story lines around them and an endorsement of their viewpoint will necessarily attract a young audiences. The *Brookside Companion* suggests a correlation between the two, claiming that the concentration on young characters ensures 'a higher-than-average appeal to the notoriously elusive teenage audience'.[8] *EastEnders* has been notoriously popular with relatively young children[9] to the extent that, as Julia Smith and Tony Holland point out,

> teachers found that they could use the show as a way of communicating with students . . . Enthusiasm for the programme as a teaching device reached such a pitch, that a teacher from the Inner London Education Authority was eventually seconded to the show for a six-month period, in order to prepare teachers' notes.[10]

David Buckingham's research into young viewers' responses suggests that the children he interviewed watched the programme not so

much for the younger characters but for the glimpse it gave them of
the forbidden adult world:

> These children's enthusiasm for *EastEnders*, was not primarily based
> on their identification with its younger characters – although this was
> at least partly the producers' intention in including them. On the
> contrary, much of their fascination – and particularly that of the
> younger children – arose from its inclusion of aspects of *adult* life from
> which they were normally 'protected.'[11]

For our purposes though, the success or otherwise of the introduction of younger characters into prime time soaps is less important
than its effect on the space given to women characters. As with the
development of male characters, the attention and time devoted to
the teenage characters and the importance attached to their viewpoints has had its effect on the weight given to women in these soaps.

Women for the male viewer?

If the introduction of male and teenage characters has tended to
undermine the dominance of women in the programmes, the representation of women themselves has in certain cases also changed.
These changes are most marked in *Dallas* and *Dynasty* and can be
seen as a part of an attempt to accommodate the male viewer by
representing women in a rather different way from that usually
found in soaps. In looking at *Dallas* and *Dynasty* in this context, we
once again need to recognise references from another genre, in this
case the film noir of the 1940s.

The major shift is from the open and knowledgeable women in
soaps to the glamorously ambiguous women more characteristic of
film noir. We saw in chapter 3 how important it is that women are
presented as the norm in soaps, that they are knowable and that the
audience is invited to understand the logic of their actions. I argued
there that soaps invite us to see things from the women's viewpoint
and that while the behaviour of the women might be ill-advised or
wrong, it is nevertheless understandable. In film noir however, the
audience is invited to share the viewpoint of the male protagonist,
the baffled but dogged investigator whose pursuit of the truth is
confused and delayed by the enigmatic femme fatale. These American films of the forties presented, as Janey Place argues, 'a remarkably potent image of woman'[12] which is a source for contemporary
films even now but it is an image based on duplicity and ambiguity.
The heroine misleads both the hero and the audience; she cannot be

trusted and while apparently frank and open, she manipulates the truth to suit her purposes. The audience is given no means of judging the stories she tells. As Annette Kuhn indicates, the narrative structure of film noir is marked by the hero's inability to understand the woman: 'it is very common for a woman character to be set up as an additional mystery demanding solution, a mystery independent of the crime enigma.'[13] Very often this investigative structure, while it resolves the crime enigma, fails to get to the truth of the woman since her character is presented as unknowable. Her very glamour is constructed and stylised and her sexuality is marked as threatening and in the end self-destructive. The audience shares the hero's lack of understanding since, as Christine Gledhill points out, 'not only is the hero frequently not sure whether the woman is honest or a deceiver, but the heroine's characterisation is itself fractured so that it is not evident to the audience whether she fills the stereotype or not.'[14]

Film noir, as feminist critics have argued, offered pleasures to women which were not necessarily deflated by the unhappy endings inflicted on them in the interests of reasserting patriarchal order. Instead the contradictions in characterisation and the excesses of visual style overwhelmed the restraints of narrative and, according to Janey Place, 'it stands as the only period in American film in which women are deadly but sexy, exciting and strong.'[15] I would share this view that there are pleasures offered to the women in the audience for film noir but would however want to place more emphasis on the construction of the audience in the position of an observer of the woman's action, with little more knowledge than that of the male hero who guides us through the plot and on the way in which the punishment of the femme fatale is presented as the inevitable consequence of her actions. In concentrating on the subversive pleasures offered to women in film noir, it is worth bearing in mind that the male spectator is well accommodated not merely by the objectification of the glamorous woman but by the destruction of the troublesome one. Although not always in control, the male protagonist is ultimately in charge of the narrative and able to destroy what he does not understand. Film noir offers to men also the pleasure of observing strong, sexually active women but allows them to do so within the relatively safe parameters of a narrative structure which reasserts its control.

Such pleasures for the male viewers are very different from those of traditional soaps where the position of identification is offered via women whose power lies not in ambiguity and duplicity but in control of the personal sphere. In their presentation of women, however, *Dallas* and *Dynasty* have adopted some of the characteristics of film noir heroines and changed the audience's relationship with these characters. There has, for instance, been an increasing emphasis on the way that the women in the programmes look. Even though *Dallas* and *Dynasty* from the beginning emphasised wealth and power, the glamorising of the central women characters over the years has been marked. In the early episodes of *Dallas*, Pam was an attractive girl-next-door, a country girl brought into the Ewing mansion. Over the years she has been regroomed into a stylised sex object. Similarly, in *Dynasty*, the original Fallon, played by Pamela Sue Martin, was not conventionally beautiful and played on a gamine quality allied with the self-confidence of the rich to get her men. Over the years and helped by a change in the actress, emphasis has shifted to a more stylised beauty, quite evidently created by hairdressers, fashion designers and Californian-style aerobics. The emphasis on this construction of female beauty is similar to that deliberate adoption of overt sexuality by film noir heroines and distances the audience which is invited to judge the result.

It is difficult to pin down the effect of the glamorisation process which does, after all, fit in with the US soaps' presentation of an extraordinary world rather than the everyday life of the British soaps. It would also be wrong to assert that women do not enjoy the deployment of glamour and we have already seen that the clothes, hairstyles and make-up are linked with the light entertainment values which are part of the aesthetic appeal of these programmes.[16] In the case of Pam and Fallon, the audience knows the history of their characters and can use it to get behind the shell of their facade. More significant perhaps, particularly for *Dallas*, is the way in which narrative constructions have combined with objectification through glamour to give the lesser female characters strong links with their film noir counterparts.

The most extreme example of this female type was Angelica in *Dallas*. Here was a dark, glamorous and mysterious woman appearing from nowhere to lure JR with talk of huge business deals and veiled promises of sexuality. Her foreignness gave an edge to her mystery and her close relationship with her blonde co-conspirator, whom she set up to bewitch Jack Ewing, hinted at an intimacy which the audience was not invited to share. The two women wove a web of conspiracy around JR and Jack and while the audience was allowed access to some of their plans no clear insight into motivation or feeling was given. Little was revealed about Angelica's own personal life and no sympathy was granted her; she refused to allow emotional relationships to interfere in her plans. Significantly, the adventures in which she engaged JR took him to exotic locations and involved him in the chases and gunfights more characteristic of a thriller than a soap. Although it was not pre-planned, it was appropriate that Angelica turned out to be an element in a dream since she could never have been accommodated into the less exotic, more domestic dramas of Southfork.

If Angelica was an extreme example, other women in *Dallas* have been presented in a similar way. These women tend not to be the main stable characters – Sue Ellen, Pam, Donna, Callie – but the characters who drift in and out of the plots and whose primary function is indeed to cause narrative trouble. Unlike the main women characters with whom the audience is invited to share a number of conflicting emotions, these women are given one driving motivation – generally a passion for JR – which serves as an explanation for a series of machinations and treacheries. Thus Holly, whom JR has used in one of his oil deals, goes whole-heartedly for revenge, drawing him into her bed and setting the scene carefully so that Sue Ellen will find them together. Although the audience is invited to sympathise with Holly when she is initially duped, the intensity with which she constructs and uses her sexuality in revenge, leaving lipstick traces on JR's shirt collar, for example, makes her a threatening figure. There is pleasure in the way in which she manipulates JR but it is undermined by the way in which she turns the attack on to Sue Ellen.

This refusal to acknowledge a common bond between women is a key characteristic of the film noir women in *Dallas*. In the cases of Kristen Shepherd and Katherine Wentworth, it is made more intense by the fact that the women they seek to overturn are their own sisters. Kristen and Katherine are very similar characters. Their function is to cause trouble in their sisters' marriages and, like Holly, they will use their sexuality quite deliberately to get what they want. They are closed characters, driven by one burning necessity and cut off from the audiences' sympathy by their capacity to manipulate. Like the heroines of film noir, they are evasive and unpredictable; Katherine, for instance, is charming and supportive to Pam during the break up of her marriage while at the same time making plans to get at Bobby. They have the 'self-absorbed narcissim'[17] which Place ascribes to the 'dark lady' of film noir, so different from the capacity to share the feelings of other women which characterises the soap heroine. Aggressiveness is combined with sexuality in a way which constructs them as violent and threatening. The image of Katherine, hovering over Pam's hospital bed with a hypodermic needle, is made the more powerful by her appearance, which is strongly reminiscent of film noir heroines; her wavy, black hair and dark red lipstick provide a vivid contrast with the comparative fairness of her sister, Pam. The programme's key moments of violence – the shooting of JR and Bobby's 'death' – are the responsibility of Kristen and Katherine respectively. It is significant also that both women themselves meet violent deaths – Kristen drowned in the swimming pool, Katherine dying in the car in which she killed Bobby, although in the latter case Bobby's reprieve allowed Katherine also to live again.

The representation and narrative deployment of women characters like Holly, Katherine and Kristen offer different pleasures from those of identification with the more open and emotionally engaging characters such as Miss Ellie or Pam. They come from a different tradition which ascribes women's strength to the conscious use of sexual aggression, their power to ambiguity and deviousness. Far from sharing a common viewpoint with other women in the programme, these characters are specifically represented as rejecting any emotion other than overriding sexual passion and, both metaphorically and literally, will sacrifice their sisters for a man. The audience is invited to observe them rather than sympathise with them and in presenting such women so strongly in *Dallas*, the programme can be deemed to have shifted at least partly away from an identification with women into an objectification which allows rather more room than the traditional soap for the exercising of male fantasies.

Representing women

The glamorisation of the women characters and the linking of female sexuality and aggression in such a highly charged way was not a course open to the more realist British soaps in their search for a wider audience. But in the British soaps too there has been a marked change in the way that women are represented and positioned in the soap narratives. To demonstrate this and to suggest ways in which the introduction of new issues and characters has been at the cost of traditional pleasures offered to women, this chapter closes with two case studies, the first of the position of women in one of the newer British soaps, *Brookside*, and the second on the demise of one of the oldest, *Crossroads*. In the first, women remain at the heart of the programme but all too often seem to be trapped in the situations it has created for them; in the second, women seemed to be gradually eased out until the programme was no longer theirs.

Brookside is normally deemed the most progressive of the British soaps, valued for the way in which it deals with social issues and recognises class as a major factor in the fabric of British life. It is somewhat ironic then to note that it is *Brookside* which has most consistently positioned women in the home and represented them through their relationships with their families. While the programme has pursued its male characters outside into the public world, the women (with the notable exception of the career woman, Heather) have been defined by their roles as wife and mother. When *Brookside* started, its main female characters were all contained within familial relationships; the single woman, featured so strongly in *Coronation Street*, went unrepresented here and the main focus for women in the programmes was on the problems which faced the family unit. In the main, the women took traditional roles, taking responsibility for domestic arrangements and child care. It was Annabelle Collins, not her husband, who went to see Gordon's headmaster over difficulties at school; Sheila Grant who met the Educational Welfare Officer about Damon and consulted both the priest and the doctor when she was worried about Karen. When new characters were introduced, they followed a similar pattern; women like Marie Jackson, Doreen Corkhill and Chrissie Rogers see their main function as defending and promoting their families. These women want to see their husbands with a secure job, their children getting on well and their homes comfortable. Their own work outside the home, if they have a job, provides a necessary extra income, but is rarely referred to as a source of either pleasure or discontent. As with Doreen Corkhill, for example, women's work outside the family becomes an issue, not through the woman's attitude to it, but when the husband objects and it is converted into an element in family relationships. The exception to this has been Heather Haversham; we looked in chapter 6 at how her career was used as a source of problems. Here we need to note how reluctant *Brookside* was to present her as a single woman and outside a family. Once she was divorced, the story lines kept her well supplied with boyfriends, scarcely finishing, for instance, with her fiancé, Tom, before literally bumping in to her next husband, Nick. Heather may have been independent at work but the programme seemed unable to permit her to be independent in her emotional relationships.

Fans of the programme and its makers would argue that this emphasis on women's responsibilities and relationships within the family is part of *Brookside*'s realism and that to represent women as more independent of family ties would be a move towards propaganda and away from the programme's commitment to reflecting women's true position. It could also be argued that within each family the women do assert their right to their own views and argue for recognition of their contribution to the family. This is clearly true of Sheila Grant who has consistently both drawn attention to the family's undervaluing of her work within the home and tried to develop her own self-confidence by returning to education through evening classes and later the Open University. Doreen Corkhill has similarly stood up for herself when her family took her for granted and has asserted her own position against that of her husband, Billy. The role of women in the family is plainly an issue for *Brookside* and has, as when Doreen finally left Billy or Bobby walked out on Sheila, given rise to some of its most dramatic moments.

Brookside has thus continued the tradition of strong women in soaps but has tended to restrict their scope to the confines of the home. This tendency is particularly marked because *Brookside* has abandoned soaps' equally strong tradition of friendship and support between women. The programme's emphasis on class difference has meant that women rarely communicate across family boundaries. Doreen Corkhill went through the trauma of debts and marital break-up with scarcely an acknowledgement that she might look to Sheila Grant for some support or help. Sheila, herself, did have a woman close friend in Theresa but, while the audience was told about this relationship, Theresa's appearances were sporadic and had more to do with story lines centring on her husband, Matty, than her role as Sheila's oldest friend. Chris Rogers, in seeking to resolve her daughter's drinking problem, turned for support to a male GP, while Heather, fighting to save her marriage when she discovered Nick's heroin addiction, turned to an old boyfriend, Barry Grant, rather than to one of the women characters. Exchanges between women are normally confined to slightly strained neighbourly re-marks across the Close and can sometimes degenerate into outright hostility, exemplified, for instance, by Sheila's public slanging match with Doreen's mother, Julia, or Annabelle's condescension to Sheila and Doreen. The easy intimacy of long-term female friendship, characteristic of *Coronation Street*'s Mavis and Rita, for instance, or *Crossroads*' Jill and Diane, is rendered impossible in *Brookside* by the prior importance given to class relationships.

When the women do talk it is within families as mother to daughter. The representation of relationships between mother and daughter has been one of the programme's great strengths, demons-trated most movingly in the exchanges between Karen and Sheila Grant and Doreen and Tracy Corkhill. Mother and daughter discuss problems seriously, with that practical attention to emotional detail which is the mark of women in soaps. There is in these exchanges a reflectiveness and a sense of mutual responsibility which is missing from the more action-based stories. Karen and Tracy both have their own views and so the relationship is not merely with one of support from mother to daughter. Nor are the inevitable clashes underestimated and there are arguments and rifts based on generational differences. Nevertheless, there is a consistent sense of underlying and active concern for each other which is missing from the relationships between other women in the programme. Even here, though, the mother's role in the relationship is often presented as that of a mediator within the family, explaining her husband's position to her daughter. When Billy Corkhill exploded with temper against Tracy's boyfriends or her attitude towards him, it was Doreen's role to explain to Tracy that it was his emotional stress rather than her behaviour that caused such an outburst. When Karen wanted to leave home to go to college in London, it was Sheila who encouraged her to face Bobby with the news. Thus, even in the strongest female relationships in the programme, the women are still firmly placed in the home (a situation underlined by the fact that these conversations often take place slightly furtively in the daughter's bedroom) and are locked into maintaining and sustaining familial relationships.

Brookside's problems with how to present women can be seen most clearly in the character of Sheila Grant. Here, above all, the contradictions surface in a representation which endorses Sheila's position but consistently undermines her capacity to act and presents her as endlessly suffering. We saw in chapter 4 how Sheila fits into the role of the strong mother who is at the heart of British soaps. She is presented as a strong and sustaining character played with great power and resource by Sue Johnston. Sheila's role has been given a feminist slant and it is clear that she is not content with being defined through the domestic role. She refused to accept Bobby's definition of herself – 'You're my wife, you're Clare and Damon's mother' – insisting that she needed to be recognised as a person in her own right. As the programme developed, this theme was underlined by the change in characterisation of her husband, Bobby. At the start of the serial, Bobby was a character of considerable moral weight whose own difficulties in coming to terms with the move to the Close and a change in his job were given sympathetic attention. By 1987, however, the more chauvinistic elements in Bobby's character were being brought out and his hostility to Sheila's desire to learn was seen to be based on a fear that she was moving away from her role as a wife and mother. The audience's rejection of this position was ensured by his degeneration into boorish drunkenness, his violence towards his son, Barry, and his unkind rejection of Debbie after Damon's death.

We have then a clear statement of a woman's viewpoint, a desire on Sheila's part to develop as an individual and not be defined by familial relationships and the audience's sympathy engaged with her even to the extent of changing a well-respected and liked male character. Why then does the presentation of Sheila seem to be so problematic? It is because Sheila, despite her strength, is continually a victim, a woman who knows that she wants more but is continually denied it. While the intention may be to present her positively, the effect of *Brookside*'s emphasis on both realism and class is to isolate her in the family without even the support of other women which is the bedrock of more traditonal soaps. Sheila *is* defined as a wife and mother (when Bobby leaves her, she is quickly installed in the Corkhill household, once again mediating between father and children) and her protestations have the effect of reinforcing our sense of her inability to change anything.

This isolation and vulnerability become particularly marked in stories where Sheila's concerns are tied in with the more action-based, crime genre narratives, such as Damon's death and the rape story. The episodes dealing with Sheila's rape were a source of considerable controversy. No one could argue with the conviction of Sue Johnston's performance nor that the programme dealt with the subject lightly. Nevertheless, the way in which the story was set up served to emphasise her isolation and guilt as a victim and while it clearly demanded that the viewer be involved in her distress, the logic of the narrative was that she had been punished. In the first place, she agrees to meet her evening class tutor, Alan, in the pub, arguing with Bobby that it was only to discuss her educational options. It emerges in the pub that Bobby was in fact correct in his suspicions; Alan invites Sheila away for a weekend and his persistence in insisting that her interest in education betokened an interest in him upsets her considerably. In the middle of this, Matty enters the pub and publicly berates her as a hypocrite for interfering with his love affair while she is herself apparently carrying on with the tutor. Fleeing the pub, Sheila is pursued into a taxi by Matty who physically attacks her while continuing his verbal abuse. Sheila escapes from the taxi and it is immediately after this that she is dragged into the undergrowth and raped by an attacker whose identity is deliberately concealed from the audience.

This narrative treatment of an admittedly difficult subject has two important consequences. Firstly, the enigma of the narrative shifts away from Sheila and into a whodunit mode more suitable for a thriller or detective story. Not only are Alan and Matty set up as suspects for the audience; Pat, too, is in the area, drinking heavily

after a violent row with his girlfriend, Sandra; it emerges also that
the wife-battering husband of a woman whom Sheila has helped is
also on the rampage. It is easy to mock soap opera plots by
condensing them and that is not my intention here but the plethora
of suspects and the variety of motives for men who had cause,
however unjustly, to be angry with Sheila were clearly designed to
invite the audience to speculate on the identity of the rapist in a way
that seemed ghoulish and contrived. Subsequent episodes were split
between Sheila's distress and Pat's arrest, interrogation by the police
and eventual release; for a while, the audience's attention was
shifted to the question of whether Pat would be falsely charged and
the development of his story, with its police series structure of
accusation, questioning and resolution, took precedence over
Sheila's story.

The second consequence of this handling of the rape story was the
way in which Sheila was humiliated, isolated and victimised before
the rape occurred. The rape itself was the culmination of a series of
attacks on her by Alan and Matty which had undermined her faith in
her tutor, her relationship with Matty and hence with her best
friend, Theresa, who was Matty's wife, and her confidence in her
own emotional judgements. In the seconds before the attacker
appeared, the camera concentrated on her anguished and tearful
face. It is as if because the physical act of rape could not be
represented it was felt necessary to provide a visual correlation for it
in Sheila's humiliation. I am not arguing that *Brookside* should not
take on such issues as violence against women but the way it was
done was highly problematic. Ironically, by both emphasising the
question of who had done it and presenting such a powerful image of
grief and humiliation, *Brookside* ran the risk of subsuming the rape
into a detective story and undermining its most powerful female
character. We are a long way here from Terry Lovell's notion of
soap opera as 'a context in which women can ambiguously express
both good-humoured acceptance of their oppression *and* recognition
of that oppression, and some equally good-humoured protest against
it'.[18]

The story of Sheila's rape was exceptional but by no means
untypical of the way in which crisis after crisis is still piled onto her.
While the intention might be to explore the full range of her
subordination, the effect is to make viewers feel she is being endlessly battered. Sheila has gone through postnatal depression, opposition from her husband over her educational ambitions, the death of
her best friend, Theresa, continued worries over her son Barry's
flirtation with the criminal world, the death of her younger son,

Damon, the break-up of her marriage and a consequent falling out with her daughter, Karen. As with the rape sequence, the problem is not so much with these story lines which, it could be argued, are fairly typical of soaps, but the way in which they are handled. Through all of this, she is presented as isolated, suffering courageously, drawing on her own inner reserves rather than the support of the community. Her only other source of support is the Catholic Church which serves once again to emphasise her isolation from others in the Close.

This mode of presentation which foregrounds isolation and suffering is not unique to Sheila, although it finds its strongest expression with her. It was used during Doreen's battles with her husband Billy over finances and his slide into crime; it was used for Heather as she discovered that Nick was a heroin addict. In each case, the woman is trapped in the home, confused about what is going on, anguished over her own role in it and unable to discuss it with the other women from whom she is separated by class difference. The traditional soap skills of patient analysis of emotional problems, of finding support among other women who have had a similar experience is apparently useless in the face of the unsupportable situation which is being played out in the confined and isolated space of the family living room. In each case, the mothering structure we explored earlier has been pushed so far that the woman, in upholding the family, becomes its endlessly suffering victim. While one may have sympathy with the analysis, the effect has been to undermine the capacity for self-assertion and control of emotional relationships by women which offered a source of pleasure in more traditonal soap presentations.

If *Brookside* offers the clearest example of the way in which the changes in British soaps in the 1980s have affected the role women play in them, then the demise of *Crossroads* is the saddest failure of nerve in this period of change. Of all the soaps studied in this book, *Crossroads* was the programme most consistently associated with women viewers and most consistently denigrated. As we saw in chapter 2, *Crossroads'* low budget and tight production schedule made it a byword for poorly made television drama while its storylines were criticised for being both slow paced and melodramatic.[19] The programme was consistently scheduled in the late afternoon or early evening and its main audience was understood to be women engaged in the after-school, after-work tasks of preparing, eating and clearing up after tea. Its scheduling indicated its role as a bridge between afternoon viewing and the directly prime time slots occupied by the other soaps discussed in this book.

Crossroads, with its reputation established as the butt of any stand-up comic and its specific appeal to the middle-aged or elderly female audience described by Hobson, was peculiarly vulnerable in the situation brought about by the 'new' soaps of the eighties. At a time when new audiences were being sought, new issues being raised and different directions were being explored by the glamorous US prime time soaps on the one hand and the more down-to-earth British programmes on the other, *Crossroads* was in danger of being stranded, or so it seemed to its production company, Central, which had always been somewhat embarrassed by the serial's success in reaching its audience. *Crossroads* was forced into change but, unlike *Coronation Street* which has maintained a consistent image during its period of adjustment, *Crossroads* was not allowed to build on its strengths. Instead, the programme went through a series of innovations which almost seemed to form a paradigm of the options available to soaps. The problem for *Crossroads* was that, in pursuing the chimera of a new younger audience, the programme switched from one strategy to another in a way that threatened to destroy the pleasures it offered its existing viewers. The first stage of this process, the departure of Meg and the viewers' response to it, has been well-documented by Dorothy Hobson. She argues that the viewers felt betrayed that 'their' programme had been cavalierly altered by the removal of a character with whom many had identified and whose role as the caring but powerful matriarch had been a source of much pleasure. The departure of Meg certainly created a vacuum in *Crossroads* which, of all the British soaps, had relied most consistently on a central woman character for its moral equilibrium and its narrative drive. Subsequent events in *Crossroads* since 1981 proved that the stability which Meg represented was central to the programme and the apparent inability or unwillingness to find an equivalent caused the programme's downfall.

With Meg's departure, control of the Motel (and of the programme's narrative organisation) was passed not to one individual but to a group of board members who vied for her position. In some sense, this construction continually reminded the viewer of the loss of Meg since it served to demonstrate the inability of any one of the group to exercise her power. The dilemmas and difficulties which the character of Meg had held within her were now transformed into a series of plots which centred on the inability of board members to reach agreement. While this could be seen as an attempt to emulate the boardroom wheeling and dealing of the US soaps, the women characters still held a strong position in the programme, a position which relied not on Alexis-style manoeuvring but on alliances between them. Thus, while David Hunter was managing director and hence able to make final decisions on Motel matters, he could be defeated when his wife, Barbara, and Meg's daughter, Jill, came together. Such defeats were not a matter of David being outvoted but of him being convinced by the commonsense and humanity which were, in the traditional manner of soaps, connected with the women's viewpoint. When the two women disagreed, the outcome was normally fractious bickering among the board members which demonstrated clearly the fundamental importance of female unity. Other women characters, while not operating at boardroom level, continued to demonstrate the programme's consistent espousal of the woman's viewpoint, seen most clearly in Kath and Glenda Brownlow's fond patronising of the men in their family and Sharon's battle for control of the motel's garage.

More changes were on the way, however, and in 1985 the production company made a clearly articulated decision to update *Crossroads* by moving it towards the more glamorous end of the soap spectrum. Nicola Freeman was introduced, brought in narratively by a business coup to manage the Motel, and was presented as attractive and elegantly dressed, the possessor of a mysterious past and a ruthless determination to run the Motel as she saw fit. The popular press picked up on the programme's PR material and announced the arrival of 'the ravishing redhead [who] will give the series about a mythical Midlands motel a sensational new *Dynasty*-style look . . . [and will] have the men swooning at her sexuality'.[20] Familiar characters like the Hunters were despatched and *Crossroads* was thus set to change again. Nicola' reign, however, was an interesting example of the way in which a soap's own history and long-standing structures transform the best (or worst) of intentions. As producer Suzi Hush commented of *Coronation Street* in 1974, '[It] has a fictional reality which has been established over 14 years . . . It's got a reality of its own and you can't pre-empt it.'[21] In the case of Nicola and *Crossroads*, although the new boss seemed to represent change, the character in fact fitted and was co-opted into the previously established tradition of strong matriarchial control. The details were different – Nicola wore more glamorous clothes than Meg, her family was complicated by stepchildren and in a *Dallas*-style twisting of the plot, by the discovery of a lost and found daughter. In the beginning, also, Nicola seemed to be concerned about her own power and not about the Motel and its staff. But as the stories developed and as the audience could begin to identify with Nicola's feelings, it became clear that she was moving in Meg's footsteps: outwardly composed, she was susceptible to self-doubt and reflection; strong and capable of making decisions, she looked for but found little sypport from the men in her life; she cared about the staff but was also determined that individual problems and rivalries would not jeopardise the institution as a whole. Under the trappings of the glamorisation process, *Crossroads* was again giving precedence to a woman's viewpoint and offering the pleasures of identification with a woman in charge.

As if piqued by the programme's capacity to reassert itself, the production company's next set of changes were so fundamental that they offered the traditional audience no means of getting round them. Moving swiftly away from the *Dallas/Dynasty* model, *Crossroads* was pointed firmly in the direction of the more regionally based British soaps. The Motel, which had formerly existed as if on its own island, was now placed, through a new set of credits, in a small English village and scenes shifted to the village pub and the local shop, moving attention away from the Motel itself. Birmingham, previously only a venue for somewhat vague business visits, was now manifest in characters like the Grices and Mrs Tardybegg who were marked as indelibly 'Brummie' as the Beale Family were East Enders. In the manner of *Brookside* and *EastEnders*, younger characters were introduced and stories of teenage tiffs and romance began to feature in the narrative. The emphasis on comedy was increased with the introduction of stereotypically comic characters like Mrs Tardybegg and the chef, while well-established characters with comic dimensions, like Benny, drifted out of the programme.

But the most significant and perhaps in the end fatal development was the shift away from the women's viewpoint as the bedrock which sustained the programme. This was marked most clearly with the ousting of Nicola by the loud, crudely jovial 'Bomber' Lancaster who took over the running of the motel. For the first time, the programme's key position in terms of its narrative organisation around control over the Motel was held indisputably by a man. The departure of Nicola was followed by that of other key women characters who had been a reliable source of emotional and moral values – Kath Brownlow was moved away while Diane, a long-standing cast member and a consistent source of the wry good humour characteristic of women in soaps, was killed off. Jill's position became much more isolated; she was both more subordinate to Bomber in motel matters and lacking in female friends with whom to share her difficulties. New women brought into the programme failed to fill the gap. Tara's specifically feminist principles allowed her to be labelled too quickly while Debbie's role as Bomber's daughter made her vulnerable to the accusation of being an outsider.

It is possible that *Crossroads* could have ridden out these difficulties and the new women characters could have developed to fill the gap left by Nicola, Diane and the rest, had not the programmes' centre of gravity been shifted so firmly towards the men. Bomber's presence was reinforced by a host of new male characters: Charlie as manager, Paul and the chef in the kitchen, John Maddingham as the pub landlord, Ray Grice as the father of the family living in the village shop. Nor were these men the weak matinee idol figures described by Jane Root. Bomber, the chef and Ray Grice were all in varying degrees loud, crude, bullying and loutish, offering no pleasure to female viewers in their behaviour and appearance. Although these characters' attitudes were not necessarily presented as sympathetic, the narrative shifted over to their viewpoint. Thus more attention was paid to Ray Grice than to his wife, Margaret, and his casually bullying attitude toward her was largely accepted by her as the norm. Bomber's role as the head of the family as well as the Motel was acceded to by his daughters who, though sometimes critical of him, ensured that he got his own way. Specific story lines give access on occasions only to the male viewpoint. One extreme but not untypical example was provided by the story of the rivalry between the chef and Paul, his assistant, over Paloma. The exotic Paloma, who came from Poland, was literally allowed no voice in this affair, a situation conveniently rationalised by her inability to speak English. Instead the story focused on Paul's hatred and jealousy of the chef who tauntingly claimed to have had an affair with Paloma and who, while commenting favourably on her body, mockingly disparaged her mind. In one scene the chef agreed to hand over his 'rights' to Paloma in exchange for Paul's lemon chicken recipe:

Chef: You give me an ingredient for each part . . . her perfectly formed soft little ears . . .
Paul (*breathing heavily*): Two cloves of garlic, crushed.

The significance of this exchange is not in its banal humour or its lack of taste. It lies in the way the values of the programme have been reversed. No longer are women in the audience offered women's voices which express something of their own experiences or concerns; no longer are we given an image of women in control; no longer is there a sense of female friendship, of being 'down among the women.' Instead we are given access to male conversation based on crudely sexist assumptions on which women can make little impact. The nadir of *Crossroads* as women's fiction had well and truly been reached; the women's space had been taken over and the replacement of *Crossroads* by a police serial, *The Bill*, in the spring of 1988 seemed an inevitable consequence of the cavalier treatment of a female audience.

Conclusion

This book has been written out of a long-term interest in exploring the possibilities and pleasures of watching prime time soap operas. As a theoretical project, it began for me in the mid-seventies when a women and film group established through the British Film Institute turned its attention to television and to *Coronation Street* in particular. During the intervening period, much has changed. At that time, it was a struggle to get work on popular television drama treated sympathetically; now, in cultural studies circles at least, the reverse is the case. The work of 'rescuing' the objects of mass culture has continued apace and has even aroused fears that 'critics today . . . immersed in their culture, half in love with their subject . . . sometimes seem unable to achieve the proper critical distance from it.'[1] In addition, the prime time soaps themselves have been in a state of flux in the eighties, undergoing a period of feverish activity which has made change rather than stability a byword for these programmes. The one element which has remained stable in Britain, though not the United States, has been the consistently high audience figures. At the end of 1989, *Coronation Street*, the longest running soap on British television and a programme which seemed to undergo a crisis of confidence in the mid-eighties, under pressure from *EastEnders* and the more glamorous US versions, had pulled through to such an extent that it was getting audiences of over 20 million an episode.

The focus of this book has been on the pleasures available to women viewers of prime time soap operas and the way in which these pleasures have been affected by the period of change which soaps have experienced in the last decade. This book outlines the way in which these pleasures are based on the validation of women's skill in the personal sphere and a reworking of those values so that they operate, albeit sporadically, in the public sphere. These soaps offer a space for women in the TV schedules which not only acknowledges their existence but demonstrates their skills and supports their point of view. At one level, soaps do not treat women homogeneously; they present different aspects of female experience in a way which allows the woman viewer to identify with the emotional dilemmas of female characters who are rarely all good or all bad but who struggle with the demands of their families and communities and with their own high expectations of the value of personal relationships. On the other hand, prime time soaps, like their daytime counterparts, do present a version of a universal 'female condition' which cuts across age, race and class and allows women to recognise each other across the barriers. It is this essentialism which is both a source of pleasure and a problem in soaps. It allows for reassurance, support, recognition of common problems to be experienced by the woman viewer and provides a challenge to an ideology, expressed on television as elsewhere, which accords women's work in the personal sphere lavish praise but no value. It is also clear, however, that soap's pleasures are based on highly conventional notions of women's skills, their role in the family or community and the notion that they should look for fulfilment, albeit often unsuccessfully, in the personal sphere.

This book has also been concerned to explore the way in which this classical soap position has been subject to change in the eighties, both in terms of the issues which are now being taken up and the way in which they are presented. Prime time soaps have quite consciously picked up on 'new' issues and centred their stories on women at work, for instance, and on the new-found assertiveness which was deemed to characterise women in the eighties. Such stories set women characters against the grain of more traditional soap concerns and fitted uneasily into the rhythms of the narrative. In addition, issues which could not be labelled as specifically of concern to women such as class, race and age began to provide an impetus for narrative action and programmes as different as *Brookside* and *Dynasty*, at opposite ends of the soap spectrum in terms of aesthetic values, shared a common concern to use class and sexual orientation as the mainspring for key characters and story lines. If I have been critical of the way in which these 'new' issues have been handled, it is because I believe that soap operas have the potential to accommodate change, to make it interesting, acceptable or even desirable, which they have not always used bravely or well. Issues around class, sexuality and race threaten the cosier constructions of the soap community and have therefore been problematic. In addition, the move away from the concentrated examination of the personal sphere has been attempted through the adoption of more conventionally male story lines and generic codes. The breaching of the women's space which soaps provided has let in relatively little fresh air to recompense for the loss of the pleasures traditionally offered to women in the prime time soaps.

In referring to these pleasures, I have been careful to suggest that they are *offered* to women and that individual viewers may reject the possibilities which others take up and enjoy. In marking a change in the experience of writing about *Coronation Street* in the mid-seventies and in writing about soap opera now, I am conscious of my own ambiguities about the project. What then was a desire to re-evaluate a cultural form which was denigrated, at least in part, because it was associated with women, now runs the risk of celebrating an illusion – the assertion of a common sensibility between women and a set of values sustaining us simply because we are women. In this context even to write 'we' rather than 'they' becomes problematic in its assumptions and smacks of a community of interest which needs to be constructed rather than asserted. As Lynne Segal puts it 'there has always been a danger that in revaluing our notions of the female and appealing to the experiences of women, we are reinforcing the ideas of sexual polarity which feminism originally aimed to challenge.'[2] It is tempting to read off the essentialism which lurks in the programmes I have been discussing onto the female audience which is assumed 'naturally' to share the values of the personal which soaps endorse. In this context, it is not merely a question of arguing for understanding womanhood as a construction but stressing the importance of understanding that it is a construction which is inhabited differently in ways that are to do with race, class, age and experience as well as gender. The female viewer may welcome the valuing of her competencies and experiences which soaps offer but she may feel uneasy at what she perceives to be her own inadequacies in the personal sphere; she may reject the programmes as too restrictive and limiting or she may relish their more disruptive elements when the traces are broken and women like Sue Ellen, Alexis or Angie refuse to take up their domestic and familial responsibilities. The guilt which women feel about 'their' programmes may be as much to do with their own ambiguity towards the terrain which soaps map out as fear of male mockery.

The space offered women by soaps is thus a contradictory one. It allows 'women's issues' to be worked through and valued but endorses a female viewpoint only because it is so firmly based on the domestic and the personal; it allows its audience actively to enjoy the trials of the patriarch but reasserts the importance of familial relationships as a model for other kinds of love. It is not surprising then that the space offered by soaps is often perceived as a ghetto in which poor production values and bad acting give visible proof of the low esteem in which women's programmes are held. This question, 'space or ghetto?', has run through many debates in the women's movement and is central to the notion of revaluing those things which have traditionally been a source of enjoyment for women. Do we accept male judgements on the Mills and Boon romances which so many women enjoy reading, for instance, or do we resist being fobbed off with what is considered second best, formulaic writing? Are soap operas a space in which women viewers can relax and enjoy their superiority or are they a pen into which women are corralled even if they know they want something better? Such questions are not confined to the cultural arena. In debates on employment, for instance, women have been asking whether women's work is undervalued simply because it is done by women or because it is tedious, boring, hard? Soaps, perhaps more than any other fictional form available to women, stress the relationship between text and reader; their constructions are dependent on the audience to fulfil their possibilities. In the end, then, the programmes cannot answer the questions posed because they are potentially both a space and a ghetto. Soaps' capacity both to engage and distance the viewer, to involve us in a story and allow us to stand back and make judgements on its implications, means that the pleasure and use got from them depends on the viewer. The position of women is endorsed in the programmes but the space also allows for it to be dissected, exposed, celebrated, disrupted and escaped from in a neverending set of narrative puzzles. In these possibilities lie soaps' strengths. It will be up to the reader to judge whether they survive into the nineties.

Notes

Introduction

1 Jane Root, *Open the Box* (Comedia, London, 1986), p. 68.
2 David Morley, *Family Television: Cultural Power and Domestic Leisure* (Comedia, London, 1986), pp. 148–50.
3 Thomas Skill, 'Television's Families: Real by Day, Ideal by Night', in Mary Cassata and Thomas Skill (eds), *Life on Daytime Television: Tuning-in American Serial Drama* (Ablex, Norwood NJ, 1983), p. 140.
4 George Comstock, 'A Social Scientist's View of Daytime Television', in Cassata and Skill, *Life on Daytime Television*, p. xxiii.
5 Horace Newcomb, 'A Humanist's View of Daytime Serial Drama', in Cassata and Skill, *Life on Daytime Television*, pp. xxxiii–iv.
6 Robert C. Allen, *Speaking of Soap Operas* (University of North Carolina Press, Chapel Hill NC, 1985), p. 3.
7 Stuart Hall quoted in Alessandro Silj, *East of Dallas The European Challenge to American Television* (British Film Institute, London, 1988), p. 25.

Chapter 1   Soap Stories

1 Richard Paterson provides an example of this process in his essay 'The Production Context of *Coronation Street*', in Richard Dyer (ed.), *Coronation Street* (British Film Institute, London, 1981).
2 Robert C. Allen, *Speaking of Soap Operas* (University of North Carolina Press, Chapel Hill NC, 1985), p. 66.
3 Dorothy Hobson, *Crossroads: The Drama of a Soap Opera* (Methuen, London, 1982). Chapter 7 provides an analysis of the anger felt by women viewers at the departure of Meg.
4 In this context, Ien Ang gives an interesting account of viewers' divided responses to Sue Ellen and Pam in *Watching Dallas* (Methuen, London, 1985), p. 124.

5   Marion Jordan, 'Character Types and the Individual', in Dyer, *Corona-tion Street*.
6   For a summary of the strategies of such film-making see Pam Cook (ed.), *The Cinema Book* (British Film Institute, London, 1985), p. 220. For a concise account of the way in which the issue developed in theoretical writing on cinema see John Hill, *Sex, Class and Realism: British Cinema 1956–1963* (British Film Institute, London, 1986), pp. 57–61.
7   Jane Feuer, 'Melodrama, Serial Form and Television Today', *Screen*, vol. 25, no. 1 (Jan/Feb 1984), p. 15. Feuer picks up the argument again in comparing soap operas with situation comedies in 'Narrative form in American network television', in Colin McCabe (ed.), *High Theory/ Low Culture* (Manchester University Press, Manchester, 1986).
8   Tania Modleski, *Loving with a Vengeance* (Methuen, New York, 1982), p. 87.
9   This article which appeared in *Woman's Own* (31 January 1987) was chosen from the many that appear every week, mainly, but by no means exclusively, in women's magazines.
10 Christine Geraghty, 'The Continuous serial – a Definition', in Dyer, *Coronation Street*, p. 25.
11 Allen, *Speaking of Soap Operas*, p. 91.
12 John Ellis, *Visible Fictions* (Routledge & Kegan Paul, London, 1982), p. 162.
13 ibid., p. 166.
14 Modleski, *Loving with a Vengeance*, p. 92.
15 ibid., p. 93.

Chapter 2   The Aesthetic Experience

1   Dorothy Hobson, *Crossroads: The Drama of a Soap Opera* (Methuen, London, 1982), p. 83.
2   ibid., p. 158.
3   Richard Dyer, *Light Entertainment* (British Film Institute, London, 1973), p. 7.
4   ibid., p. 23.
5   ibid., p. 24.
6   Thomas Elsaesser, 'Tales of Sound and Fury', in Christine Gledhill (ed.), *Home is Where the Heart is* (British Film Intitute, London, 1987), p. 52.
7   Geoffrey Nowell-Smith, 'Minnelli and Melodrama', in Gledhill, *Home is Where the Heart is*, pp. 73–4.
8   Christine Gledhill, 'The Melodramatic Field: An Investigation', in Gledhill, *Home is Where the Heart is*, p. 11.
9   Jane Feuer, 'Melodrama, Serial Form and Television Today', *Screen*, vol. 25, no. 1 (Jan/Feb 1984), p. 9.
10 ibid., p. 10.

11 Steve Neale, 'Melodrama and Tears', *Screen*, vol. 27, no. 6 (November/December 1986), p. 6.

12 ibid., p. 7.

13 Julia Smith was appearing on BBC Television's *Open Air*, 19 February 1987.

14 For an account of young people's response to *EastEnders*, see chapter 4 of David Buckingham, *Public Secrets: EastEnders and its Audience* (British Film Institute, London, 1987).

15 John Hill, *Sex, Class and Realism: British Cinema 1956–1963* (British Film Institute, London, 1986), p. 57.

16 Andrew Higson, ' "Britain's Outstanding Contribution to the Film,": the documentary-realist tradition', in Charles Barr (ed.), *All Our Yesterdays* (British Film Institute, London, 1986), p. 95.

17 Raymond Williams, *Keywords* (Fontana, London, 1976), p. 218.

18 Richard Dyer (ed.), *Coronation Street* (British Film Institute, London, 1981), p. 2.

19 ibid., p. 4.

20 'Where *Coronation Street* has failed', *Woman*, 4 December 1982. Redmond repeated his comment in his introduction to *Phil Redmond's Brookside The Official Companion* (George Weidenfeld & Nicolson, London, 1987): 'People in modern Britain tend not to go in to the pub and announce all their private and personal business to all concerned,' p. 6.

21 *Broadcast*, 26 October 1984, p. 29.

22 Tony Holland, quoted in *Daily Mirror*, 11 October 1984.

23 Clive James, *Glued to the Box* (Picador, London, 1983), p. 92.

Chapter 3   A Woman's Space

1 Although soaps are still derided by TV critics and by many in the TV industry, the work of Brunsdon, Ang, Feuer and Modleski, among others, has, rather ironically, given soaps a higher status in the academic world of cultural studies and media theory.

2 Charlotte Brunsdon, ' "Crossroads" – Notes on Soap Opera', *Screen*, vol. 22, no. 4, p. 32. For a more extensive discussion of work in this area, see Annette Kuhn, 'Women's genres', in Christine Gledhill (ed.), *Home is Where the Heart is* (British Film Institute, London, 1987).

3 David Morley, *Family Television: Cultural Power and Domestic Leisure* (Comedia, London, 1986), p. 164.

4 Male viewer in ITV's *Watching Us, Watching You*, 6 April 1987.

5 For a fuller discussion of the way narrative variants are organised in soaps, see Christine Geraghty, 'The Continuous Serial – a Definition', and Richard Paterson and John Stewart, 'Street Life', both in Richard Dyer (ed.), *Coronation Street* (British Film Institute, London, 1981).

6 *The Sun* (28 January 1983), for instance, ran contrasting articles on Deirdre's dilemma – 'Yes, why not have a fling?' by the Women's

Editor, Wendy Henry, and 'No, don't fall for Mike's charms' by the Problems Columnist, Deirdre Sanders.

7 Tania Modleski, *Loving with a Vengeance* (Methuen, New York, 1982), p. 102.
8 ibid., p. 101.
9 ibid., p. 100.
10 ibid., p. 101.
11 ibid., p. 98.
12 ibid., p. 88.
13 ibid., p. 93.
14 ibid., p. 92.
15 ibid., p. 108.
16 ibid., p. 97.
17 ibid., p. 98.
18 ibid., p. 98.
19 ibid., p. 92.
20 Brunsdon, ' "Crossroads" – Notes on Soap Opera', p. 34.
21 ibid., p. 34.
22 ibid., p. 35.
23 ibid., p. 36.
24 ibid., p. 35.
25 ibid., pp. 35–6.
26 Laura Mulvey, 'Visual Pleasure in Narrative Cinema', in Philip Rosen (ed.), *Narrative, Apparatus, Ideology* (Columbia University Press, New York, 1986), p. 204.
27 Carl Gardner, 'Street on the Dole', *City Limits*, quoted in 'Inside Television: Soap comes Clean', the programme for the Institute of Contemporary Arts Television Season, 29 September 1982.
28 Manuel Alvarado, Robin Gutch and Tana Wollen, *Learning the Media* (Macmillan Education, London, 1987), p. 163.
29 For an analysis of how a strike story was handled in *Coronation Street*, see Paterson and Stewart, 'Street Life'.

Chapter 4 Family Matters

1 See, for instance, Thomas Elsaesser, 'Tales of Sound and Fury', and Geoffrey Nowell-Smith, 'Minelli and Melodrama', in Christine Gledhill (ed.), *Home is Where the Heart is* (British Film Institute, London, 1987). See also Jon Halliday, *Sirk on Sirk* (Secker and Warburg, London, 1972) and Paul Willeman, 'Towards an Analysis of the Sirkian System', *Screen*, vol. 13, no. 4 (Winter 1972/3) and 'The Films of Douglas Sirk', *Screen*, vol. 12, no. 2 (Winter 1977/8). Christine Gledhill provides a useful overview of this area of film theory in 'The Melodramatic Field: an Investigation', in Gledhill, *Home is Where the Heart is*.
2 Laura Mulvey, 'Notes on Sirk and Melodrama', in Gledhill, *Home is Where the Heart is*.

3 ibid., p. 75.
4 See Colin McCabe's highly influential article 'Realism and the Cinema: Notes on some Brechtian Theses', *Screen*, vol. 15, no. 2 (Summer 1974).
5 Mulvey, 'Notes on Sirk and Melodrama', p. 75.
6 ibid., p. 75.
7 ibid., p. 76.
8 ibid., p. 76.
9 See Mark Finch, 'Sex and Address in *Dynasty*', *Screen*, vol. 27, no. 6 (November/December 1986) for further discussion of Blake's character.
10 Gillian Swanson, '*Dallas* Part 1', *Framework*, issue 14 (1981), p. 34.
11 Terry Lovell, '*Frieda*', in Geoff Hurd (ed.), *National Fictions* (British Film Institute, London, 1984), p. 33.
12 Finch, 'Sex and Address in *Dynasty*', p. 26.
13 Marion Jordan, 'Character Types and the Individual', in Richard Dyer (ed.), *Coronation Street* (British Film Institute, London, 1981), p. 72.

Chapter 5 The Construction of a Community

1 Richard Dyer (ed.), *Coronation Street* (British Film Institute, London, 1981), p. 4.
2 Helen Franks, 'Why they're Cleaning up with Soaps', *Woman's Own*, 12 February 1982.
3 Marion Jordan, 'Realism and Convention', in Dyer, *Coronation Street*, p. 29.
4 David Buckingham, *Public Secrets: EastEnders and its Audience* (British Film Institute, London, 1987), pp. 94–6, describes the well-established image of the cockney and gives some detail of the literary and televisual tradition on which *EastEnders* draws.
5 *The Daily Express*, 11 October 1984 and *The London Evening Standard*, 10 October 1984.
6 Dyer, *Coronation Street*, p. 5.
7 Geoff Hurd (ed.), *National Fictions* (British Film Institute, London, 1984), provides a wealth of examples of this practice and offers an account of the reasons for the tenacity of this source.
8 Dyer, *Coronation Street*, pp. 3 and 4.
9 Buckingham, *Public Secrets*, p. 91.
10 Richard Paterson and John Stewart, 'Street Life', in Dyer, *Coronation Street*, p. 85.

Chapter 6 Utopian Possibilities

1 Janice A. Radway, *Reading the Romance Women, Patriarchy and Popular Literature* (University of North Carolina Press, Chapel Hill, NC, 1984), p. 93.

2 For examples of women's enjoyment in watching alone or with women friends see David Morley, *Family Television: Cultural Power and Domestic Leisure* (Comedia, London, 1986), and Ann Gray 'Behind Closed Doors: Video Recorders in the Home', in Helen Baehr and Gillian Dyer (eds), *Boxed In: Women and Television* (Pandora Press, London, 1987).

3 Radway, *Reading the Romance*, p. 122.

4 ibid., p. 162.

5 Alison Light, ' "Returning to Manderley" – Romance Fiction, Female Sexuality and Class', *Feminist Review* 16 (Summer 1984), p. 22.

6 Tania Modleski, *Loving with a Vengeance* (Methuen, New York, 1982), p. 37.

7 Radway, *Reading the Romance*, p. 124.

8 Modleski, *Loving with a Vengeance*, p. 44.

9 Radway, *Reading the Romance*, p. 147.

10 Modleski, *Loving with a Vengeance*, p. 45.

11 Radway, *Reading the Romance*, p. 147.

12 ibid., p. 140.

13 Light, ' "Returning to Manderley" ', p. 22.

14 Modleski, *Loving with a Vengeance*, pp. 58 and 60.

15 Radway, *Reading the Romance*, p. 151.

16 ibid., p. 215.

17 Modleski, *Loving with a Vengeance*, p. 58.

18 Radway, *Reading the Romance*, p. 151.

19 ibid., p. 215.

20 ibid., p. 217.

21 Pam Cook, 'Melodrama and the Women's Picture', in Sue Aspinall and Robert Murphy (eds), *Gainsborough Melodrama* (British Film Institute, London, 1983), p. 14.

22 Maria LaPlace, 'Producing and Consuming the Woman's Film Discursive Struggle in *Now Voyager*', in Christine Gledhill (ed.), *Home is Where the Heart is* (British Film Institute, London, 1987), p. 138.

23 Mary Ann Doane, 'The "Woman's Film": Possession and Address', in Mary Ann Doane, Patricia Mellencamp and Linda Williams (eds), *Re-Vision Essays in Feminist Film Criticism* (American Film Institute, USA, 1984), p. 68.

24 See E. Ann Kaplan, 'Mothering, Feminism and Representation: The Maternal in Melodrama and the Woman's Film 1910–40' and Christian Viviani, 'Who is Without Sin? The Maternal Melodrama in American Film, 1930–39,' both in Gledhill, *Home is Where the Heart is*.

25 See Doane, 'The "Woman's Film" '.

26 LaPlace, 'Producing and Consuming the Woman's Film', p. 151.

27 Christine Gledhill, 'The Melodramatic Field: An Investigation', in Gledhill, *Home is Where the Heart is*, p. 36.

28 Doane, 'The "Woman's Film" ', p. 69.

29 Cook, 'Melodrama and the Women's Picture', p. 20.

30 Doane, 'The "Woman's Film" ', p. 70.

31   LaPlace, 'Producing and Consuming the Woman's Film', p. 164.
32   ibid., p. 165.
33   Doane, 'The "Woman's Film"', p. 80.
34   Linda Williams, ' "Something Else Besides a Mother" *Stella Dallas* and the Maternal Melodrama', in Gledhill, *Home is Where the Heart is*, p. 320.
35   Richard Dyer, 'Entertainment and Utopia', in Rick Altman (ed.), *Genre: The Musical: A Reader* (Routledge and Kegan Paul, London, 1981), p. 177.
36   ibid., p. 177.
37   ibid., pp. 183–4.
38   ibid., p. 189.
39   Hans Magnus Enzensberger, 'Constituents of a Theory of the Media', *Dreams of the Absolute* (Radius, London, 1988), pp. 36–7.
40   Jane Root, *Open the Box* (Comedia, London, 1986), p. 40.
41   Dyer, 'Entertainment and Utopia', p. 180.
42   ibid., p. 180.
43   ibid., p. 180.

Chapter 7   Sex, Race and Class: the Pressures for Change

1   Peter Buckman, *All for Love: a Study in Soap Opera* (Secker & Warburg, London, 1984), p. 60.
2   Mary Cassata, 'The More Things Change, the More They Are the Same: an Analysis of Soap Operas from Radio to Television', in Mary Cassata and Thomas Skill (eds), *Life on Daytime Television: Tuning-in American Serial Drama* (Ablex, Norwood NJ, 1983), p. 100.
3   Robert C. Allen, *Speaking of Soap Operas* (University of North Carolina Press, Chapel Hill NC, 1985), p. 70.
4   Dennis Porter, 'Soap Time: Thoughts on a Commodity Art Form', in Horace Newcomb (ed.), *Television: the Critical View* (Oxford University Press, USA, 1979), p. 96.
5   Buckman, *All for Love*, p. 38.
6   ibid., p. 93.
7   ibid., p. 64.
8   Antony Easthope, *What a Man's Gotta Do* (Paladin, London, 1986), p. 130.
9   Ien Ang, *Watching Dallas* (Methuen, London, 1982), p. 31.
10   Cassata, 'The More Things Change, the More They Are the Same', p. 99.
11   Issues of ideology and realism have been subject to intense interrogation in media theory and in film study in particular. Terry Lovell, *Pictures of Reality* (British Film Institute, London, 1980) offers a complex account of the histories of the terms while John Hill, *Sex, Class and Realism: British Cinema 1956–1963* (British Film Institute, London, 1986), provides a cogent overview.

12 Charlotte Brunsdon considers the construction of the independent heroine in cinema of the 1970s in 'A Subject for the Seventies...', *Screen*, vol. 23, no. 3–4 (Sept/Oct 1982).

13 Mark Finch, 'Sex and Address in *Dynasty*', *Screen*, vol. 27, no. 6 (Nov/Dec 1986).

14 See Stephen Bourne, 'Coming Clean: Introduction', in Therese Daniels and Jane Gerson (eds), *The Colour Black* (British Film Institute, London, 1989), for a brief history of black characters in British soaps.

15 For comments on the programme's potential, written in the first six months of its life, see Christine Geraghty, '*EastEnders*', *Marxism Today*, vol. 29, no. 8 (August 1985).

16 Quoted in an interview, *London Daily News*, 30 April 1987.

17 Quoted in an interview, *New Muscial Express*, 11 July 1987, reprinted in Daniels and Gerson, *The Colour Black*, p. 157.

18 David Buckingham, *Public Secrets: EastEnders and its Audience* (British Film Institute, London, 1987), pp. 100–4.

19 'Where *Coronation Street* has Failed', *Woman*, 4 December 1982.

20 Jane Feuer, 'Melodrama, Serial Form and Television Today', *Screen*, vol. 25, no. 1 (Jan/Feb 1984), p. 14.

21 Manuel Alvarado, Robin Gutch and Tana Wollen, *Learning the Media* (Macmillan Education, London, 1987), p. 163.

22 Finch, 'Sex and Address in *Dynasty*', p. 33.

23 ibid., p. 42.

24 A viewer speaking on Channel 4's *Right to Reply*, 4 June 1988, commented 'It is unfortunate that many gay people find it hard to identify with any of the ... gay characters currently seen in British soaps ... Why are the gays in these series shown as bland, two-dimensional characters?'

25 Buckingham, *Public Secrets*, p. 113.

26 Finch, 'Sex and Address in *Dynasty*', p. 31.

Chapter 8   Women's Fiction No More?

1 Jane Root, *Open the Box* (Comedia, London, 1986), p. 72.

2 For an analysis of these programmes, all produced by Euston Films, see the essays by Jim Cook, '*Out* and *Fox*: Better Popular Television Than We Deserve' and Michael Winterbottom, 'In Production: *Minder*', both in Manuel Alvarado and John Stewart (eds), *Made for Television Euston Films Limited* (British Film Institute, London, 1985).

3 David Buckingham, *Public Secrets: EastEnders and its Audience* (British Film Institute, London, 1987), p. 111.

4 Root, *Open the Box*, p. 72.

5 Mary Cassata, 'The More Things Change, the More They are the Same: an Analysis of Soap Operas From Radio to Television', in Mary

Cassata and Thomas Skill (eds), *Life on Daytime Television: Tuning-in American Serial Drama* (Ablex, Norwood NJ, 1983), p. 99.

6 Tony Pearson, 'A Serial Drama with a Difference?', in *Phil Redmond's Brookside The Official Companion* (George Weidenfeld & Nicolson, London, 1987), p. 112.

7 Buckingham, *Public Secrets*, p. 114.

8 Pearson, 'A Serial Drama with a Difference?', p. 112.

9 See chapter 4 of Buckingham, *Public Secrets*, in which young people's comments on *EastEnders* are recorded and analysed.

10 Julia Smith and Tony Holland, *EastEnders: The Inside Story* (BBC Books, London, 1987), p. 205.

11 Buckingham, *Public Secrets*, p. 200.

12 Janey Place, 'Women in Film Noir', in E. Ann Kaplan (ed.), *Women in Film Noir* (British Film Institute, London, 1980), p. 36.

13 Annette Kuhn, *Women's Pictures* (Routledge & Kegan Paul, London, 1982), p. 35.

14 Christine Gledhill, '*Klute* 1: a Contemporary Film Noir and Feminist Criticism', in Kaplan, *Women in Film Noir*, p. 18.

15 Place, 'Women in Film Noir', p. 54.

16 A number of Ang's correspondents comment on the pleasure they get from the *Dallas* women's clothes and hairstyles. See, for instance, Ien Ang, *Watching Dallas* (Methuen, London, 1982), p. 47.

17 Place, 'Women in Film Noir', p. 47.

18 Terry Lovell, 'Ideology and *Coronation Street*', in Richard Dyer (ed.), *Coronation Street* (British Film Institute, London, 1981), p. 51.

19 See chapter 8 in Dorothy Hobson, *Crossroads: The Drama of a Soap Opera* (Methuen, London, 1982), for an account of criticisms of the programme by the Independent Broadcasting Authority and the television profession and Root, *Open the Box*, for examples of the way in which *Crossroads* was set up in the press as a national joke.

20 *The Sun*, 1 March 1985.

21 From an interview with Susi Hush by Robin Thornber in *The Guardian*, 26 December 1974.

Conclusion

1 Tania Modleski, *Studies in Entertainment: Critical Approaches to Mass Culture* (Indiana University Press, Bloomington, 1986), p. xi.

2 Lynne Segal, *Is the Future Female? Troubled Thoughts on Contemporary Feminism* (Virago Press, London, 1987), p. xii.

Index

(Because women characters in soaps change their names so frequently through marriage, fictional characters are indexed by their first names)